MODERNITY AS EXCEPTION AND MIRACLE

SUNY series, Intersections: Philosophy and Critical Theory
―――――――
Rodolphe Gasché, editor

MODERNITY AS EXCEPTION AND MIRACLE

Eduardo Sabrovsky

Translated by
Javier Burdman

With an Introduction by
Peter Fenves

English translation of *De Lo Extraordinario: Nominalismo Y Modernidad*, 2nd rev. ed. (Ediciones Universidad Diego Portales, 2013).

Translation and indexing (provided by Tristan Bradshaw) were supported through funds the Mellon-Foundation program, Critical Theory in the Global South at Northwestern University.

Cover photo: Thomas Ledl, *The Austrian Postal Savings Bank building* (cropped).

Published by State University of New York Press, Albany

© 2020 State University of New York

All rights reserved

No part of this book may be used or reproduced in any manner whatsoever without written permission. No part of this book may be stored in a retrieval system or transmitted in any form or by any means including electronic, electrostatic, magnetic tape, mechanical, photocopying, recording, or otherwise without the prior permission in writing of the publisher.

For information, contact State University of New York Press, Albany, NY
www.sunypress.edu

Library of Congress Cataloging-in-Publication Data

Names: Eduardo Sabrovsky | Javier Burdman, translator. Peter Fenves, Introduction.
Title: Modernity as Exception and Miracle / Eduardo Sabrovksy, translated by
   Javier Burdman. With an Introduction by Peter Fenves.
Description: Albany : State University of New York Press, [2020] | Series:
   SUNY series, Intersections: Philosophy and Critical Theory | Includes
   bibliographical references and index.
Identifiers: ISBN 9781438479156 (hardcover : alk. paper) | ISBN 9781438479170
   (ebook) | ISBN 9781438479163 (pbk. : alk. paper)
Further information is available at the Library of Congress.

Library of Congress Control Number: 2020937135

10 9 8 7 6 5 4 3 2 1

Contents

Preface to the English Edition   vii

Preface to the Spanish Edition   xi

Introduction: From the Transcendental, through the Extraordinary, to "Perpetual Peace"   1
   Peter Fenves

1   Musil's Death   7

2   The Extraordinary, History   17

3   The Extraordinary, Myth   27

4   The Works of Science   37

5   Nietzsche: The Incombustible in Reason   49

6   The Truth Is That There Is No Truth   61

7   The Endless Sacrifice: Art and the Production of the Extraordinary   67

8   Outline for an Ethics of Immortality   85

9   Politics of Space and of the Gaze   101

10	Notes on the Spectrality of Objects	117
11	Psychoanalysis: The Future of an Illusion	127
Notes		147
Bibliography		187
Index		193

Preface to the English Edition

For the third time now, I am writing a preface to this book—a book that was initially published in Spanish in Chile in 2001 under the title *De lo extraordinario: Nominalismo y modernidad*. The Pinochet dictatorship was already a decade back in time; nonetheless, the local publishing industry was still undergoing its aftereffects. So was I, and so were many of my fellow philosophers and friends. We were scholars without a fixed academic address: while I wrote this book, I was still laboring as a part-time university professor, hopping between universities in Santiago and Valparaíso, a hundred kilometers away, just to make ends meet; relief, in the form of a full-time academic position, would only come almost at the same time this book was being published in its initial form.

The translation I am presenting now is based on the book's second revised and expanded edition, published in 2013 by Universidad Diego Portales, the university in which, after those difficult and interesting years, I have been teaching for almost two decades now. This second and definitive edition includes an introduction that, as well as containing introductory remarks regarding each of the book's chapters, gives a global perspective on it, organized around four keywords: decision, exception, miracle, and "*lo extraordinario*," the nominalized form of the Spanish adjective "*extraordinario*" ("extraordinary"), a form that does not translate well into English and that for that reason was dropped from this book's title, with "exception" and "miracle" taking its place.[1]

There is another word I would now add to that list of keywords: "event." Exceptions, miracles, fundamental historical discontinuities ("decisions," if we follow this word's Latin etymology, "caedere," hence "cut") are not part of a historical world's normal states of affairs but are extraordinary historical-metaphysical events that, in the way of a big bang, constitute the very origin of a world's normalcy. Besides this complement, there is nothing I would add to my introductory remarks of the 2013 Spanish edition. Nonetheless, and anticipating certain quite plausible reactions, I deem it necessary to explain why, in a book written by a Chilean intellectual and philosopher, almost no mention is made of Chilean or Latin American realities and issues; almost no attempt to engage in a critical and philosophical reflection with those realities and issues as its visible subject.

In my defense, I might point out that, in fact, one chapter does engage with the work of an important Chilean conceptual artist: Gonzalo Díaz, who was awarded with the Chilean National Visual Arts Prize in 2003. This engagement is intertwined with a reflection on modern art as such, and on the practice of sacrifice as a negative path to secular glory (see chapter 7). I would also call to the reader's attention chapter 8, which dives deep into "The Immortal," a fiction by the Argentinian writer Jorge Luis Borges. However, in this fiction, Borges deals with ancient manuscripts, with death and immortality and repetition in life and literature, and not at all—alas!—with gauchos, tangos, or the disputable legacy of Juan Domingo Perón. And so do I, distilling from it the notion of an *avant-la-lettre* poststructuralist literary aesthetics.

These, however, are only feeble excuses. The actual contested issue, the frequently and occasionally fiercely contested issue, is the one Borges himself faced in the Argentina of the 1950s, under the fire of right-wing and left-wing nationalism unified under the leadership and legacy of Juan Domingo Perón. Was Borges, as his nationalist critics claimed, less of a Latin American writer, essayist, intellectual, for his preference for so-called European and cosmopolitan literary topics? And where does all this leave me, and my fellow Europhylic Latin American philosophers?[2]

In an essay published at the beginning of the 1950s ("The Argentinian Writer and Tradition") Jorge Luis Borges offered a solid argument against what he understood as a false dilemma. Analyzing the devotion of nationalist writers towards "gauchesca," a literary gender allegedly deep-rooted in firsthand experience of life in the Argentinian lowlands ("*la pampa*") and in the language of its inhabitants, *gauchos*, Borges wrote:

> The nationalists tell us that *Don Segundo Sombra* is the model of a national book; but if we compare it with the works of the gauchesque tradition, the first thing we note are differences. *Don Segundo Sombra* abounds in metaphors of a kind having nothing to do with country speech but a great deal to do with

the metaphors of the then current literary circles of Montmartre. As for the fable, the story, it is easy to find in it the influence of Kipling's *Kim*, whose action is set in India and which was, in turn, written under the influence of Mark Twain's *Huckleberry Finn*, the epic of the Mississippi. When I make this observation, I do not wish to lessen the value of *Don Segundo Sombra*; on the contrary, I want to emphasize the fact that, in order that we might have this book, it was necessary for Güiraldes to recall the poetic technique of the French circles of his time and the work of Kipling which he had read many years before; in other words, Kipling and Mark Twain and the metaphors of French poets were necessary for this Argentine book, for this book which, I repeat, is no less Argentine for having accepted such influences.[3]

For Borges, each and every item in the library of the literary tradition shares the fate of Güiraldes': under close scrutiny, it is revealed to be a hybrid, a biblical coat of many colors. And the condition of the Latin American writer, neither settled in the *pampas* nor in Europe, but on the edge, as "a writer on the edge,"[4] is understood by him as the nutritious ground, the privileged observation point from which such deconstructive conception of literary and cultural productions may arise. In fact, he assimilates this condition to the position of Irish writers towards British culture and of Jews towards the whole Western culture. In relation to the latter, he writes:

> What is our Argentine tradition? I believe we can answer this question easily and that there is no problem here. I believe our tradition is all of Western culture, and I also believe we have a right to this tradition, greater than that which the inhabitants of one or another Western nation might have. I recall here an essay of Thorstein Veblen, the North American sociologist, on the pre-eminence of Jews in Western culture. He asks if this pre-eminence allows us to conjecture about the innate superiority of the Jews, and answers in the negative; he says that they are outstanding in Western culture because they act within that culture and, at the same time, do not feel tied to it by any special devotion.[5]

According to Borges's sweeping argument, nationalism would be nothing but a European artefact. Of course, that might be just a ruse for getting even—of turning the indictment back to the indicter and deviously rejoicing in our shared destiny as colonized subordinates to the metropolis. Nonetheless, it is the very relation between these poles that is being placed in question. To wit: with the legitimacy provided to it by its "legislators," *les philosophes*, the European Enlightenment launched a radical campaign, a sort of internal colonization effort, with the intention of wiping out vernacular cultures and languages in its own soil.[6] In other words, the classical Latin American dilemma—"Culture or Barbarism," in the Argentinian nineteenth-century intellectual José de Sarmiento's famous words—was previously rehearsed in Europe; it was later to be the substance of the Enlightenment romanticism dispute that most Latin American essentialist debates tend to reproduce. In other words, Europe had to colonize itself before becoming the modern, enlightened Europe it somehow still is; and the colonization effort directed from without may be understood as the continuation of the shock wave that had already disassembled the European traditional culture, and, certainly, a shock wave that still endures, as the midwife of the present modern world that now encompasses most of the planet; a world, moreover, intrinsically related to the discovery/ingestion/creation of the New World.

So, finally, this is all about the legacy of the modern world; for many, an unsought legacy, but to which, however, the whole human kind is now entitled: to cultivate with reverence; to submit to criticism and deconstruction; to carnivalize or even to straightforwardly reject. Besides, writing on the edge is not equivalent to abstract cosmopolitism; many of Borges' fictions, essays, and poems deal with his native city and country, Buenos Aires, Argentina, with its history, literature, and politics, with the edge understood now in its historical and geographical sense. But even in his most "local" pieces, Borges never ceases to self-reflectively interrogate the conditions of possibility of his own writing and of literature in general. Metaliterature, sometimes associated with postmodernism—Borges takes care to show, however, that it is as old as Valmiki's *Ramayana* or Cervantes' *Don Quixote*—would thus constitute the most straightforward approach to literature for writers on the edge. And this approach, to which the label "deconstruction" is also frequently attached, may be extended to Latin American cultural production as a whole, and especially to philosophy.

The cast of characters in this book includes the likes of Robert Musil, Adolf Loos, Friedrich Nietzsche, Hugo von Hofmannsthal, Ludwig Boltzmann, Theodor Adorno, Walter Benjamin, Georges Bataille, and Sigmund Freud. But, as I hope to have argued rather persuasively, it is no less Latin American, less Chilean, "for having accepted such influences."

Santiago de Chile, March 2019

Preface to the Spanish Edition

A little over a decade has gone by since the publication of this book. During this time, I have frequently returned to it, either with a view to its translation into French, a project which ended successfully in 2012 with its publication by L'Harmattan; or otherwise, and more fundamentally, due to a sort of gravitational pull from which it is still not easy for me to escape.

However, to write a prologue for a new edition can be the occasion to make a balance and establish a distance: to read the book as if it were, as it already is somehow, someone else's. I give an account of this in what follows. I use as a guiding thread the word that is visible in the title: extraordinary, *the extraordinary*.

As far as a I can explain at this point, I recall that the notion appeared to me—to that other—imperiously, as an obsessive idea, after listening to a conference on the so-called "ordinary language philosophy." I was deeply interested in the way the speaker managed to play two incompatible games at once: on the one hand, to adhere to a philosophy that asserts its ability to reduce each and every metaphysical terms to ordinary language (in *Philosophical Investigations*, Wittgenstein calls them "super-concepts," and claims that they could not refer to anything more elevated than what is referred to by words like "table," "lamp," or "door");[1] on the other, to maintain the professorial, "business-as-usual" claim to philosophical truth, Olympically ignoring the abyss he was approaching.

Both the philosophers of ordinary language (led by Nietzsche as their precursor) and the speaker just mentioned can be accused of falling into the very frightening "performative contradiction": what the enunciation does—to assert truth—contradicts its content: "in truth, there is no truth." However, one of the main philosophical intuitions in this book, which I have persistently developed afterwards, is that such contradiction, *pace* rationalists like Apel or Habermas, represents no refutation at all. Rather, as a reading of Aristotle or Leibniz shows, the performative contradiction is precisely the hinge that opens the path for the fleeting production of the extraordinary. This path does not lead to a God commensurable with the human intellect, as philosophers and theologians once wanted to believe, or make believe. It leads to that supplement of height that modern human beings, immersed in what simply "is the case," demand in order to acquire a certain substance, paradoxically and fleetingly, a certain support in being. ("Man, in order to be what he is, must believe that he is more than he is," Robert Musil wrote in *The Man without Qualities*; one of the epigraphs in this book repeats it.) In other words, condensing here my critique of the candid partisan of "ordinary language philosophy," the modern immersion in the ordinary is to be understood, and can only be understood, as a sort of spring mechanism that, by means of the performative contradiction, projects the human being toward the extraordinary. This is how Modernity, in its militant choice for a reality that is primordially ordinary, formless, and lacking intrinsic order, turns out to be rather the vehicle of a minimalist religiosity, which is as silent as it is severe. In other words, Wittgenstein's claim that there is nothing elevated in the world is precisely *the* metaphysical-theological claim that, through the performative contradiction inherent to it, institutes the elevation that it would want to negate. Reciprocally, for Modernity there may be no other elevation, no other metaphysics than the one instituted by such negation: as in a fragment by Kafka that I quote somewhere in the book, we moderns, in order to build our Tower of Babel, have to dig a pit. The modern subject is precisely the one who digs it; the one who writes—this is the case with modern science—"I do not write, I am written," and who, precisely by virtue of this negation, sovereignly does write, does speak. Through contradiction, then, he performs himself as a subject of enunciation that sovereignly excepts himself from the content of the enunciation.

What I say here is not different from the movement that follows from the third antinomy in the *Critique of Pure Reason*. Kant shows there that the aspiration to causally explain the totality of the universe necessarily leads to a first cause, which cannot be itself an effect of a cause—that is, to freedom, which causal totalization would want to disprove. Kant deduces from this that the understanding must remain within its boundaries, or otherwise fall under the spell of the "transcendental illusion." However, the subsequent tradition will identify here a performative contradiction, following from a ban (on the knowledge of the real) that it cannot but transgress in the very act of its enunciation. This is the essence of the "dialectic of the limit," *Dialektik der Grenze*, which Hegel, in his *Science of Logic*, develops in opposition to the ban, to the limit that Kant had established upon our capacity to know. Essentially, the problem is that whoever draws a boundary, knows already what is on the other side; in Kant, it is the enigmatic "X," the "thing in itself." However, Hegel wants this leap to infinity to be entirely rational: only thus can the wedding between Freedom and Reason be celebrated on the stage of history (in Kant, by contrast, the event would have been no more than a Platonic affair). Nonetheless, it will be shown later that the marriage was unhappy and infertile.

Indeed, history is the instance in which the paradoxical production of *the extraordinary* frequently shows its tragicomic face. History is the topic of chapter 2 ("The Extraordinary, History"), in the series of eleven chapters in which I analyze instantiations, *apparitions* of *the extraordinary*. The issue there is history, read under the optics of German idealism and its inheritor Karl Marx, as a gigantic "pious work" leading to salvation, to the ultimate end of all fracture in human existence; to the fulfillment of what Kant, in a writing with an axiomatic, normative style, lacking the verbal twists of his romantic successors, called *Idea for a Universal History with a Cosmopolitan Aim*. Section 9 of this essay is peculiar. Its long title is perhaps symptomatic of the difficulty that the author must face in it: "*A philosophical attempt to work out universal world history according to a plan of nature that aims at the perfect civil union of the human species, must be regarded as possible and even as furthering this aim of nature.*"[2] Here, Kant, in a self-reflective move, turns upon his own *philosophical attempt* and, aside from considering it *possible*, grants it a *furthering* effect. We are here in the midst of the philosophy of the will. Unlike the legend that describes him as the guardian of the fortified frontiers of the island of the Enlightenment, the "spider of Königsberg"—this is how Nietzsche once called him—shows his venom, that of a discourse hiding its performativity under the thick fabric of "mere reason." And indeed, Kant himself admits a few lines down that his attempt could be read as a novel. The argumentation that follows, which concludes the essay, does not refute this hypothesis—rather, it puts it under the sign of "the useful"; of the uninterrupted power of an elite ("only a *learned public* that has endured uninterruptedly from its beginning up to our time can accredit ancient history," Kant writes in a footnote);[3] of the need for consolation facing a chaotic reality, as it essentially is for the moderns; last, of the ambition of the powerful ("the heads of state as well as their servants") for securing the "glorious remembrance down to the later age."⁴ In sum, even if with a different and even opposite sign, Kant's motives are essentially similar to those that led the German romantics to write historical novels; Nietzsche to develop a philosophy oriented not to truth, but rather to rhetoric and to what he called "perspectivism"; and the famous Kantian Hans Vaihinger (founder of the famous and erudite journal *Kant-Studien*) to formulate his philosophy of the "as if" ("*Philosophie als ob*"), in which he made explicit the continuity between Kant and Nietzsche and asserted without hesitations the political need to produce fictions in order to instruct the people.

At this point, we are still in the wake of Plato's "noble lie"; of myth and rhetoric (especially of that powerful trope: unconditional truth); of fiction as an instrument of politics. However, a new seriousness soon replaces the romantic irony, which had understood the novel self-reflectively as a novel, poetry as poetry: as "poetry of poetry," and which relied on self-reflectivity and the ensuing opening to infinity in order to relativize the finitude of historically crystalized forms. For Fichte and for Marx, it was no longer enough to narrate history in an edifying manner, with all the possibilities that the imagination could provide, either by means of nationalism or by means of the "proletarian" revolution. History itself would be an edification, constructed no longer as a novel (*Bildungsroman*), but rather as a concrete actualization. Ordinary history, with all the trivial things that Kant, in the writing just mentioned, still acknowledged and difficultly reconciled with his "novel," had yielded to a new history of salvation—history as a "pious work," as the temporal objectification *of the extraordinary*.

It was given to my generation to be the witness of the bitter conclusion to this process. Witness of the erosion that sediments and brings to light the true form, of the dusty and gray reality of such exalted projects. Specifically, the pious work that was the State in Hegel, classless society in Marx, and collective will and the Communist Party in Lenin and Gramsci, was progressively reduced to what is most prosaic and also most essential: in the last instance, no more than a wall, which vanished in the air the night of November 9–10 of 1989, without anyone firing a single bullet to defend it. Thus, the extraordinary abandoned history, so as to recover its narrative, mythical, theological character.⁵

A decisive turn follows from this. For my generation (and one need not be in the Left to believe this), the October Revolution had cut history in half, into a before and an after. Communists and fascists, social democrats and liberals, we all had to realize that we shared a common ground: we were ultimately, by destiny, moderns. From that point on, Modernity becomes a primordial explanatory category both in the social sciences and in philosophy, as it had been for Max Weber's generation before. The so-called post-Modernity, in fact, was nothing but Modernity turning self-consciously upon itself—the "postmodern condition" belongs to the one who knows that he is historically modern and can no longer forget it.[6]

By means of a powerful image, which I also bring up at one point in the book, Robert Musil accounts for the metaphysical gesture that defines the modern world. Following this gesture, this world would not be, as it is often presented, the outcome of the unhindered progress of reason, and thus a progress against which the stubborn clusters of unreason that still stand might be measured and normatively rejected. With Musil, we are transported into the Austro-Hungarian Empire, in the years immediately before the Great War, when a big part of the Kakanian society—*kayserlich und königlich*, *K&K*, is the seal that government buildings naively display—is getting ready to celebrate, in 1918—but the date will never arrive—the seventieth anniversary of Emperor Franz Joseph's happy reign. Musil's image adequately refers to this "metaphysical gesture" through another gesture. In one of the many chapters of his historical fiction, we are presented with a group of prominent scientists who, invited to an aristocratic ceremony that is already part of the celebration, "looking at a beautifully glazed, luxuriantly curved vase," yields to "the thought of smashing it to bits with a single blow of one's stick."[7] This blow condenses everything: for a Modernity that already knows that "all ornamentation is crime" (Adolf Loos, another Kakanian), the issue is to expose what deceitfully presents itself as *extraordinary* as no more than a modality of the *ordinary*, understood as ontologically primordial. The goal would be then to generate form—complexity, order, difference—on the basis of the blind interaction between simple and undifferentiated elements; on the basis of the accumulation of infinitesimal variations whose slow sedimentation would make up the "low" origin of the aura of necessity—substantiality—that often surrounds things.

This violence (a sort of modern protest against the tyranny of the existent), Musil concludes, would account for "the peculiar predilection of scientific thinking for mechanical, statistical, and physical explanations that have, as it were, the heart cut out of them."[8] We arrive thus at the metaphysical, theological-political core of Modernity. Indeed, Modernity is characterized by the Weberian disenchantment of the world. A disenchanted world is opaque to human reason: no longer a Cosmos of rational forms, but rather the effervescence of an infinite singularity in which, in the absence of an immanent order, the very modern will to order can exert its planetary task; in which autonomy thus becomes possible, as the subject is freed from the tutelage of "objective" morality or politics—and there is technology, the market, and modern bureaucracy.

In terms of a history of ideas, which one should not oppose to a "materialist" history (ideas can be historically effective forces; "material" changes acquire historical significance only through human agents), disenchantment follows from the nominalist theology of the late Middle Ages. Its main elements will be deployed later on in the public sphere by the Reformation, as highly explosive theological-political weapons.[9] For the power of the medieval-ecclesiastic institution was grounded upon its self-conferred privilege not only to interpret the Scripture, but also to decipher the Creation, translating everything in it into ethical-political norms that from that point on became unavoidable. Against this power-knowledge device, nominalism, and then the Reformation, emphasize the idea of divine omnipotence, of a divinity whose designs are inaccessible to human reason. The attempts to rationally apprehend such designs thus become mere anthropomorphic projections: idolatry, which seeks to build a god in a human scale.

The other side of this prohibition, concerning not merely images but also each and every anthropomorphic projection (of the humble [?] human reason and its world toward the universe), is God's indifference to this world, which transpires in the exclusion of the miracle. That is, Modernity excludes the miracle because, within itself, it concentrates all *miracleness*. In his *A Lecture on Ethics*, which explains the theology implicit in the *Tractatus Logico-Philosophicus*, Wittgenstein addresses the disenchanted world of Modernity and the paradox inherent in it to "absolute judgment of value." He coins for that two powerful, Borgesian images: the "book of the world" and "a book on Ethics which really was a book on Ethics."[10] The former, written by "an omniscient person . . . [who] knew all the movements of all the bodies in the world dead or alive and that he also knew all the states of mind of all human beings that ever lived" would contain "facts, facts, and facts but no Ethics."[11] That is to say: no statements with an absolute value; no miracles. Science does not show that there are no miracles; on the contrary, their exclusion constitutes its grounding *a priori*, its Law ("the truth is that the scientific way of looking at a fact is not the way to look at it as a miracle").[12]

The "book on Ethics," by contrast, would indeed contain (and only contain) statements with absolute value. Wittgenstein adds, enigmatically: "this book would, with an explosion, destroy all other books in the world."[13] The enigma is cleared away if we understand that statements of absolute value (or better: the statement of absolute value; the plural here can only be understood as a rhetorical figure) lack meaning, and that therefore such a "book" could only be the mind of God—the mind of an arbitrary, nominalist God who, by means of the unavoidable "transcendental illusion," becomes present to us each time we try to rationally reach the eminent historical decision (understood in its fundamental meaning, according to its etymology: *caedere*, to cut), the exception that, by giving the modern world its initial kick, is also the forgotten source of its normality. This book is then the mind of a God that intervenes by giving a first push, a historical direction, to the modern world and then leaves the scene. Otherwise, its intervention would possess once again the character of an exception (of the miracle) that transcends all rationality—the catastrophe.

"Decision," "exception," and "miracle" appear scarcely or not at all in this book (six, two, and one time, according to the useful and quick search function of the word processor). "Decision" appears in almost all cases in connection to modern science, to the decisions (even economic decisions, for experiments often end when they run out of funds) that make a "fact" out of something. More fundamentally, "decision" appears in connection to the historical *decision* that, with Galileo, turned mathematics into the language in which the book of the universe is written. "Exception" refers almost always to a change of level or power (as in arithmetic): either to the transfer of control between organizational or technological "black boxes" within hierarchical systems, or to the questions that becomes present and unavoidable when there is no longer a higher power to which one can resort. This happens when, either in thought or in life, the comforting idea of an "infinite regress" (of an infinite time) yields to the disquieting finitude of life and reason; the idea of the tomb as the only point at which art and architecture converge, in Adolf Loos's architectural conception; the idea of the decision beyond all decisionism, beyond all subjective will, like freedom in Kant's third antinomy, which fatally becomes present *in extremis* when reason has exhausted its set of ruses.

Regarding the miracle, its absence can be understood along the lines of what Borges claims in connection to the Quran ("The Argentine Writer and Tradition"): the absence of camels in it would be precisely what makes it the Arab book *par excellence*. Analogously, if in this book there are no miracles, it is because the entire book is connected to them—to the religion of the moderns, to their (our) religiosity, concentrated in a virtual point, and silent to the point of atheism; to the exclusion of the miracle in a world that, as I said before, would concentrate in itself all *miracleness*, in such a way that its desire—desire for the extraordinary, for the impossible that is at the same time unavoidable—as a sort of metastasis, would spread all over the place.

"Decision," "exception," and "miracle" are words that belong to Carl Schmitt's terminology. The contemporary philosophical-political, or rather theological-political debate, insofar as it takes upon itself the inquiry into "ultimate things"—that is, into the eschatology of a modern world no longer veiled by the false dichotomy between capitalism and communism—can hardly avoid them.[14] In one way, or rather in many ways, this book prefigures this debate, as well as a philosophical-political position in it, which I can only outline here (it is also part of a book whose provisional title is *El tigre cautivo*).

The attention that the intellectual left devotes today to Schmitt, a Catholic, anti-Enlightenment thinker who actively supported the Nazis, stems from the peculiar symmetry between the situations, then and now. Facing a left that, in the first decades of the twentieth century, essentially linked its success to progress and the development of the forces of production, the Schmittian right defended the decisionism it associated with the figure of the sovereign, as well as the irreducible conflictual nature of the political. Today, faith in progress has moved to the "neoliberal" right, while those who are discontent put their hopes in the reestablishment of the primordial conflictivity neutralized by the liberal State, and which they link to the political by means of a revival of Schmitt.

However, things were already more complex in Schmitt's time. For there was a Leninist Left that, although lacking metaphysical depth, reclaimed for itself the primacy of the moment of intensified political will, not embodied in the person of the sovereign, but rather in a politicized elite—"few, but good," Lenin wrote soon before his death—the Bolshevik Party, which in 1917 had been ready to carry out a revolution "Against *Capital*" (these are the words of a young and irreverent Antonio Gramsci, in an article published in response to the October Revolution). "Against *Capital*," that is to say, in a country like Russia, where the "objective conditions" for the establishment of socialism were almost completely absent.

Beyond the surprising mutual admiration between the two, it is possible to see in the figures of Carl Schmitt and Walter Benjamin in those years a turn toward political theology (and toward a "methodological extremism" concomitant to political theology in modern conditions), stemming from the failure of the revolution from either left or right in Germany after the Great War, and from the establishment, with Weimar, of a liberal republic.

But there is an additional element, at least in Benjamin, which can be identified in an essay that was published almost simultaneously with Schmitt's *Political Theology*: his *Towards a Critique of Violence*. In this essay, Benjamin defends, against the violence associated with sovereignty, a "divine violence" that, although its immediate precedent is the idea of "general strike" in Georges Sorel, can be also understood as a theologization of Leninism in its revolutionary phase. In fact, Georg Lukács, shortly before joining the Hungarian Communist Party in 1918, and writing from a perspective similar to Benjamin's (at the intersection of Jewish Messianism, philosophy, German literature, and the ambiguous intellectual legacy of Max Weber),[15] had not hesitated to link the Leninist revolution to the *"credo quia absurdum est"* of the early Christians, and consequently to the urgency—salvation now!—of making heaven come to earth.

From that point on, however, Lukács's and Benjamin's trajectories diverge. Lukács joined a project that, as with early Christians, was forced to make peace both with the world and with scientific, calculating reason, which not only interprets the world, but also projects its transformation in terms of *possibility*. Like Saint Paul, who in his Second Letter to the Thessalonians introduced the enigmatic figure of the *katheion*, "the postponer" (who, with the aim of preventing the coming of the Antichrist, preserves the political order, and thus also avoids the ensuing Second Coming and Salvation—Dostoyevsky's figure of the Great Inquisitor is already visible there), the Bolshevik Revolution, in its struggle for survival, had to relegate communism, in a katechonian manner, to an indeterminate future. It replaced it with "socialism in one country," geopolitics, and the distribution of the world in spheres of influence. To Benjamin, by contrast, a trip to the Soviet Union, driven by emotional rather than political reasons, sufficed to leave aside the idea of joining the Communist Party. And, in fact, beyond his activity as a man of letters, he has not known concrete political activism, not even the distribution of pamphlets or the participation in a demonstration. Therefore, it is not at all surprising that Benjamin replied to the Soviet Union's supreme katechonian act (its pact with Hitler in 1939 to *postpone* the imminent German invasion) with an expression of radical messianism, disregarding actual history and *Realpolitik*. In them, in the manner of the early Christians, Benjamin sees nothing but ruins. And this is his celebrated and posthumous *On the Concept of History*.

Thesis IX of this manifesto, the allegory of the Angel of History, is well known. Benjamin has rejected the easy consolation of symbols and intellectual intuitions, as well as the one provided by secular theodicy, either under the epic form that the first Lukács opposed to the novel or as expressed in Hegelian Marxist dialectics. Thus, with truly allegorical style, he presents us with a vision (the angel's vision) that, in truth, should be beyond the reach of any representation. So, even if we can know with certainty what the angel does not see ("where we perceive a chain of events": the causal linkage of facts characteristic of human understanding), what he does see, as Benjamin tells us ("one single catastrophe which keeps pilling wreckage upon wreckage and hurls it in front on his feet"),[16] constitutes, above all, a rhetorical strategy that allows the author to present, by means of the angel, what he himself would like to make us see. And regarding the difference between "what we call progress" and the angel's alleged experience ("a storm . . . blowing from Paradise; irresistibly propels him into the future . . . , while the pile of debris before him grows skyward"),[17] it is worth making a remark that, from the perspective of the reinterpretation that I am here bringing to conclusion, is not insignificant.

Indeed, the idea of progress, beyond the value judgment that it implies ("today we are well, and tomorrow we will be even better"), is indebted to a conception of time as a unidirectional, irreversible arrow. But this is also the angel's temporality (or rather Benjamin's): "a storm [that] irresistibly propels him into the future." Now, in a chapter that I have included as an addition to this second edition (chapter 4, "The Works of Science"), I examine the question of the irreversibility of time in the context of the second law of thermodynamics, where it receives a mathematical formulation that, at least in a first reading, is paradoxically Platonic and eternal. However, relying on an interpretation by French Israeli biologist Henri Atlan ("matter," he writes, "only lets itself be constrained and dominated up to a certain point"),[18] I identify in this law the very historical expression of the will to order characteristic of the Modern Age. This will, although visibly expressed in the development of techno-science (in this case, in the effort to build machines capable of transforming caloric into kinetic energy: the First Industrial Revolution) permeates the totality of the modern world. By the way, there is another achievement that I recognize in this book (in the course of becoming its first reader): I understood that the outmost expression of the spirit of Modernity lies not in science, but rather in Nietzschean perspectivism and its byproducts (poetic or poietic art).

Some authors (Ilya Prigogine and Isabelle Stengers, *Le temps et l'éternité*) have wanted to see in the second law of thermodynamics the expression of a creativity stemming from the nature of things, which classical physics, with its reversible conception of time, would have ignored. But this edifying interpretation, with its blindness regarding the constitutive role ("transcendental") of mathematics, and more specifically of statistics, for the observation/constitution of what counts as real, is as unhistorical as it gets. And the optimism that derives from it, reduced to its historical aspects (those of a Modernity that, starting with the apriorism of mathematics, projects a world), is but the clearest expression of an already anachronic faith in progress (the Adamic time of invention, which is then followed by the eternal repetition of the same).

What remains, if we bracket Prigogine and Stengers's scientific progress, as well as Benjamin's messianic catastrophism, is the bare arrow of time, no longer as an a-historical reality of time "in itself," but rather as an expression of the specifically modern temporality that, as I have said above, flows irreversibly from the exception at its origin toward the normalization in which this origin is forgotten. "Irreversibly," because given the complexity and the stability of forms ("objective spirit") by which the modern world systemically differentiates itself, the reestablishment of its fluidity and reversibility is necessarily beyond any subjective will, whether individual or collective,[19] so that it can only be thought under the anonymous form of the catastrophe, where the heavens no longer bring their joy to the earth, but rather collapse onto it. In other words, it can only be thought in terms of the emergence of a pure exteriority, of a "signification without context," as Emmanuel Lévinas says in explicit connection with eschatology understood as "rupture of the totality," in his *Totalité et infini*.

This systemic self-differentiation of modern society, along with the irreversibility implied by it, led Schmitt, in the wake of Weber, to think Modernity as "the age of neutralizations and depoliticizations." Indeed, the modern state, in order to end the wars of religion unleashed by the Reformation, protects religious freedom under the condition that all substantive faith become private, that is, that it be transformed into belief, confined to the interiority of an individual or of a community of believers that have given up the aspiration to impose it upon others as faith. But this process, which begins with religion, does not stop at it. On the contrary, it expands until, as in our time, it encompasses political convictions, which become progressively hollowed-out "positions." Thus, and here lies the secret of what Schmitt called "the incredibly coherent systematics of liberal thought,"[20] "the political" (political sovereignty and its concomitants, decision and exception) withdraws, shrinks into a virtual point, while at the same time politics becomes technified "policy," interrupted by sporadic and inorganic explosions of discontent; meanwhile, in the intellectual sphere, it becomes the intellectualized messianism that, despite displaying the tinsels of an idealized revolutionary messianism, is not but the B-side of the katheionic temporality of the age. This B-side is the depoliticized and passive waiting for a messianic event that, because it can always take place ("every second of time was the straight gate through which the Messiah might enter," Benjamin writes in the appendix that concludes his "Theses on the Philosophy of History"),[21] it actually never takes place.

It is also the case that the "divine violence" incarnated by Benjamin's Messiah draws no boundary. As Benjamin had written in *Critique of Violence*, divine violence "boundlessly destroys."[22] In other words, the figure of the sovereign, situated in the exception (in that virtual point that is his substance), establishes limits, order. By excluding himself from it, the sovereign grounds this order, in such a way that his exteriority constitutes what Jacques-Alain Miller calls *extimacy*—an excluded interiority; an intimate exterior.[23] Benjamin's Messiah—the angel, his messenger—by contrast, insofar as he draws no boundary at all (insofar as he abolishes the Law once and for all), avoids this paradox, which is also the paradox of the production of the extraordinary. He becomes thus an encapsulated figure: confined either to a beyond that is excessively distant (an exteriority that is never intimate), or otherwise to an interiority that is rather ordinary and opaque, like a dissected exotic bird for display as part of a collection.

Introduction

From the Transcendental, through the Extraordinary, to "Perpetual Peace"

PETER FENVES

In the following paragraph of the *Critique of Pure Reason*, where Kant, reflecting on how we speak of the difference between appearances and reality, recapitulates the basic argument he formulates in favor of transcendental idealism, the word *extraordinary* assumes the extraordinary function of explicating the meaning of the word *transcendental*:

> If, therefore, we say: The senses represent objects to us as they appear, but the understanding as they are, then the latter is not to be taken in a transcendental but merely an empirical way, signifying, namely, how they must be represented as objects of experience, in the thoroughgoing connection of appearances, and not how they might be outside of the relation to possible experience and consequently to sense in general, thus as objects of pure understanding. For this will always remain unknown to us, so that it even remains unknown whether such a transcendental (extraordinary [*außerordentlichen*]) cognition is possible at all, at least as one that stands under our ordinary [*gewöhnlichen*] categories. With us understanding and sensibility can determine an object only in combination. If we separate them, then we have intuitions without concepts or concepts without intuitions, but in either case representations that we cannot relate to any determinate object.[1]

Nowhere else in all of his extant writings does Kant explain the cardinal attribute of his technical vocabulary, *transcendental*, with reference to the colloquial term *extraordinary*. As if the substitution of *transcendental* by *extraordinary* were not extraordinary enough, he emphasizes the point by describing the categories of the pure understanding as nothing less than "ordinary." Since, however, the demonstration of the objective reality of these categories derives from a transcendental deduction—this is, of course, the cornerstone of the critical program, which Kant considers so important that he accomplishes it twice—the passage cited above can be rephrased as following: the extraordinary yields the ordinary; more precisely, only by virtue of an extraordinary deduction can the ordinariness of the categories be recognized. Even as Kant denies the possibility of extraordinary cognition, at least for human beings, he admits, if only by way of substitution, that the ordinariness of cognition derives from the extraordinary.

De lo extraordinario—which was first published in 2001 and appears here under the title *Modernity as Exception and Miracle*—makes us acutely sensitive to the subtle semantic event that happens in this brief passage of the *Critique of Pure Reason*. A new kind of "hermeneutics of suspicion" emerges from the pages of Sabrovsky's production of a new table of quasi-categories, which, congruent with the Kantian one, derives from a "transcendental (extraordinary)" deduction. Whereas the genealogical inquiries of a Nietzsche or a Foucault prompt the suspicion that power is everywhere implicated in even the most apparently neutral ends or benign techniques, the analysis that ensues in this volume alerts its readers to the fact that the forms and functions of contemporary order and ordinariness derive from the extraordinariness and out-of-ordered-ness of Modernity itself. It is for this reason—and in contrast to the Kantian program of grounding the sciences in the "transcendental (extraordinary)" unity of apperception—that Sabrovsky's study does not present Newtonian or classical mechanics but, rather, statistical thermodynamics as the exemplary modern science: every semblance of order is understood in advance to be extraordinary, a deviation from the state of equilibrium toward which bodies and fields, matter and energy move. And it is for the same reason that Sabrovsky's analysis takes its point of departure from a general conception of language that is so altogether ordinary within the context of Modernity, including and especially its exact sciences, that we fail to recognize its extraordinariness—the conception, namely, that denies without the slightest compunction the possibility that certain words acquire their meaning and thus become words in the proper sense of the word only because they are ultimately grounded in the order of reality. In other words, Sabrovsky precisely locates the Modernity of Modernity in the total victory of late scholastic nominalism over early scholastic realism. It is for this reason, finally, that the original publication of *De lo extraordinario* bore the subtitle *nominalismo y modernidad*: the quasi-categories of modern philosophy, science, literature, art, and politics derive from a generally occluded memory of nominalism's triumph, which required each of these spheres of knowledge, action, and judgment to represent a version of the extraordinary—the exceptional, the miraculous—in which the battle would continue, and the victory could be repeated and forgotten *ad infinitum*.

What Sabrovsky discerns in the following passage drawn from the eleventh and final chapter of *Modernity as Exception and Miracle* precisely captures what Kant admits almost as an aside in the passage quoted above from the *Critique of Pure Reason*:

> [T]he nominalist, who asserts the radical unknowability of the Real (its primordial alterity in connection to our language), knows, however, of the Real—precisely as something unknowable, as other. In other words, nominalism seeks to exclude the projection of the forms of reason into the Real and thus to ban, once and for all, the passage between being and thought. But insofar as its unknowability is in itself an unverifiable postulate (for in order to verify it, a sort of "thinking of thinking" would be necessary, which would face again the same problem), it can be nothing but a projection. Thus . . . the nominalist postulate is violated at the very instant that it is asserted. However, nominalism, as well as the modern world instituted by it, are not "refuted" by this paradox. Rather, the paradox is the source of energy that keeps modern reason working. (142)

Just as Sabrovsky concisely restates the epistemic aporia around which Kant's critical program revolves, in which the unknowability of things-in-themselves is of a different order of knowledge than the knowledge of the object of experience in general, so does he subtly indicate the exact point at which Modernity becomes exceptional from within the context of its exemplary science. Because the "postulate" from which Modernity emerges remains only a demand, not an axiom that can be demonstrated through some form of intuition, the "source" of its "energy" is inexhaustible. Modernity is thus akin to a perpetual-motion machine, which statistical thermodynamics, emerging from the industrial revolution as the crux of the modern sciences, does not so much disallow in accordance with some metaphysical principle as declare inadmissible in the real world, including its ideal models of energy transfer. By virtue of the inexhaustibility of its dynamic source, however, Modernity must view itself as an infinitely unlikely exception to the probabilistic laws and thus the only legitimate miracle. Of course, the same argument proceeds in the opposite direction: since we cannot know, after all, whether or not the source of Modernity's energy is in fact inexhaustible, there is no end to the number of ways in which its end can and will be imagined. Insofar as such speculation is itself a source of energy, however, the anticipation of its exhaustion results in its replenishment.

To my knowledge, there is only one previous attempt to understand Modernity as a *perpetuum mobile*, namely, Kant's little treatise of 1795, *Zum ewigen Frieden*, which is often, and for good reason, translated as "Perpetual Peace." In certain passages, Kant suggests that an end to warfare—not only political but also metaphysical—can be accomplished without a total exhaustion of living forces only through the establishment of a system of mutually sustaining and enlivening states that would represent the analogue in the sphere of freedom to a perpetual-motion machine in the sphere of nature. Even if Sabrovsky never mentions "Perpetual Peace" in *Modernity as Exception and Miracle*, the passage of the *Critique of Pure Reason* in which Kant first speaks of a lively peace maintained in perpetuity is the point of departure not only for his analysis of the extraordinary quasi-category of history in the second chapter but, in retrospect, for all of the subsequent quasi-categories, insofar as each of them, as modern, is historical in the relevant sense.[2] For Kant, of course, Newtonian science, along with arithmetic and Euclidean geometry, is the exemplary science. Even as his very first book, *Thoughts on the True Estimation of Living Forces*, written some fifty years before "Perpetual Peace," gingerly enters into the century-long debates concerning what eventually would be called the first law of thermodynamics, he had no access to the kinds of investigation Sabrovsky analyzes in his fourth chapter, "Works of Science." Nevertheless, he was well enough aware of the relevant conjectures and experiments to recognize that he could associate his proposal for perpetual peace with the idea of a *perpetuum mobile* only if he self-consciously adopted an attitude of ironic detachment, for it is not only princes and politicians but also natural philosophers and protoscientists who would scoff at any such proposal.[3] Here, if anywhere, a hermeneutics of suspicion is warranted since what else could be behind a proposal that everyone familiar with the modern sciences knows to be impossible—a system of forces that mutually sustains and enlivens each and all of its members?

Despite all of this justified mockery and suspicion, however, the proposal stands unrefuted and, indeed, irrefutable. *Modernity as Exception and Miracle* is one of its genuine successors, for it retrieves that infinitely fine balance of argument, style, and tone through which "Perpetual Peace" retains the possibility that global Modernity as a whole—however little this "whole" can be represented by a universal term, including *Modernity*—may be its own miracle, an exception to the laws that govern the universe.

Chapter 1

Musil's Death

"And one day Ulrich stopped wanting to be promising."[1] With this simple sentence, written in one of the initial chapters of *The Man without Qualities* (a novel whose first volume was published for the first time in Germany in 1930), Austrian writer Robert Musil provides an account of the change in the trajectory of the main character. It is the years immediately prior to World War I. Ulrich, who enjoys a comfortable economic situation, has decided to leave in suspense his promising career as a mathematician and to "take a year's leave of absence from his life in order to seek an appropriate application for his abilities."[2]

Thus, and in the best tradition of the *Bildungsroman*, this novel, written throughout two decades (since the beginning of the twenties until the very day of Musil's death in 1942) seems to invite us to follow a vital trajectory, at the end of which—such is the "plausible" of the genre—the crisis would be overcome by a new equilibrium. However, what has been left in a state of suspense turns out to be something more than Ulrich's scientific career. Time itself seems to have slowed down or stopped. Lacking movement on the temporal axis (is this not what happens every time that the hour of truth comes near?), the novel must turn to space and the interiority of its characters. This way, *The Man without Qualities* is a kind of walk without a fixed itinerary through the social and psychological landscape of the Musilian "Kakania": a past world, that of the ancient Austro-Hungarian Empire, whose public buildings display on their facades, proudly and candidly, the initials K&K ("*Kayserlich und Koeniglich*"; "imperial and royal"), and whose governing elite gets ready to celebrate, in 1918, the seventy years of Emperor Franz Joseph's reign. This date, however, is never to arrive.

Despite this ramshackle look, Kakania is also "the first country in our present historical phase from which God withdrew His credit":[3] a place—anticipation of the global Kakania of our time—where, in the absence of the guarantee provided by the divinity, ethical and cognitive accounts show an alarming tendency to the red. It is a world in which everything vanishes in the air; where objects and even subjects are but occasional aggregates of qualities, lacking any fixity, any substantiality. In order to save his most intimate self from dissolution, the "man without qualities" will seek shelter in a virtual space, at the edge of the world. Ulrich, the Musilian Ulysses, will end up traveling in circles, trapped by the vortex of a narcissistic and incestuous relationship with his female alter ego, namely his younger sister Agathe, from whom he has been distanced for a long time, and with whom he is going to meet again after the death of their father.

These are, in broad terms, the circumstances in which Ulrich discovers his lack of qualities and stops wanting to be promising. The crisis is unleashed by a characteristically banal fact: a commentary in the press, whose author, surely an ignoramus in Ulrich's mind, foregrounds the achievements of a "racehorse of genius."[4] Suddenly, Ulrich will understand that he inhabits a world in which, for better or worse, the performances of the emerging "geniuses" of soccer, boxing, tennis, and even equestrian sports have begun to displace traditional virtues. Such virtues have been reduced to mere ornaments, to residues that come out to shine only in after-dinner conversations and edifying speeches.

Unlike "the fainthearted, the softheaded who comfort their souls with spiritual nonsense,"[5] Ulrich, a mathematician and a careful reader of Nietzsche, understands that admiration for sports, with all its banality, is inseparable from the virtues of the modern world. Science itself, Ulrich reflects, "has developed a concept of hard, sober intelligence that makes the old metaphysical and moral ideas of the human race simply intolerable."[6] These notions, as well as the old powers that they legitimated, have been dislodged by the spirit of exactitude: the demand that all argument be supported not by authority (whatever it may be) but by verifiable evidence. But, in this way, Ulrich continues, it was almost inevitable that, as he reached the goal, "the horse had beaten him to it."[7] Even more: it would be necessary to acknowledge that "a psychotechnical analysis of a great thinker and a champion boxer would probably show their cunning, courage, precision and technique, and the speed of their reactions in their respective fields to be the same" (and it would also be necessary not to underestimate "how many major qualities are bought into play in clearing a hedge").[8]

But to Ulrich's eyes, which were just recently opened, the boxer and the horse show even an advantage: "[T]heir performance and rank can be objectively measured, so that the best of them is really acknowledged as the best. This is why sports and strictly objective criteria have deservedly come to the forefront, displacing such obsolete concepts as genius and human greatness."[9] Games, we may say, are that territory of dreams in which, unlike what happens in everyday life, one either wins or loses, plain and simple. Sports are connected to this binary character—"yes / no"; to win or to lose against a rival or, eminently, against oneself—to the display of psychophysical skills that are most appreciated by modern individuals. It is not odd, we might conclude with Ulrich, that sports should occupy such a prominent place in the consciousness of the mass societies of the twentieth century.

Here, I speculate, the novel and the destiny of its author—the life and death of Musil—converge. Like Ulrich, Musil, who had served in the military before turning first to physics and then to literature, devoted "one hour daily . . . a twelfth of a day's conscious life . . . to keep a trained body in the condition of a panther alert for any adventure."[10] Also like Ulrich, he had been educated to distrust—himself before anyone else.

Let us now imagine a man, somewhat older, who devotes an hour each day in solitude to an exhausting physical exercise (let us think of gymnastics, jogging, or swimming). Evidently, his body is not the same every day. There are occasions (let us suppose that our man slept badly, committed some gastronomical, alcoholic, or amatory excess, or that he simply caught an unspecified virus) in which it seems to request a pause in its demanding routine. Nevertheless, and except in the agonies of pain or pleasure (always too late), the body can no longer demand nor give anything to a man without qualities. The body saturated with signification (female, or literally hysteric body, as psychoanalysis, that typically Kakanian invention, would say) is also the channel through which power can make its way until it reaches the soul, with the weapons of pleasure or pain. For Musil, however, the body of the modern individual—free and stoical, the product of a social process of "objectification" whose prototype is sports—is bound to lack signification: it is no more than an indifferent notation in the "book of the world" imagined by his contemporary and fellow-*Kakanian* Ludwig Wittgenstein.[11] In other words, for a subject educated in suspicion, as Musil was (as Ulrich is, eternally ruminating in the pages of *The Man without Qualities*), it is no longer possible to know if it is the body that asks for a truce, or if it is mere laziness, indulgence, or scarcity of will. The only certainty that remains is the abstract measure: three hundred sit-ups, running five kilometers, seventy laps in the pool . . .

Musil died suddenly on April 5, 1942, during his daily session of calisthenics. It is said that, when his dead body was found shortly after, his face expressed "mockery and slight surprise."[12]

The Utopia of Exact Living

Musil's death—sudden and lacking witnesses who might provide pathetic or miserable details—is a metaphysical death, which took place in the name of what Ulrich calls "the utopia of exact living" in one of his reflections. This utopia would consist in taking "those daytime hours they call not their life but their profession"[13] out of their confinement, the attitude that characterizes the practical life of scientists, businessmen, administrators, sportsmen, and technicians. More precisely,

> to cut down to the minimum the moral expenditure (of whatever kind) that accompanies all our actions, to satisfy ourselves with being moral only in those exceptional cases where it really counts, but otherwise not to think differently from the way we do about standardizing pencils or screws. Perhaps not much good would be done that way, but some things would be done better; there would be no talent left, only genius; the washed-out prints that develop from the pallid resemblance of actions to virtues would disappear from the image of life; in their place we would have these virtues' intoxicating fusion in holiness. In short, from every ton of morality a milligram of an essence would be left over, a millionth part of which is enough to yield an enchanting joy.[14]

However, the moral minimalism of the utopia of exact living is far from exciting to the sensible men who inspire it. "This man," Musil remarks, "given to taking everything seriously and without bias, is biased to the point of abhorrence against the idea of taking himself seriously, and there is, alas, no doubt that he would regard the utopia of himself as an immoral experiment on persons engaged in serious business."[15] It is as if, paradoxically, the everyday sensibility of bourgeois existence were inhabited by a principle of insaneness that secretly rules over it. As in the psychology of neurosis, the bourgeois psyche would fruitlessly attempt to protect itself from this principle by raising prohibitions, which would be immediately overcome inasmuch as one would recognize in them the trace, the phantom of what was purportedly excluded.

The Musilian formula of an "utopia of exact living," bordering the oxymoron (can exactitude leave room for the utopian excess?); the promise of a disturbing unification of virtues in *sanctity*; the messianic hope that seems to be the secret and paradoxical engine behind "the point of view of exactitude"; within all this is unveiled the principle of insanity that lurks under the smooth surface of modern everydayness.[16] What, at bottom, does this principle consist in? A reflection on modern science should allow us to go deeper into this question.

The Man without Qualities provides elements for this reflection. Science is presented there as animated by a demonic drive, similar to that which, "looking at a beautifully glazed, luxuriantly curved vase," feels "a nasty itch . . . at the thought of smashing it to bits with a single blow of one's stick."[17] Nasty itch; drive to make the *extraordinary* a modality of the *ordinary* understood as ontologically primordial: to produce form—complexity, order, difference—out of the blind interaction of simple and undifferentiated elements; of the accumulation of infinitesimal variations whose slow sedimentation would constitute the "base" origin of the aureole of necessity (substantiality) often displayed by things. This violence (a sort of modern protest against the tyranny of the existent) would attest "the peculiar predilection of scientific thinking for mechanical, statistical, and physical explanations that have, as it were, the heart cut out of them":

> The scientific mind sees kindness only as a special form of egotism; brings emotions into line with glandular secretions; notes that eight or nine tenths of a human being consists of water; explains our celebrated moral freedom as an automatic mental by-product of free trade; reduces beauty to good digestion and the proper distribution of fatty tissue; graphs the annual statistical curves of births and suicides to show that our most intimate personal decisions are programmed behavior; sees a connection between ecstasy and mental disease; equates the anus and the mouth as the rectal and the oral openings at either end of the same tube—such ideas, which expose the trick, as it were, behind the magic of human illusions, can always count on a kind of prejudice in their favor as being impeccably scientific.[18]

It is possible to date the demystifying prejudice of modern science back to Galileo, with his abandonment of the aspiration to unravel the intrinsic rationality of nature characteristic of Aristotelian science in favor of quantification. The truth is that for Modernity, whose first steps are already recognizable in Galileo, reason and nature have come to be incommensurable elements. Even if the book of the universe is written in mathematical characters, as in Galileo's famous image, the real as such has become illegible.[19] Regarding the radical intellectual revolution of the seventeenth century, of which Galileo is a central figure, Alexander Koyré writes:

> This scientific and philosophical revolution—it is indeed impossible to separate the philosophical from the purely scientific aspects of this process: they are interdependent and closely linked together—can be described roughly as bringing forth the destruction of the Cosmos, that is, the disappearance, from philosophically and scientifically valid concepts, of the conception of the world as a finite, closed, and hierarchically ordered whole (a whole in which the hierarchy of value determined the hierarchy and structure of being, rising from the dark, heavy and imperfect earth to the higher and higher perfection of the stars and heavenly spheres), and its replacement by an indefinite and even infinite universe which is bound together by the ideality of its fundamental components and laws, and in which all these components are placed on the same level of being. This, in turn, implies the discarding by scientific thought of all considerations based upon value-concepts, such as perfection, harmony, meaning and aim, and finally the utter devalorization of being, the divorce of the world of value and the world of facts.[20]

The question of the legibility of the real concerns the relationship between words (concepts), which constitute the "medium" of thinking, and things. This is a metaphysical question, undecidable, insofar as its answer would require an observer situated outside the magic circle of existence (to whom, on the other hand, the same problem would be posed anew). But the question is indispensable, insofar as diverging models of legitimation in the ethical-political realm (in which ideas become intertwined with human pain and frequently acquire their deadly materiality) follow from its answer. Indeed, from the thesis of the legibility of the book of the universe follows the possibility of its "translation" in terms of ethical-political norms—of a ladder of "pious works" that those who are faithful are to climb, thus justifying the pain of existence and securing salvation.

But there where theology and medieval metaphysics had reached their utmost expression (in the idea of a *logos*, of a cosmological master plan that could not but be commensurable with human reason), the nominalism of the late Middle Ages, further projected into the historical stage by the Reformation, descried a relapse into paganism. An intelligible divinity, they argued, must be an anthropomorphic monstrosity, an idol. There is no translator, and thus no mediator, between the individual and a transcendence turned opaque, concealed. The uncertain task of interpreting the Scripture is reserved to the individual, and only to him. In this way, the individual becomes subject (*subjectum*, ground): the only and problematic source of order and intelligibility, as well as the vanishing point toward the modern, abyssal alterity of the real, of which he is a potential prey and witness. Here, the well-known episode of April 18, 1521, in the Diet of Worms, finds its place: Luther, facing the demand of Emperor Charles V for a retraction, rejects any authority beyond his own conscience.[21] And from this death or retraction of God (a God that ceases to be the warrantor of the commensurability of being and thinking) follows the emergence, or rather the legitimation, of instrumental spheres of action and self-affirmation, such as techno-science and the market.

The idea of the complete intelligibility of the real reached its most developed expression in the physics and metaphysics that medieval scholastics extracted from Aristotle through a Platonizing reading. In this medieval Aristotle, genres and natural species are not just arbitrary taxonomic constructions (pragmatically valid, we would say), nor are they, as in Nietzsche or the second Wittgenstein, the sediment of practices, of life-forms slowly placed and hypostasized into language. On the contrary: in their universality, under which individual differences remain sublimated, genres constitute the very life of nature (*physis*). The intelligible character of beings transpires in their form (*eidos*); however, in the case of *physis*, such form is not the result of any external intervention. Therefore, it is even possible that the metaphor of the legibility of the world does not do justice to the organic character, that is, to the concrete universality of the forms of the medieval universe. Indeed, as the Egyptian king Thamus observes in a famous anecdote that Socrates mentions in the *Phaedro*, writing already assumes that a world of living forms has been left behind. "Father of writing," Thamus says to god Theuth—a prolific inventor: chess seems to be indebted to him as well—who has come to offer him such a prodigious invention, "it will introduce forgetfulness into the soul of those who learn it: they will not practice using their memory because they will put their trust in writing, which is external and depends on signs that belong to others, instead of trying to remember from the inside, completely on their own. You have not discovered a potion for remembering, but for reminding."[22]

The universe of the Middle Ages is one in which natural forms keep a perfect record of the differences sublimated in them. It constitutes a kind of living memory, an extraordinary animal in which, as Thamus wanted, *traces* have not yet been dissociated from their *spirit*. To this formidable living memory (whose least improper expression, I speculate, would be nonverbal representation: the visual image, music), Modernity opposes the gray severity of writing: the abstract universality of a culture of the book, in which the possibility of reestablishing the life of the spirit, of reanimating the flame out of the ashes preserved in its pages, depends at each moment on interpretation, which is capable "of awakening reminiscences." Modern freedom, as shown by the episode of Luther in Worms, is primordially freedom of interpretation. But interpretation can only be inserted there where memory leaves cracks, where the crushing weight of the living totality has yielded to the gray lightness of writing. From there, Modernity remains thrown into an infinite interpretation—into the infinite of interpretation, which bestows its specific dignity to the Modern Age.

In any case, from that point on, it will be difficult to eschew the issue of violence, of the *forgetfulness* that universality would exert upon the particular—violence and forgetfulness whose conscience and corresponding discontent constitute the patrimony of the ubiquitous nominalism of Modernity ("no one says 'I am a nominalist,' because no one is anything else," as Borges writes).[23] To this nominalism, let us say, reality appears as the boiling of an infinite singularity,[24] a singularity that contrasts with the arbitrariness, the poor universality of language. Thus, Modernity will be split into two wings. A memorious wing (here lies the principle of insanity that lurks behind Musil's utopia of exact living), whose protest, aimed precisely against the tyranny of *reified* being ("all reification is forgetfulness," Adorno asserts), inexorably concludes with silence and paralysis. The paradigmatic expression of this silence and paralysis is the Angel of History, the figure imagined by Walter Benjamin in the ninth thesis of his *Theses on the Philosophy of History*: where others see a causal chain (History), the Angel cannot but see a heap of ruins that raise up to the sky. The other wing attempts to somehow reconcile singularity with universality, raising it to the extraordinary level of a "concrete universal."[25]

For this wing of Modernity, concrete universality can no longer be the fabulous *extraordinary animal*, the living memory of the Aristotelian cosmos. It is to be rather an *extraordinary work*: the paradoxical, shattered attempt through self-affirmational activity to take off from the nominalist cultural ground, which at the same time provides the only nourishment for the modern self-affirmation. We are dealing now with the workmanship of history and with art.

Chapter 2

The Extraordinary, History

Kant stands at the center of the intellectual and political landscape of the modern age.

On the one hand, he succeeded in assimilating and superseding the ideas of those who would become his predecessors: Hobbes, Descartes, Leibniz, Hume, Locke, and so on. On the other hand, starting with Herder and Fichte, and going through German idealism and then through Schopenhauer and Nietzsche, up to twentieth-century phenomenology and the so called "neo-Kantian" philosophy, the Frankfurt School and French philosophy, the philosophical discourse of Modernity has remained under the spell of the ideas that Kant bequeathed to his posterity. And, although academic specialists tend to split his work into three different bodies (Cognition, Morals, Aesthetics), its deep significance is political, as implied by the very first paragraphs in the prologue to the first edition of his *Critique of Pure Reason*: How are the unsociable and inherently skeptical individuals scattered throughout the land by the collapse of the closed and hierarchically ordered medieval world to be made sociable, in the absence of any transcendent and (from a modern viewpoint) external and heteronomous law?[1]

In fact, each one of Kant's three Critiques explores this question from a different angle. Modern unsociality as a philosophical problem was already at the center of Thomas Hobbes's institution of sovereignty as the *ur*-dialectical product of his state of nature. The foundations of this formation, as the structure of Hobbes's works shows very clearly, are cognitive and moral.

However, it is only in Kant's *Critique of Pure Reason* that we find the in-depth exploration of the essence of modern cognition that Hobbes and the empiricist tradition had been unable to carry to its completion. This is the task of Kant's critique:

> The critique . . . which derives all decisions from the ground-rules of its own constitution, whose authority no one can doubt, grants us the peace of a state of law in which we should not conduct our controversy except by **due process**. What brings the quarrel in the state of nature to an end is a **victory**, of which both sides boast, although for the most part there follows only an uncertain peace, arranged by an authority in the middle; but in the state of law it is the **verdict**, which, since it goes to the origin of the controversies themselves, must secure a perpetual peace.[2]

Kant's practical philosophy goes even deeper: political sovereignty has to be complemented by a structure of subjectivity capable of putting the unsocial individual's infinite impulses under the control of an internal sovereign. A vast number of Kant's essays, from his *Critique of Practical Reason* up to his later works, such as *Religion within the Boundaries of Mere Reason* (1793), aim to show how this controlling instance can arise in the absence of a heteronomous morality. In these essays, we learn that modern autonomy should not be reduced to mere freedom of choice. This freedom is just the executive side of the will; its legislative side, however, commands that passions and impulses, considered heteronomous, be placed under the control of a purely rational instance. But these two somehow contradictory faces of the will (*Willkür* versus *Wille*, as Kant calls them using a distinction in the German language) find their unity within a disposition (*Gesinnung*) that, although made of an individual's inherited traits and biographic experience, is a realization of autonomy, as long as the individual willingly acknowledges it as the product of his choice.[3]

Finally, as Kant observes in his *Critique of Judgment*, most of our cognitive approach to nature consists not in applying concepts to phenomena, but rather in inductively, reflectively searching for concepts. Thus, the approach is grounded on the a priori assumption of an intrinsic commensurability between our cognitive faculties and external reality. Aesthetic pleasure and beauty suggest that this may be the case and make us confident that the modern production of a humanized world is a feasible task. Nonetheless, in the final analysis, the required commensurability calls for a teleology of nature that cannot be asserted by human understanding; it can only be postulated in the manner of an "as if," as the content of a minimalist "religion within the boundaries of mere reason."

In any case, universal history is the stage in which the drama of modern sociability takes place and in which these principles have to display their effectiveness. In fact, in Kant's *Idea for a Universal History with a Cosmopolitan Aim*, history represents an enlightened mediating instance between the facticity of social being and the normativity inherent to universality. In the face of the dispersion and irrationality of human behaviors ("everything in the large is woven together out of folly, childish vanity, often also out of childish malice and the rage of destruction"),[4] Kant relies on the idea of a secret "aim of Nature," which would find its fulfillment in the species and its political organization. Thus, we read in his Second Proposition: "*In the human being* (as the only rational creature on earth), *those predispositions whose goal is the use of his reason were to develop completely only in the species, but not in the individual.*"[5] And then, in the Fifth Proposition: "A society in which *freedom under external laws* can be encountered combined in the greatest possible degree with irresistible power, i.e. a perfectly *just civil constitution*, must be the supreme problem of nature for the human species."[6]

For the sake of reason's glory, that secret aim should be capable of integrating even those phenomena that are opposed to it. Thus, they come to be mere appearances, means that Nature would require in order to fulfil its essential plan. In this way, wars become "only so many attempts (not, not be sure, in the aims of human beings, but yet in the aim of nature) to bring about new relationships between states," which ends up in a "civil commonwealth."[7] And unsociability (which leads man "to direct everything so as to get his own way")[8] morphs into "social unsociability."

Kant has written a kind of godless theodicy, apparently capable of recycling or "adjusting" (theodicy: *justice* of God) waste (thus, for example, the innocent victim), of forgetting it for the sake of the species, the medium through which "the aim of Nature" spreads into human society. Nevertheless, and in agreement with the profound logic of transcendental philosophy, it is now an "as if" theodicy, a sort of fiction whose ground can only be pragmatic.[9] In fact, regarding the first two principles of his theodicy, Kant writes:

> For if we depart from that principle, then we no longer have a lawful nature but a purposelessly playing nature; and desolate chance takes the place of the guideline of reason . . . Because

otherwise the natural predispositions would have to be regarded for the most part as in vain and purposeless; which would remove all practical principles and thereby bring nature, whose wisdom in the judgment of all remaining arrangements must otherwise serve as a principle, under the suspicion that in the case of the human being alone it is a childish play.[10]

These two principles refer to the finalist character of Nature and to the primacy of the species over the individual. Nonetheless, their ultimate foundations are negative and fragile. Thus, it should not be surprising that, in the Ninth Proposition, Kant acknowledges that with his justifying efforts "only a *novel* could be brought about,"[11] whose truth would have a rather pragmatic status: "[I]f, nevertheless, one may assume that nature does not proceed without a plan or final aim even in the play of human freedom, then this idea could become useful,"[12] says Kant, thus showing his game, that is, the pragmatic "secret clause" through which his critical project arises, at the edge of paradox.[13]

In its turn, Hegelian philosophy can be understood as the attempt to actually write such a novel, which was only dubiously drafted by Kant. It is not in vain that in its center lies, as a fundamental piece, that *Bildungsroman* (educational novel) titled *Phenomenology of Spirit*. There, indeed, Hegel attempts the reconciliation of the universal and the particular in a universality capable of absorbing each and every singularity as a moment of its own becoming.

If we pay attention to the writings of the Frankfurt period (1797–1800), gathered in *The Spirit of Christianity and Its Fate*, it is possible to speculate that the horror in the face of abstract universality—whose historical figure is Judaism—would constitute the primordial scene that feeds Hegel's thought in its unfolding. Eloquent and violent passages testify to this horror. Already with Noah and the Flood, Judaism would have acquired "the most prodigious disbelief in nature,"[14] its spirit would have become "the spirit of self-maintenance in strict opposition to everything—the product of [its] thought raised to be the unity dominant over the nature which he regarded as infinite and hostile."[15] Abraham "wanted *not* to love, wanted to be free by not loving,"[16] and "the whole world [he] regarded as simply his opposite; if he did not take it to be a nullity, he looked on it as sustained by the God who was alien to it. Nothing in nature was supposed to have any part in God; everything was simply under God's mastery."[17] The horror reaches its dramatic climax when Hegel refers to Pompey's frustration as he penetrates the Temple's *Sanctasantorum*: expecting to "gaze on a Being as an object for his devotion," he would have found himself "in an empty room."[18]

Under the traits of the mosaic cult (the ban on images: "the infinite subject had to be invisible, since everything visible is something restricted";[19] the abstract severity of the Law) we can recognize the very contemporary Kantian *Moralität* and its purported abstraction, as well as modern science and the Protestant creed, in whose theology Hegel had been raised. These are the immediate experiential items that trigger the *horror vacui* that the philosopher transfers to his character Pompey. Nevertheless, is not a matter of indifference that the figure chosen by Hegel is precisely that of the "people of the Book." Indeed, as we have noted above in connection to the metaphor of the legibility of the world and the precautions of Egyptian king Thamus, writing and the specter of abstraction are associated.

In the *Phenomenology of Spirit*, however, Hegel has disregarded with remarkable imprudence the Egyptian king's admonition. On the one hand, it is a work that does not conceal its conceit of constituting an extraordinary scriptural object, a sort of Absolute Book: we would be dealing, no more and no less, with the Spirit's autobiography (its *Odyssey*, as Hegel himself suggests in the prologue). However, it cannot be but one among the books that awaken Thamus's suspicion—one among the infinite entries in the Borgesian library; a fairly extensive collection of material characters (483 pages in the Spanish translation by Wenceslao Roces that lies on my desk), whose very extension evidences its finitude, its arbitrariness, its misery.[20] Thus, at the very moment of its fulfillment, philosophy is paradoxically disclosed as a variety of writing: of fantastic literature, or of the "fable of individuals" (as Borges defines the modern novel),[21] to whose catalogue of inventions the Hegelian Absolute Knowledge would belong. Indeed, throughout the *Phenomenology* we witness the thorough weaving process of a universality that, having dialectically overcome the particular moments of its becoming, would be exonerated of the accusation of obliviousness. Absolute Knowledge is the figure that Hegel suggestively describes precisely in terms of a memory without loss:

> As this fulfilment consists in perfectly knowing what it is, in knowing its substance, this knowing is its withdrawal into itself in which it abandons its outer existence and gives its existential shape over to *recollection*. Thus absorbed in itself, it is sunk in the night of its self-consciousness; but in that night its vanished outer existence is preserved, and this transformed existence—the

former one, but now reborn of the Spirit's knowledge—is the new existence, a new world and a new shape of Spirit. In the immediacy of this new existence the Spirit has to start afresh to bring itself to maturity as if, for it, all that preceded were lost and it had learned nothing from the experience of the earlier Spirits. But *recollection*, the inwardizing, of that experience, *has preserved it* and is the inner being, and in fact the higher form of the substance. So although this Spirit starts afresh and apparently from its own resources to bring itself to maturity, it is none the less on a higher level that it starts. . . . The goal, Absolute Knowing, or Spirit that knows itself as Spirit, *has for its path the recollection of the Spirits as they are in themselves* and as they accomplish the organization of their realm.[22]

But "the night of self-consciousness" has turned out to be more complex than Hegel had foreseen. Immersed in it, modern reason does not succeed in rescuing the "recollections of the Spirits as they are in themselves"; it is rather lost in a labyrinth without origin or end. The maximization of memory leads to dispersion and to the violent destruction of communicative language. Literature after Hegel provides plenty of examples of that. Remarkable among them are the novels of James Joyce: *Ulysses*, with its excessive attempt to fictionalize a day of experience ("splendid agony of a literary genre," says Borges), to draw a map that coincides with the territory it maps; *Finnegans Wake*, in which the quest for literary realism ends up exploding language. *In Search of Lost Time*, Proust's novel—in the way it is read by Walter Benjamin—constitutes the document of the destabilizing irruption of unconscious memory (a memory not yet woven by the forgetfulness inherent to reason), which drags writing in its whirlwind.

Bouvard and Pécuchet, Gustave Flaubert's posthumous novel, may be understood as a ferocious parody of Hegel's *Phenomenology of Spirit*. It is about two humble copyists that decide to retire, move to the countryside, and, through study and practice, acquire an absolute knowledge. Their failure, the confusion that results each time the two friends try to fulfill their projects, cannot be attributed to them, but rather to the very knowledge they try to assimilate. Indeed, specialists—this is their defining trait—disagree: thus, for each truth dwelling on the bookshelves that Bouvard and Pécuchet thoroughly look over, there is, here or there in the same library, a countertruth. Bouvard and Pécuchet experience the Babelic character of knowledge.

Driven by its own internal dynamics, the philosophical fable of individuals dissolves into a kind of mystical fog. As mystical traditions know, the claim to an Absolute Book—to the extraordinary as Book—can only be upheld insofar as it contracts into a virtual point: into a pretext, against and from which the infinitude of interpretation is performed.[23] However, "philosophers have hitherto only interpreted the world in various ways; the point is to change it," as Marx says in his *Theses on Feuerbach*. In other words, given that Hegelian historiography has failed, its promise of human emancipation has now moved to factual history, with the transformative forces harbored by it—to the historical work as such, beyond all writing—with the prospect of finding in it the modern equivalent of the extraordinary Aristotelian animal.

Indeed, nature has been already disenchanted, objectified. Hegel says: "Organic Nature has no history; it falls from its universal, from life, directly into the singleness of existence."[24] In other words, assuming that this expression is still meaningful, the *immanent order* of nature has become unfathomable to reason. In their universality, the genres of scholastic theology made up the very life of *physis*, providing conceptual universality with the model of a concrete universality; however, there is no place for them in the disenchanted nature of Modernity. Nonetheless, at the very foundation of Marx's theoretical project, we find an impulse that, without transgressing the modern ban on the enchantment of nature (*malgré* Engels, there is no dialectics of nature in Marx), reaches out toward the Aristotelian idea of genre, in order to ground in it the idea of history as an extraordinary work aimed at reconciliation. Indeed, in Marx's *Economic and Philosophical Manuscripts of 1844*, we find a peculiar use of the concept of genre (*Gattung*). The peculiarity consists in that Marx claims that only the human being is *Gattungswesen*, capable of belonging to a genre—and this not by virtue of its naturalness but, on the contrary, of its transformative praxis: "[I]n his fashioning of the objective man really proves himself to be a *species-being* [*Gattungswesen*]. Such production is his active species-life."[25]

More precisely, Marx had inherited this peculiarity from the Young Hegelians (Strauss, Ruge, Bauer, Stirner, Nauwerck, Feuerbach), and specially from the latter's critique of Christianity, which Marx deeply admired.[26] In their essays, these left-wing Hegelians had turned the dialectical logic of their master against his later writings, and specially against his *Philosophy of Right*. In these writings, in the interest of preserving social order, Hegel had chosen to bring the all-dissolving task of his dialectics to a halt. He believed that, with the emergence of the Prussian state and its paternal protection of civil society, which is the sphere of unsocial private interests, the works of the Spirit were basically completed.

Feuerbach's participation in the undoing of the Hegelian legacy is contained in his writings on religion. He shows there that the figure of God is nothing but an inverted, abstract, and alienated image of humankind's species-being and of its main power, that is, the power to produce itself and its world. The task of a critique of religion would then consist in taking that power back from God and restoring it to a liberated humankind. Feuerbach writes:

> Hence this attribute of the species—productive activity—is assigned to God; that is, realised and made objective as divine activity. But every special determination, every mode of activity is abstracted, and only the fundamental determination, which, however, is essentially human, namely, production of what is external to self, is retained. God has not, like man, produced something, in particular, this or that, but all things; his activity is absolutely universal, unlimited.[27]

Other Young Hegelians, like David Strauss and Arnold Ruge, followed Feuerbach's steps but shifted his critique of alienation toward the state and political society. Marx was even more radical: he understood that self-productive human activity was not confined to the sphere of ideas but, rather, material production in the real, historical world of economic labor and production. Consequently, critique should be aimed at political economy. In his celebrated *Economic and Philosophical Manuscripts* (1844), he wrote:

> It is therefore in his fashioning of the objective that man really proves himself to be a species-being. Such production is his active species-life. Through it nature appears as his work and his reality. The object of labour is therefore the objectification of the species life of man: for man reproduces himself not only intellectually, in his consciousness, but actively and actually, and he can therefore contemplate himself in a world he himself has created. In tearing away the object of his production from man, estranged labour therefore tears away from him his species-life, his true species-objectivity, and transforms his advantage over animals into the disadvantage that his inorganic body, nature, is taken from him.[28]

Marx sought to build a bridge between Aristotelian metaphysics and political economy. The Hegelian sacred history of the constitution of Absolute Knowledge, in whose flawless memory each and every particular moment is preserved without loss, is subordinated in Marx to profane history, to the history of the concrete devices through which universality and generic man have been produced. These devices are labor, market economy, capitalist relations of production, and money. In its "apparent" irreducibility, individuality would only be a moment in a dialectical becoming: insofar as the protohuman animal hominizes itself historically and forms itself concretely, it acquires a genre. At the end of history, we discover that this acquisition was always the real force, the necessity that acted behind the scenes. Thus, at the core of this history, there would be no opposition between the individual and humanity—the progress of the genre would coincide with the progress of each one: "[T]he object of labour is therefore the *objectification of the species-life of man*."[29] Along the way, there are obstacles to be removed: "In tearing away the object of his production from man, estranged labour therefore tears away from him his *species-life*, his true species-objectivity."[30]

Marx strived to reduce all alienation to alienated labor.[31] This way, it was possible for him to make a gigantic "pious work" of human history,[32] whose positivity (its concrete, material traits) would be dissolved and redeemed in a universality without waste. Nevertheless, at the very moment when "real socialisms" purported to realize this extraordinary aspiration, the nominalist consciousness of Modernity could not but discern in it a consummated form of forgetfulness, a false reconciliation. The promise was the production of an extraordinary work, the reenchantment of life emerging from the very guts of Modernity. However, the positivity of such a work, its limited here and now, the same dense veil—a whole Wall—of apologetic discourses that attempted to disguise it, betrayed its misery. The modern public showed itself disappointed, and from then on it preferred to turn its gaze away, toward the box of myths, television.

Chapter 3

The Extraordinary, Myth

The nominalism of Modernity has opened up an abyss between facts and values, between *is* and *ought*. This abyss has been canonically articulated in the tradition of Anglo Saxon thought, from Hume to Moore. "From an is does not follow an ought," Hume had written in his *Treatise on Human Nature*. Wittgenstein, halfway between Cambridge and Vienna, excluded from his "book of the world" the propositions of ethics, which were to be confined to silence.[1] Now, this interdiction is generally understood as referring only to ethics—in fact, such is the terrain in which it is originally formulated. However, it is possible to extend it until it encompasses all universality. Indeed, every universality is normative: concepts, words, are not learned by induction nor applied after empirical verification. Rather, as Wittgenstein thoroughly shows in *Philosophical Investigations*, they are figures in a game (the language game of speaking about this or that), forms that are applied *a priori* to experience and that, consequently, do not merely say that something is, but rather how it must be in order to correspond to some of the entries in the encyclopedia of a certain linguistic community. When I claim that the animal that just ran by me is a dog, I am not making an empirical report (which, in any case, could not but leave the differences out: in good empirical rigor, the dog at three-fourteen, seen from the side, is not the same as the dog at a quarter past three, seen from the front): I am forgetting differences ("to think is not to forget differences"),[2] "producing" the dog so as to be able to speak. With all the violence that Modernity acknowledges in this, the existent is produced and reproduced in language, and although this tyranny is not at all foreign to the essence of modern subjectivity, it is also inherent to it that, in its self-affirmation, the modern subject should resent it. Thus, silence ("what we cannot speak about we must pass over in silence"),[3] which seemed to affect only ethics—which seemed to be confined to its own sphere—violates this sanitary barrier and expands toward language as a whole.

"Human beings, in order to be what they are, must believe that they are more than they are" (Musil). In this paradoxical distance—from "what they are" to "what they are": a distance always crossed, always reproduced—the essence of what is human is at stake. Man is *Gattungswesen*, "*capable of having a genre*," but such capacity vanishes precisely to the extent that genre, essence, turns into full presence, possession.

The divinity was traditionally the provider of the required supplement of entity. When, with Modernity, this role was left vacant, man was left immersed in his empirical being, in that which strictly *is*. Conversely, only at this point could his own-most being make itself present to him as unconditioned (nonconditioned: what is conditioned is now fallen, uncertain, and inessential), extraordinary.[4] However, man is the *zoon logon echon*, the Aristotelian linguistic animal, and if human essence hangs uncertainly from above, the same is to happen with language. To speak presupposes universality, ought: a bridge to the extraordinary. In its most elemental form, this bridge is built with myth, which Enlightened Modernity disenchants. Nonetheless, myth does not disappear, nor could it disappear. Rather, it goes underground—or otherwise it lives a degraded public existence in mass culture. In fact, the world of mass media is populated with myths: they constitute the decomposed remainders of the wreck of traditional society, which keep on circulating, adrift.

It is in relation to the myths of mass culture (cars and design objects, news and sentimental magazines, movie stars, and famous figures) that Roland Barthes developed his *mythology*, his critical semiology of myth.[5] Myth, whose operation Barthes's analysis dismounts in detail, is that semiotic device by virtue of which the existent exerts its tyranny; that device—"a theft of language," Barthes would say—through which things lose the memory of their profane history and are imposed to us as nature, as value. Myth, the linguistic representative of reification, of forgetfulness, transforms facts into values, "history into nature."[6] "[M]yth has the task of giving an historical intention a natural justification, and making contingency appear eternal . . . Myth is constituted by the loss of the historical quality of things: in it, things lose the memory that they once were made."[7] Thus, facing the cover of a glossy Parisian magazine from the 1950s, *Paris-Match*, which shows a black soldier saluting the French flag—this is Barthes's example—a mythical reading comes to the fore (the legitimation of the French colonial imperiality), above the here and now of the situation impressed upon the filmic sheet. Empirics is not negated by myth, but rather sublimated. It constitutes something like its reserve of evidence, the "alibi" that allows it to present itself precisely as nature: "The signification of myth is constituted by a sort of constantly moving turnstile which presents alternately the meaning of the signifier and its form, a language-object and a metalanguage, a purely signifying and purely imagining consciousness,"[8] in such a way that, more precisely:

> Myth is speech *stolen and restored.* Only, speech which is restored is no longer quite that which was stolen: when it was brought back, it was not put exactly in its place. It is this brief act of larceny, this moment taken for a surreptitious faking, which gives mythical speech its benumbed look.[9]

However, where does the critical thinker, the mythologist, speak from? How would it be possible for him to avoid the mythical turnstile? The difficulty of this question is insinuated in what we have already said about myth. Indeed, the aspiration of the mythologist is, inevitably, to situate himself at the level of a "language-object," of a purely signifying consciousness. Referring to the reading and deciphering of myth, Barthes inquires further into the question. He writes:

> If I focus on a full signifier . . . I undo the signification of the myth, and I receive the latter as an imposture: the saluting Negro becomes the *alibi* of French imperiality. This type of focusing is that of the mythologist: he deciphers the myth, he understands a distortion.[10]

The full signifier would be that which, in its plenitude, does not leave that gap of ambiguity, of semantic emptiness through which the mythical *poiesis* infiltrates. But how could a signifier be full? (What would be the univocal meaning of a picture such as that of *Paris-Match*?). Symptomatically, Barthes's answer relies on a language in which things themselves would take up the word: a sort of language of the Genesis, prior to the linguistic dispersion of Babel: while "myth always comes under the heading of metalanguage . . . , trained to *celebrate* things, and no longer to '*act* them,' " "the language-object . . . '*speaks things.*' "[11]

In Barthes, this language of things is associated with the proletarian's speech (thus, if I am a woodcutter, "I 'speak the tree,' I do not speak about it"), the speech of the oppressed, whose surrogate, we would say, is the mythologist. And beyond Barthes's problematic attempt to situate his mythological knowledge on the left, it is essential that, as he says, "the speech of the oppressed is real . . . it is quasi-unable to lie."[12] The signifying fullness of the object-language, to which the mythologist aspires, associates it with mathematical language and with poetic language. In the case of the former, it is a language that "cannot be distorted, it has taken all possible precautions against *interpretation*: no parasitical signification can worm itself into it."[13] Contemporary poetry, in its turn, would be "a *regressive semiological system*. . . . Its ideal . . . would be to reach not the meaning of words, but the meaning of things themselves."[14] The poetic resistance to myth, Barthes adds further down, ends up in silence, in "a murder of Literature as signification":[15] in a kind of crime of passion, in which language is annihilated because of an excessive love for it. Nevertheless—and this admonishment could not but turn against the mythologist—"when the meaning is too full for myth to be able to invade it, myth goes around it, and carries it away bodily. . . . Myth can reach everything, corrupt everything, and even the very act of refusing oneself to it."[16] Myth responds to the resistance of the full signifier, we would say, by proposing a kind of *liaison dangereuse*: "[W]hoever here resists completely yields completely,"[17] Barthes asserts. The myths of the scientist ("Einstein's brain") and of science ("$E=mc^2$"), as well as the myth of the poet, testify to this tendency. But, what about the myth of the mythologist? Barthes sees the danger: "[T]he best weapon against myth is perhaps to mystify it in its turn, and to produce an *artificial myth*: and this reconstituted myth will in fact be a mythology. Since myth robs language of something, why not rob myth?"[18] Nevertheless, this mythopoetic possibility, Nietzschean in a certain sense (more about Nietzsche later on), which Barthes sees realized in the Flaubert of *Bouvard and Pécuchet*, is no more than a digression in a text where the mood of the Enlightenment predominates, with the ensuing mythical-critical call to the extraordinary language that "speaks things."

The Barthesian language of things is related to the name in the mystical theory of the young Walter Benjamin ("the name is that through which nothing is communicated any longer and in which the language itself is communicated absolutely"), and also to the conception of language in the *Tractatus Logico-Philosophicus*. When he was nineteen years old, reading Francis Bacon's critique of the *idola* that capture consciousness (and anticipating the

Lord Chandos Letter, a document of the nominalist discontent in language published in 1902, on which I will comment later), the Viennese poet Hugo von Hofmannsthal left the following comment for the registry: "The concepts of language (*Begriffe der Sprache*) are *idola* of the same genre." The *Tractatus* is not understood if it is separated from the task of demystification of language undertaken by Bacon (which took place, suggestively, in the same Trinity College of Cambridge that would later be Wittgenstein's point of arrival), and continued by the Viennese generation of von Hofmannsthal, Krauss, and Mauthner, to which Wittgenstein belonged.

In their *Dialectic of Enlightenment*, Horkheimer and Adorno call attention to the manner in which modern reason recognizes its adversary, myth, not outside but within itself. They say:

> The latest logic denounces the words of language, which bear the stamp of impressions, as counterfeit coin that would be better replaced by neutral counters. The world becomes chaos, and synthesis salvation. . . . Causality was only the last philosophical concept on which scientific criticism tested its strength, because it alone of the old ideas still stood in the way of such criticism, the latest secular form of the creative principle. . . . [The categories] were left behind as *idola theatri* of the old metaphysics.[19]

This tendency is fulfilled in the *Tractatus*. "Superstition is nothing but belief in the causal nexus" can be read in Proposition 5.1361.[20] The *Tractatus* is transcendental philosophy (the "logical space," which is one of its central concepts, is the condition of possibility of the facts that make up the world), but turned against itself in a secularized way, and therefore reduced to its zero degree: there is nothing left but logical necessity ("and outside logic everything is accidental"),[21] and the very transcendental subject has been reduced to a virtual point, to a "limit of the world."[22] If causality is a superstition that reason must enlighten, it should pay much more attention to the resources of language that allow us to seamlessly construct mythical entities such as "the current King of France," as well as propositions with a deceitful empirical aspect, such as "the current King of France is bald." To exclude this possibility is the function of the "theory of descriptions," which Wittgenstein took from Russell. In his *Tractatus*, Wittgenstein deduced from this theory the logical necessity of the existence of certain semantic atoms, the names or simple objects whose nature is logical (that is, immune to myth) and which are to exist by themselves, aside from all empirical observation.

Thus, the Barthesian ideal of the full signifier, immune to mythical seduction, is fulfilled in the perfect language of the *Tractatus* (a quite paradoxical fulfillment: these signifiers are to be empirically empty; by contrast, regarding the signifiers endowed with empirical content, one never knows). The ideal of the language of the oppressed, "incapable of lying," is also fulfilled. Indeed, the logical atomism of the *Tractatus* leads to the definition of propositions with meaning as those having a true/false polarity. The goal, in the words of a commentator, is to "allow no possible situation to be such that we would deny that the proposition was right, was true, without *ipso facto* making it false."[23] Lies, by contrast, avoid this filter: they operate within the mythical knot, always at the threshold between the true and the false. But not only lies. Strictly speaking, only identity applies to the elements or simple names of the *Tractatus*: "A is A." To say that "A is B" presupposes indeed that somehow A yields to non-A: it presupposes a gap in identity, which is excluded by names or simple elements in their striving to make themselves immune to myth.

The ancient interdiction formulated by Parmenides rules over the Wittgensteinian or Barthesian *Ursprache*: from untainted being, only identity can be said—"being is" or, even better, "is." In the object-language of the mythologist, words reduplicate the real—or rather, they have sunk again into the muteness of things. The Kabbalah contains the disquieting hypothesis that, in the day of Redemption, words will set themselves loose from the serfdom of meaning and will turn "like stones in our mouths." Myth can be then understood as the temporal suspension and postponement of that catastrophic but inevitable event in which the word, a faint but extraordinary fluttering in the smooth surface of things, is reabsorbed into it.

Modernity requires myth in order to keep talking—this constitutes its deep dialectics. But it speaks primordially about its radical enterprise of disenchantment, and consequently, its complex dependency on myth necessarily constitutes its blind spot. Thus, in the modern world, myths are destined to live the degraded existence mentioned above in connection to mass culture—or otherwise, to put on masks that hide their true nature. One of the most suggestive representatives of myth mentioned by Barthes is that of the grammatical example, or paradigm *"ego nominor leo"* ("for I am called lion"). On the one hand, it is an example of a grammatical rule in Latin (concordance of the attribute). On the other, it is an "exemplar," a paradigm. A paradigm constitutes a kind of nonempirical consensus, that is, the outcome of the conversion of a mere empirical indication into a norm ("what Latin exemplarity distorts [Barthes says] is the naming of the lion, in all its contingency"),²⁴ with the mythical knot in the middle. This way, we can understand why Thomas S. Kuhn, when he had to explain the functioning of scientific communities, had to rely on this notion (*The Structure of Scientific Revolutions*). Indeed, science, as Popper had already understood in his critique of induction (*The Logic of Scientific Discovery*), does not operate inductively. Moreover, a scientific community is defined by a consensus, which could not be merely inductive, regarding certain objects and procedures. Without these objects and procedures (that is, at the mercy of *logos* in its raw state, not mythically cushioned), there would be no scientific language, but rather Babelic dispersion or mere tautology. In the last instance, as Kuhn himself shows when it comes to specifying the notion of paradigm, such notion contains both "the constellation of group commitments" and, mainly, the idea of "shared examples."²⁵

Kuhn's position is often close to the one of the "second Wittgenstein," and with good reasons. Indeed, in the *Philosophical Investigations*, Wittgenstein turned to considering the multiplicity of "games" that make up the "ancient city of language." He addressed there the nature of those elements of "language games" that, like the simple names in the *Tractatus*, cannot be negated (nor affirmed) without contradiction. The existence of these elements does not seem to be an empirical question but, rather, to be included metaphysically in their essence, which could not but exist. But it is no longer something sublime, crystalline, profound: "What looks as if it *had* to exist is part of the language."²⁶ These are the elements, the rules, the pieces through which different language games are played and that make up their deep grammar. Thus, if the game of measuring is played, the measuring standard (the meter-model kept in Paris) lacks itself measure: its existence, in connection to this game, does not belong to the *a posteriori* character of the empirical but to the *a priori* of the rule.

We are once again in front of the murky knot that leads from being to ought to be, of the more or less resigned acceptance of local myths (Kuhn's normal science and its paradigms; Wittgenstein's ancient city and its rules) through which the existing prolongs its tyranny but without which the atrocious promise of redemption mentioned above would reach its fulfillment. The enterprise of disenchanting the world, whose radical wing is modern science, consists ultimately (Foucault has seen it this way in his *History of Sexuality*) in the staging of a compulsion to speak of experience—to bring entities into presence by means of the word, with growing clarity and distinction. But the word is wrapped in a murky commerce with myth. In this way, the inner truth of the Enlightenment consists in myth, and, conversely, beyond any lineal contrast, myth is but a resource of enlightened reason—a ruse, we would say.²⁷ Thus, Modernity, which goes to the bottom of this experience (through Nietzsche's thought, for example), could be defined as a *knowledge regarding myths: mythology*. A knowledge for which myth would be a kind of specular double, the nocturnal side that such knowledge would require in order to develop later its auroral aspect: the dream of disenchanted humanity which, always at the edge of losing the word, would be in need of myth in order to retake it.

In this knowledge, Modernity reencounters its distant origin. Barthes's notion of myth thematizes the performative power of language—its mobilizing power, which enlightened reason cannot but see with distrust. Nevertheless, this performativity is what the West has thought in the classic notion of *mythos*, which alludes to a "magic of the word" that, in an oral culture, "stimulates its public to an affective communion with the dramatic actions recounted in the story"²⁸ and that the *logos* associated with writing seeks to invoke:

> By deliberately foregoing drama and the marvelous, the *logos* acts upon the mind at a different level from an operation involving *mimēsis* or emotional participation (*sumpatheia*) on the part of the audience. . . . It is only when it has thus assumed the written form that a discourse, divested of its mystery and, at the same time, of its suggestive force, loses the power to impose itself on others through the illusory but irrepressible constraint of *mimēsis*. Its status is thereby changed: It becomes something "common," in the sense that this term had in Greek political vocabulary. No longer is it the exclusive privilege of whoever possesses the gift of eloquence; now it belongs equally to all the members of the community.²⁹

Nevertheless, *mythos* and *logos* are connected in their origin:

> The Greek word *muthos* means formulated speech, whether it be a story, a dialogue, or the enunciation of a plan. So *muthos* belongs to the domain of *legein*, as such compound expressions as *mutholegein* and *muthologia* show, and does not originally stand in contrast to *logoi*, a term that has a closely related semantic significance and that is concerned with the different forms of what is said. Even when, in the forms of stories about the gods

or heroes, the words transmit a strong religious charge . . . *muthoi* can equally well be called *hieroi logoi*, sacred speeches.[30]

Thus, it will not be possible for *logos* to set itself free from the performativity (power of suggestion, mimetic magic) that constitutes the mark of its impure origin—not unless it relies on the Barthesian object-language, on the perfect language of the Genesis (another myth!): language in its zero-degree, equivalent to silence. The dialectic of Enlightenment, that is, of the self-referential *logos* implacably turned over and against itself in search of the mythical remainders that contaminate and constitute it, ends up then in silence: in the mystical ascesis to which we arrive, not by virtue of a weakening of reason, but rather of its rigorous implementation. Modernity, both in its critical wing and in its most positive and instrumental aspects, is animated by a mystical impulse: by a disproportionate desire for the extraordinary (perfect or original language, Absolute Book) that, from the shadows, presides its daily and sensible ceremonies.

In order to understand the deep mythical core of Modernity—regarding which there is no "freedom to err," following a magnificent expression by Father Ribadeneira, theologian and polemicist from the sixteenth century[31]—there is perhaps nothing better than reading closely Jacques Monod, the twentieth-century biologist who was awarded a Nobel Prize in 1965. In his book *Chance and Necessity*, Monod presents a strong critique of all animism, understood precisely as the positing of a commensurability, or an alliance ("the ancient covenant"), between being and thinking. He opposes to this animism the "austere censorship" that constitutes the "principle of objectivity."

> The cornerstone of the scientific method is the postulate that nature is objective. In other words, the *systematic* denial that "true" knowledge can be got at by interpreting phenomena in terms of final causes—that is to say, of "purpose" ("teleonomany and the principle of objectivity").[32]

However, Monod is aware that the postulate of objectivity is a postulate: "ironclad, pure, forever undemonstrable. For it is obviously impossible to imagine an experiment which could prove the *nonexistence* anywhere in nature of a purpose, of a pursued end."[33]

But then—reading Monod beyond Monod—we should be able to understand that the postulate of objectivity, whose content is only the exclusion of all animistic projection, is in itself but another projection. Thus, the core of the very sensible modern scientific reason would be inhabited by a kind of ineffable, torn animism, turned toward and against itself: animism's zero-degree, condemned to recognize, once and again, its enemy within itself. A self-reflexive consideration of Modernity can only bump into this animism and conclude that there exists in Modernity (and here lies its legitimacy) a kind of mystical core of religiosity, which is silent to the point of atheism—a religiosity lacking images, watchful of the Name, in which monotheism would reach its paradoxical fulfillment. Thus, Monod's final words in *Chance and Necessity* acquire their just, Pascalian resonance:

> The ancient covenant is in pieces; man knows at last that he is alone in the universe's unfeeling immensity, out of which he emerged only by chance. His destiny is nowhere spelled out, nor is his duty. The kingdom above or the darkness below: it is for him to choose.[34]

In Modernity's ineffable and primordial myth, being and ought to be, facticity and validity, essentially converge. But, like parallel lines, their encounter is deferred to infinity. It happens then as in the Kafkian parable about the law (in the story *Before the Law*): we have come across the door, reserved only for us, which would lead us to the law. But it is to be always inaccessible to us. Modernity lives in the heartbeat of that inaccessibility, of that waiting.

Chapter 4

The Works of Science

The biologist and mathematician Henri Atlan is undisputedly a central figure in the area of complexity. In its masterful vagueness (all words are vague, Wittgenstein used to say: "complexity" simply does not conceal its blurry, inexhaustible character), this area makes possible that once again, as with other tremors experienced by the building of the "exact" sciences in the last one hundred years or more, a fascinating junction took place between sciences that are forced to go back to their foundations and philosophical reflection.[1]

In what follows, I shall discuss the relationships between science and technics, relying essentially on some of Atlan's ideas. In short, my claim is that both disciplines are identical at the core, in such a way that, with true conceptual rigor, we should think in terms of "techno-science," rather than dealing with each one of them separately. And my intention is to ground this claim, not only upon the already traditional philosophical discourse about it (for example, the one that we could extract from some of Heidegger's writings, which I will later describe in passing), but rather upon a text by Atlan ("Ordres et significations," from his book *Entre le cristal et la fumée*). It is possible, I claim, to extract from this text an argument from within science (and not from the philosophical tradition which, justly or not, can always be disregarded for being "exterior" to it) that supports the identity of science and technics that I am proposing. And, in the last instance, my argument revolves around the meaning of the scientific notions *order* and *disorder*, and *work*, which is very close to *energy*.

It is important to begin by briefly stating the "traditional" philosophical position, as it can be found in Heidegger. This position was laid out in

Being and Time and further developed in his remarkable conference "The Age of the World Picture" ("Die Zeit des Weltbildes"), which took place in 1938 in Freiburg im Breisgau. For Heidegger, modern technics (or technology) is not "applied science," as it appears to common sense.[2] Rather, the "world picture" that Modernity, and particularly its Cartesian-scientific wing, projects, is technological from the start.[3] One of the arguments offered by Heidegger, which I find the most adequate to be summarized here, begins by paying attention to the Greek root of our word "mathematics," which for us presupposes a numerical, quantitative approach to phenomena. But Heidegger makes clear that this usual meaning is rather derived, secondary, nonprimordial.

Modern physics, Heidegger writes, is called mathematical because it applies a very specific mathematics in an eminent sense. But it can only proceed in this manner, mathematically, because it is already mathematical in its most profound sense. For the Greeks, *ta mathemata* meant *that* which man already knows beforehand when he contemplates entities or has contact with things: the body-character of bodies, what plants have of the plant, animals of the animal, human beings of the human.[4]

In other words, paradoxically (but attention! not so much), "mathematical" is originally that which we know before "knowing" in the specialized sense of the word. Before "knowing," we know in fact the language and the practices in which we have been socialized: we know (that is the essence of the Kantian "a-priorism") of space, of time, of categories such as causality, which have not been extracted from our individual experience but which constitute the culturally determined lenses through which we approach the real. Going back to Heidegger's argument, the mathematical is not intrinsically numerical. The numerical, however, is essentially mathematical, because numbers, the mathematical entities in general, can be considered as the prototype of that which we know before "knowing." According to Heideggerian (and also Kantian) reasoning, even enclosed in a completely isolated cell, without any empirical input, we could nevertheless build the entire mathematics, if the length of our life and the power of our neurons would allow it. Heidegger says:

> If we come upon three apples on the table, we recognize that there are three of them. But the number three, threeness, we already know. This means that number is something mathematical. Only because numbers represent, as it were, the most striking of always-already-knowns, and thus offer the most familiar instance

of the mathematical, is "mathematical" promptly reserved as a name for the numerical.[5]

This is Heidegger. His argument is strong, but there are those who are not convinced or do not let themselves be convinced by it. And there is a powerful and respectable motivation for this refusal (for example, by a segment of the scientific community), given that from this perspective the truths of science cease to be unconditioned, "pure," and seem to become one way or another mere instrumental truths, capable of being conditioned, for example, by economic, political, and social interests, which operate behind technology and, less evidently, behind science. The scientist enclosed in his office, or sitting in the garden while thinking and listening to Bach, transported to the Platonic world of ideas, can legitimately ask himself: what does technology (big data, TV, the culture or arms industry) have to do with what I do?[6] And it is true that this question stems from his immediate experience. But in the same manner, absolute calm is the immediate experience of the one who is situated in the eye of the storm. That is precisely Heidegger's position, which I want to develop by moving closer to the language of science: regarding the turbulent world of technology (in connection, for example, with mass and business culture), science would be precisely the very eye of the storm.

Unconditionality (of truth in this case) as a topic is not only a concern of science. It is also a concern of ethics and aesthetics, which would not want to be reduced to the expression of interests (thus, ethics would not want to be mere chatter masking economic or power interests; similarly, an artist wishes that his work be different from a simple decoration or a mere commodity). The aesthetic phenomenon, in modern or postmodern conditions (it does not matter: post-Modernity is nothing but self-reflexive Modernity, conscious of itself), tends to fleetingly establish its aspirations to unconditionality by means of what I will call, a few chapters below, "the infinite sacrifice": the constant staging of its own impossibility. And as far as ethics is concerned, a contemporary discussion (I will go back to this at the end) concerns the way in which it would be possible, without naiveté, to uphold some aspiration to ethical unconditionality[7] within a culture (ours) that has already collectively learned that everything is reducible to constructions, manipulations, and interests.

Let us say, to summarize, that the objection to the identity of science and technology is legitimate insofar as one can understand the concern with unconditionality that lies behind it. The response to this objection would be to ascertain that there is the unconditional; however, it is not up to science to guard it, but it is rather up to ethics and aesthetics; or otherwise to reframe the entire question of unconditionality without abandoning it. I will address these alternatives at the end of this chapter.

In order to show the identity of science and technics from within techno-scientific language, my strategy will be, following Atlan, to enter the discussion about the scientific definition of order and disorder. Then, by following Atlan in his discussion of Boltzmann's statistical formulation of the second law of thermodynamics, I will show that this law could only emerge in the context of Modernity and the Industrial Revolution. Finally, I will suggest that the concept of "work" might be the missing link that allows the assimilation of science to techno-science, to technology.

I start with a rather long quotation from Atlan who, at the beginning of the chapter "Ordres et significations" in *Entre le cristal et la fumée*, takes an example once proposed by Bateson:

> The story of the office and the shelves packed with books and documents is well-known. The books seem to be stacked up without any order. However, their owner knows how to find any document if he needs to. If by any chance it occurs to anyone to "put things in order," the owner will perhaps become incapable of finding anything there. It is evident in this case that the apparent disorder is an order, and vice versa. The issue here is the relationship between the documents and their user. The apparent disorder concealed an order determined by the knowledge of each document and of its possible utilitarian meaning. But what did the appearance of disorder in this order consist in? It consisted in that for a second observer, who wants to "put things in order," the documents have no longer the same signification individually. At the limit, they have no signification other than the one linked to their geometric form and to the place they could occupy in the office and on the shelves, so as to coincide, *altogether*, with a certain a priori idea, with a "pattern," considered as *globally* ordered. We thus note that the opposition between order and appearance of order proceeds from the documents being considered globally with their signification, or from being considered globally with a different individual signification (determined, for example, by their size, their color, or any other principle of location applied from outside and without the user's assent), or even without any signification whatsoever.[8]

In other words, what Bateson and Atlan show with this example is that statements containing the words "order" or "disorder" are not of the same kind as those that state objective qualities of some object—for example: "this table is made of wood and metal." In this case, one can assume that a random observer (presupposing a certain culturally given knowledge of furniture and materials) will agree with this statement, which comes to be in this sense "independent of the observer." In the case of order and disorder, by contrast, it is not possible to "dispense" with the observer: what the statement states is not an objective quality but rather the existence (order) or inexistence (disorder) of *a relationship between the object and an observer, in this case the user*—in other words, we are dealing here with the commensurability between the user's representations and the real.[9] We might say that, unlike statements that refer to objective qualities, those that refer to order (and to disorder) are second degree statements: they do not refer directly to the object, but rather to the possible relationship between the object and its user, its observer.

Opposing this "relativization" of the concepts of order and disorder, or so it seems, stands the objectivity of the measurement of order in thermodynamics, given by its statistical formulation presented by Boltzmann:

$$S = k \sum_{i=1}^{\Omega} P_i, \ln P_i \tag{1}$$

$$\sum_{i=1}^{\Omega} P_i = 1 \tag{2}$$

where S is the so called "entropy," K is a universal constant (called "Boltzmann's") equal to 3,3 x 10^{-24} calories/degree, and the probabilities p_i correspond to the probabilities of finding a fragment of matter (a gas, for example) in each one of its Ω possible states.

Originally, entropy was a macroscopic magnitude established by scientists and builders of machines (Carnot, Clausius, Kelvin) during the first Industrial Revolution (machines that transformed caloric energy into kinetic energy and mechanical "work").[10] This magnitude accounted for the observable fact that, in every machine of this kind, there is a waste of energy due to a phenomenon that Galileo and Newton's physics still considered possible to ignore (because it is a tiny causal magnitude, "negligible," as it is, or as it was said, in scientific jargon), but that now appears as irreducible: friction.

Thus, no matter how efficient a machine is, it is impossible for it to recover without loss of the heat that was originally invested in the production of motion (kinetic energy). There is always friction, and so an amount of heat is irreducibly lost. Boltzmann's merit consisted primarily in establishing a link between classic physics and this law, which at the beginning looked merely practical, inductive-observational. In order to establish such a link, however, he had to make inherent to physics the statistical, probabilistic way of thinking, which had originally emerged in the study of human populations.[11] After this incorporation, classical physics was never the same, for the fundamental questions, such as "Does God play dice?," broke into it.

In its microscopic or statistical expression, the second law of thermodynamics (or the law of entropy) has its ground in the fact that, as Atlan says, "matter only lets itself be constrained and dominated up to a certain point."[12] In microscopic-statistical terms (statistics provides the tools that make it possible to deal with a very large number of aleatory interactions between microscopic molecules, as it typically happens with a gas), this means that, again in Atlan's words:

> The transformations imposed by machines imply an orientation and an *ordering* of matter and of its constitutive elements (molecules, atoms). Matter left to itself ignores this order imposed by the maker of machines. In particular, the main source of natural energy, heat (from fire and the sun), has the effect of agitating molecules in a disorderly way, that is to say, in an aleatory way, in all directions, without any of them having any privilege, even in average or statistically. In order for there to be motion, displacement of matter, work, it is necessary that all the molecules in the piece of matter be displaced together in the same direction.
>
> To transform heat into work implies that an order is produced in the disorderly motion of molecules, so as to reach an oriented motion, such that the average of molecules is displaced in a same direction. This transformation, imposed from within, cannot be complete: a certain part of molecular disorder will always exist, which translates into non-usable heat. That is what the second principle of thermodynamics says, in its statistical expression.[13]

It is immediately worth noticing in these quotations the relationship that they tacitly establish between the formulation of the second principle of thermodynamics and a primordial historical *factum*: the emergence of the modern planetary enterprise of domination of matter and the Industrial Revolution. The context for a claim such as the one reproduced above, "matter only lets itself be constrained up to a certain point," can only be provided by this enterprise of planetary domination. Only in this context, in which the order inherent to the medieval cosmos has been replaced by a "will to order,"[14] by the human affirmation in the midst of a universe that has become chaotic,[15] is it possible to conceive of machines seeking to maximize the transformation of caloric energy into mechanical work; that is, to introduce order "in the disorderly motion of molecules, so as to reach an oriented motion, such that the average of molecules are displaced in a same direction." From this viewpoint, the second principle of thermodynamics ceases to be unconditionally objective, although this does not mean that one must fear that it should become merely subjective: above the objective and the subjective lies the a priori (scientists often ignore this). This is the lens through which a collective observer (society, the culture of Modernity in this case), shaped as such by socialization processes within practices, life-forms, and languages, observes reality. In the case of Modernity, this lens presupposes, as an indisputable datum and "groundless ground,"[16] the magnus enterprise of "disenchantment" of nature—Max Weber's *Entzauberung* (demagnification)—and its consequences: instrumental rationality and market economy; freedom of the enlightened individual, emancipated from the tutelage of the old ecclesiastical-state institution. The purported unconditional objectivity of the second law of thermodynamics (that is, of the measurement of order) turns out to be, following Atlan, the result of a view upon reality through a lens: a view through the sociocultural lens of Modernity, and only through it.

Somewhere in his writing, Atlan seems to want to distinguish the conception of order that depends on the observer from the supposedly objective (because it is expressed mathematically) conception of order in physics. Atlan says:

> Thus, the definition of order and disorder in nature presents evident differences with the one implicit in the example of the office and its disorder. The first characteristic that distinguishes it is that here the definition seems objective, mediated by means of a physical magnitude: entropy. In the example of the office, on the contrary, the ordered character depended on the possible signification of order, different for different users.[17]

However, in the paragraph, it becomes evident that this return to the strong distinction between objective order and the one dependent on an observer is no more than a rhetorical means ("the definition seems objective") to emphasize precisely the opposite. Thus, Atlan immediately adds:

> And yet entropy, which is a physical magnitude, is defined only in relation to the *possibilities of observation and of measurement*, as shown by the example of the entropy of the mixture of two different gases. The spontaneous formation of a homogeneous mixture of two gases evidently comes with an increase of entropy that is eventually capable of being measured. This phenomenon is conceived differently if it is observed either before or after the discovery of radioactivity. If radioactive molecules of a same gas are used, it is no longer the same gas, and there is an entropy in the mixture. *This means that for the same system of two recipients of a same gas, one radioactive, the other one not, which can be mixed, there would be no entropy before the discovery of radioactivity, but it does exist after its discovery!*[18]

That which drives Atlan to this exclamation (what he wanted to emphasize through his rhetorical effect) is that there are two measurements for the entropy of the gas mixture, *both accurate*, depending on an element that could only be classified as techno-scientific (and that legitimates the use of this term): the discovery of radioactivity. Only this discovery, in Atlan's example, makes it possible to distinguish molecules of a same gas located in different and connected containers. This distinction, produced by "possibilities of observation and measurement," is the source of all entropy, and also of energy and mechanic work.

Let us remember that energy is defined as the capacity to produce work. The paradox then comes up (but again, this is not so paradoxical) that a distinction, which is in principle purely observational, makes it possible to obtain energy and work where there was none. Because, although the distinction is observational, it stems from a complex theoretical-empirical development in the natural sciences, inseparable from the general development of the forces of production (the discovery of radioactivity, in this case).

It is therefore possible to define the technological, techno-scientific role of science on the basis of science's fundamental task: to introduce new *distinctions* (and, as I proposed above, to explain the apparent unworldliness of the pure scientist, his or her distance from the technological whirlwind, not as the quiet of the margins, but rather as belonging to the very center of the vortex). And, counterintuitive as it may be, it is this drawing of distinctions that makes it possible to extract new energies and sources of work from nature. Thus, a task that is apparently of a purely theoretical, contemplative kind (in Greek, *theorein* is connected to vision, to contemplation), but unmistakably inserted in the complex of forces of production through the division of labor, becomes the main source of energy and work required by the industrial or postindustrial mode of production,[19] to which science (and not as mere "applied science," for reasons I have already presented) is central.

With this conclusion, the task proposed at the beginning of this chapter—to reduce (or stretch out) science to "techno-science," to technology—is essentially accomplished. It only remains to take on the philosophical questions that follow from such a conclusion, as I also proposed at the beginning to this chapter. Indeed, the identity of science and technics that I have established, based on the scientific problem of order and disorder has, in principle, the consequence of deflating science's claim to unconditional truth. This is equivalent to asserting (as I have also clarified above) that scientific knowledge as such would be immersed (though not in an immediate and crude way) in the turbulent waters of modern technology and economy.

It also becomes important to address this question (which, at its core, is the question of the nonunconditionality of truth), given that Atlan is a follower of Spinoza's thought in connection with biology. Spinoza (together with Nietzsche, who acknowledged Spinoza's greatness) may be considered the highest representative of a philosophical monism that leaves no space for any sphere of unconditionality whatsoever. For Atlan, indeed, "the will and the understanding are one and the same thing."[20] It is not hard to find claims of a similar kind in Spinozist *ethics*. Thus, for example, in Proposition 22 (Etica, Pars Quarta, "De Servitude Humana seu de Affectuum Viribus"), it is said: "No virtue can be conceived as prior to this one, namely, the conatus to preserve oneself."[21] And from here, a few lines down, Spinoza draws the following corollary: "The conatus to preserve oneself is the primary and sole basis of virtue. For no other principle can be conceived as prior to this one . . . , and no virtue can be conceived independently of it."[22]

Spinoza is struggling to take distance from the Cartesian dualism that distinguishes ontologically between *res cogitans* and *res extensa*, between human beings (and God) and nature. By contrast, Spinoza naturalizes human reason, and in particular practical reason, or ethics: virtue, the good, is not but a mask for self-preservation. But given that there is no difference between ethics and the interests linked to self-preservation, there is no place from which these interests can be questioned. Spinoza anticipates contemporary utilitarianism and pragmatism. If we follow his point of view, works like Sigmund Freud's *Civilization and Its Discontents* (and possibly psychoanalysis as a whole) would be impossible, mere absurdity. For the attempt is made there to establish a balance between the costs and benefits of culture, understood as self-preservation, in a moment (the world wars, the *Shoah*) in which all the pain, ruin, and barbarism intertwined with culture as its shadow seemed to have burst onto the stage of history.[23]

From a Spinozist point of view (which would be in principle strengthened by the identity of science and technics, of truth and instrumentality, which I derived earlier following Atlan), it does not make sense to consider, for example, "the indefinite postponement of the hour of reason." How to postpone it, and why, if the will lacks autonomy? This postponement, however, constitutes for Emmanuel Lévinas the essence of what is human ("infinitesimal difference between man and non-man").[24] I will go back to Lévinas at the end of this text.

Kant has been the starkest opponent of Spinozism in the Enlightenment era. Although in the *Critique of Pure Reason* he already sees in Newton and Galileo's science a moment of unconditionality,[25] this unconditionality might still be reabsorbed by Spinozism and considered to be a mask for "heteronomous" cognitive interests, that is, in Kantian terms, imposed from the outside. That is why Kant turns directly to ethics. His *Groundwork of the Metaphysics of Morals* begins with this "innocent" sentence: "[I]t is impossible to think of anything at all in the world, or indeed even beyond it, that could be considered good without limitation except a **good will**."[26] That is to say, everything empirical is a-valoric: no good that is truly good, and not a mere mask for mundane interests, can be found there. Kant is often criticized for carrying his position to absurdity (he does so himself sometimes), given that if the good must remain uncontaminated by empirics, a greedy philanthropist would have more value than a pure philanthropist, a lover of humanity, with a good heart (given that, if he had a good heart, he would be extracting epicurean, heteronomous enjoyment, from his philanthropic act). Thus, Kantian ethics seems to be subtracted from any connection with reality: it is reduced to a call to sanctity, to the abandonment of mundane interests by the philosopher, and to the related abandonment of the world to the crudest instrumentality. This ethics appears differently if we understand that the choice that it imposes upon us does not take place between a pure, uncontaminated subject and a subject that does not even come to be one, because it is nothing but the toy of causality, whether external or internal (his passions). The choice is rather between an empirical subject and a modern subject, which is torn, permanently split between the fulfillment of its duty and its interests and passions.[27] Or as Max Weber used to say in reference to political activity, there is a constitutive split in Modernity between an "ethics of responsibility" (an ethics of calculus and of the consequences of actions) and an "ethics of convictions" or of the heart, whose demands are unconditional. The political man (is not everyone political?) was, according to Weber, constantly torn between these two logics.

Although much can be drawn even today from Kant, commonsense approaches to the history of philosophy tell us that the aspirations to unconditionality in Kantian ethics were crushed by that Spinozist that Nietzsche was. For him (in *The Genealogy of Morals*, for example), the autonomous, ethical, Kantian subject is only the result of a domestication: the "breeding" of an animal capable of making promises, that is, of postponing the satisfaction of its empirical interests to favor a superior interest. "The [Kantian] categorical imperative smells of cruelty," says Nietzsche.[28] According to his continuator in the twentieth century, Michel Foucault, it smells of social technologies of discipline and punishment, of which the social sciences would be an eminent part. Finally, the only defense for a subject whose behavior might be isolated from empirical explanations consists in transforming this subject into a virtual point. This is the case with the first Wittgenstein (in his *Tractatus Logico-Philosophicus*), in which the subject does not disappear but is transformed into a limit of the world: a virtual point, a zero dimension.[29]

This line of reasoning leaves science in the hands of Spinozism, so to speak, with the goal of saving ethics (and aesthetics). From the viewpoint of the cognitive discourse, the human being is a mere puppet, controlled behind the scenes by some version of causality. In other words, the human being does not speak—rather, circumstances (physical-chemical, genetic, sociological, economic, even psychological) "speak" ventriloquistly through it. The discourse of science (and the discourse of philosophy, at the peak of its self-consciousness) says, "There is no truth," "The truth is that there is no truth." Unless one distinguishes languages and metalanguages, which is difficult within natural language, this constitutes a performative contradiction, like the one that says, "I lie." This is how the scientific discourse of Modernity and a large part of the philosophical discourse seem to end up: in a self-contradictory declaration of aphasia.

"Civilization of aphasics," Lévinas remarks in connection to this conclusion. However, from the Lévinasian point of view, it is not indispensable to sacrifice reason's cognitive interests in favor of a very problematic salvation of its ethical interests (from the start, the clear distinction between these two interests is problematic). For Lévinas, all discourses are ethical at their core, insofar as speaking (even if only to say "I do not speak") is always the response to the other's interpellation, who from the height, or in any case from an asymmetric position (which prevents the equivalence or the interchageability between them), interpellates a Self that is inherently separated from, and irreducible to, even a generic unity with its interlocutor. The unconditionality of the ethical is grounded precisely upon this "dialogic" character (but it is a dialogue that is never symmetrical), where I am unconditionally interpellated to answer for my utterances, even for my cognitive and negative utterances, facing my interlocutor face to face. The social, duality and pluralism, by contrast to the monism of Spinozist reason, is not an accident but the "very curvature of being," Lévinas has said. And he has also said: "Objectivity is not what remains of an implement or a food when separated from the world in which their being comes into play. It is *posited* in a discourse, in a *conversation* [*entre-tien*] which *proposes* the world. This *proposition* is held between [se tient entre] two points which do not constitute a system, a cosmos, a totality."[30]

Chapter 5

Nietzsche

The Incombustible in Reason

> There is a wolf in my guts
> That strives to be born
> My sheep-heart, slow creature
> Bleeds for it.
>
> —Manuel Silva Acevedo, *Wolf and Sheep*

In Nietzsche, knowledge about myths (the mythology at the core of Modernity that we have identified before) becomes exemplarily clear. Indeed, in his work, consciousness of myth coexists with its critique—Zarathustra's mythical *poiesis* together with the mythoclast furor of *On the Genealogy of Morals* and other texts.

The first of these two aspects—that which Nietzsche in *The Gay Science (fröliche Wissenschaft)* calls his "perspectivism"—is already present in an early and decisive writing, *On Truth and Lying in a Non-Moral Sense*, and goes on until his later writings and posthumous fragments. Along these lines (strictly speaking, the lines of a radical empiricism or nominalism), Nietzsche repeatedly stresses the impossibility of logically grounding the relationship between words and things. This implies the radical contingency of our language and the forgetfulness (joyful, healthy forgetfulness, up to this point) of the "things in themselves"—of that which makes up, so to speak, the shadow of our words, the shadow of the world we build through them, and that we should leave behind with joy. With the emergence of language, Nietzsche claims, nature "has thrown away the key": if it were possible for us to look through the keyhole ("fateful curiosity," he says), we would see that we dream on "the back of a tiger." Let us note, however (and this is not trivial at all), that Nietzsche is indeed the one who is capable of looking. The "fateful curiosity" is first of all his own, which casts a discordant (fateful) note upon the joyfulness, the celebration with which the perspectivist individual receives, in principle, the world-producing powers of language, which are in this sense poetic.

There is a forgetfulness that is inherent to language's "legislative power," which Nietzsche links, for example in *On Truth and Lies* . . . , to the exit from the state of nature and the emergence of the social (the end of the "*bellum omnium contra omnes*": the promise of peace). However, above this first-order forgetfulness, there is a consummated, second-order forgetfulness: the one that characterizes metaphysics and science. This is a forgetfulness of forgetfulness itself, by virtue of which metaphors (fiction, myth) are taken to be reality itself. Thus, "only through forgetfulness could human beings even entertain the illusion that they possess truth."[1] Against this objectification, in a way necessary, the perspectivist philosopher and the poet are destined to exert a critical labor, which consists in giving back to metaphors their primordial fluidity. "What, then, is truth?," Nietzsche asks in *On Truth and Lies*. And he responds with these famous and eloquent words:

> A mobile army of metaphors, metonymies, anthropomorphisms, in short a sum of human relations which have been subjected to poetic and rhetorical intensification, translation, and decoration, and which, after they have been in use for a long time, strike a people as firmly established, canonical, and binding; truths are illusions of which we have forgotten that they are illusions, metaphors which have become worn by frequent use and have lost all sensuous vigour, coins which, having lost their stamp, are now regarded as metal and no longer as coins.[2]

The question that opens up now concerns the place that Nietzsche and the perspectivism of his "will to power" (*Wille zur Macht*, an essential concept in Nietzschean thought) take in connection to Modernity's philosophy of the subject. Heidegger has essentially explained this ("Nietzsches Wort 'Gott ist tot,'" *Holzwege*): the subject is primordially *sub-jectum* (the Greek *hypokeimenon*): ground. Once the ancient covenant that secured the human being a place in the transcendent order of the universe is broken, it is the subject who must (and who only then can) unfold as will to order, turning itself into the measure of all things.

Notwithstanding the frequent claims found in the critical approaches to Cartesianism inspired by Heidegger, this ground-giving, fundamental subject reaches its fulfillment, that is, its purified figure, not in the mere cognizant, Cartesian subject, but in in the myth-creating poet. Along this line, the will, understood as will to illusion, would be the ultimate truth of the modern subject. And indeed, as Nietzsche often shows, the scientist and science itself are but modalities of the mythic poet, which are ontologically subordinated to him. Thus, causality, a basic principle of the order that science reads, or believes that it reads, in the world, would only be "a hypothesis through which we make the world accessible both to our eyes and to our calculations."[3] The difference between the poet and the scientist is reduced here to a question of more or less self-reflexivity. From this stance, as Nietzsche often suggests, it would even be possible to make Kant his predecessor. For what is a text like the *Critique of Pure Reason*, if not the magnus modern myth of the phenomenal world, written within the radical estrangement of the things in themselves?

We could even claim that the typical gesture of metaphysics—the transformation of effective history (*wirkliche Historie*) into sacred history—is, *malgré lui*, repeated by Nietzsche. Indeed, history as it is metaphysically told, as the genealogist Nietzsche himself teaches us, is always the history of an origin that would be fullness, followed by a fall (the present whose miseries would be thus rationalized and justified) and a promise of redemption. In this self-conscious consummation of the metaphysics of Modernity, which is condensed in the perspectivism of Nietzsche's *Wille zur Macht*, these positions are taken by the metaphoric, the fantastical, and the fantasizing animal, whose praise Nietzsche seldom omits; by the reification, the forgetting, and the crystallization of metaphors; finally, by the promise of the artistic reappropriation of the poietic potencies inhabiting the origin.

Just a single fact should be enough to identify the modern nature of Nietzsche's perspectivist will to power. The peak of our late Modernity is not occupied by the scientist (this is already stated by Heidegger in his writings and presentations on technics) but rather by the expert in marketing, by the designer (also the politician) to whom the mythical-poetic powers of the *Overman* (*Übermensch*) seem to have migrated. "Everything is built and destroyed in language": this is the motto of the knowledge that puts the will to power in motion today. Neither the scientists who study the phenomena of semiconduction nor the technicians who build chips are the ones leading the game, but rather entities such as Microsoft, which envelope all that with mythical packages for mass consumption. They are the ones who unfold the mythical-poetic powers of language—not the poets, whom no one reads, and who for a long time have occupied a different place.[4] Poetry is no longer a joyful game, but rather the "murder of language," as Barthes has said (*Writing Degree Zero*), following Blanchot.

With Nietzsche the mythologist, the opposition between scientific positivism and hermeneutic ontology—with the "perspectivist" Nietzsche that is our concern here, and also with Heidegger and Gadamer as its outmost exponents–becomes illusory, even though philosophical thinking has lived from it during much of the twentieth century. Indeed, we read in the following passage, which explicitly summarizes the fragments gathered under the title *The Will to Power*: "*Recapitulation:* To *stamp* Becoming with the character of Being—that is the supreme *will to power*."[5] Drawing attention to this passage in his lectures on Nietzsche, Heidegger comments: "Becoming only is if it is grounded in Being as Being."[6] What can "to stamp Becoming with the character of Being" mean? Along the lines of the Heideggerian reading of Nietzsche, but taking it further (until it encompasses Heidegger himself, as Lévinas does), we might answer this question by remembering that becoming is precisely that against which, since the dawn of Greek thought, identitarian, world-constructing powers have measured themselves: reason and word. "Ontology" is the general name with which Lévinas designates philosophical thought since Socrates (whose "teaching" was "the primacy of the Same"). Thus:

> To know ontologically is to surprise in an existent confronted that by which it is not this existent, this stranger, that by which it is somehow betrayed, surrenders, is given in the horizon in which it loses itself and appears, lays itself open to grasp, becomes a concept. To know amounts to grasping being out of nothing or reducing it to nothing, removing from it its alterity.[7]

This nihilism ("to grasp Being on the basis of nothingness or to carry it to nothingness") is precisely the operation executed by Heideggerian ontology—and that retrospectively justifies the expansion of the name "ontology" to the entire tradition of philosophical thought. Lévinas says, with Heidegger once again on target:

> It is the Being of existents that is the *medium* of truth; truth regarding an existent presupposes the prior openness of Being. . . . Its intelligibility is due not to our coinciding, but to our non-coinciding with it. . . . Since Husserl the whole of phenomenology is the promotion of the idea of *horizon*, which for it plays a role equivalent to that of the *concept* in classical idealism; an existent arises upon a ground that extends beyond it, as an individual arises from a concept. . . . *Being and Time* has argued perhaps but one sole thesis: Being is inseparable from the comprehension of Being (which unfolds as time); Being is already an appeal to subjectivity.[8]

Lévinas explicitly links the buffering of experience produced by the mediation of Being to the exercise of the will to power:

> The relation with Being that is enacted as ontology consists in neutralizing the existent in order to comprehend or grasp it. It is hence not a relation with the other as such but the reduction of the other to the same. . . . "I think" comes down to "I can"—to an appropriation of what is, to an exploitation of reality. Ontology as first philosophy is a philosophy of power. It issues in the State and in the non-violence of the totality, without securing itself against the violence from which this non-violence lives, and which appears in the tyranny of the State.[9]

The operation of "*stamp*[ing] Becoming with the character of Being" is inherently ontological. Thus, within its *horizon,* alterity, which is here designated by becoming, dissolves and becomes commensurable with *logos.* The Nietzschean "supreme will to power" consists in that this operation goes unnoticed—in that becoming remains entirely subsumed within being, and the equivalence between thinking and being prevails without gaps. But in order for this to be possible, it is necessary for thinking to leave behind its Cartesian narrowness and reencounter its original affinity with myth. Hermeneutics corresponds to this widening of thinking. By turning Being into "interpretation, from top to bottom," hermeneutics brings back into the philosophic republic the mythic potencies that a much too narrow version of *logos* had left outside.[10]

But positivism is precisely that position of thought which, beyond its varieties, would erase all traces of alterity; a position that, freed from all "fateful curiosity," has "thrown away the key" and immersed itself once again in facticity, in the normal (nonrevolutionary, non"transvaluing") exercise of power.[11] Given what I have said, however, this position is the one occupied today by the trends that I am calling here "hermeneutic," in a broad sense.[12] Scientism, by contrast, has been left behind. Indeed, its aspiration to a purely referential language, capable of constraining linguistic polysemy, can be seen today as a nostalgic call to alterity, to a reality (an "X") that is beyond the identity of being and thinking.

Only a few years after Nietzsche's death, Hans Vaihinger noted and celebrated the relationship between positivism and Nietzschean perspectivism. This took place mainly in an essay ("The Will to Illusion in Nietzsche") published as an appendix to a book by him, whose title is extremely eloquent from this perspective: *The Philosophy of "As If": A System of the Theoretical, Practical and Religious Fictions of Humanity* (published in German in 1913; translated into English in 1925). In the essay, Vaihinger grounds his "idealist positivism" upon a rigorous and documented reading of Nietzschean perspectivism and concludes: "[T]he consummation of the history of philosophy is therefore, according to Nietzsche, the philosophy of illusion: the realization of its indispensability and justification."[13]

The "philosophy of illusion" is characterized by its aspiration to interpret all differences as "perspectives" articulated by fiction and myth—as "moments" of an Absolute Knowledge that, unlike the one dreamed by Hegel, does not rise dramatically above the nominalist split between being and thinking but simply ignores it. Thus, this philosophy prefigures the imaginary of contemporary globalization. Beyond the technological paraphernalia that sustains it, this imaginary is driven by a provocation to discourse (as Foucault shows in connection to sexuality), by virtue of which the dark continent of the human psyche becomes a landscape populated by secrets that, undisclosed, become "differences" within an apparently limitless discursive field that lacks exteriority.

If Nietzsche had limited himself to prefiguring this present, we could consider ourselves already satisfied. But there is something else. It is one thing to build myths, and another thing to know that one is doing so. Nietzsche's thought, the peak of Modernity's thought, can be characterized (this is what I proposed at the beginning of this section) as a knowledge about myth. "This is the game that is being played" (the sentence, out of context, is Wittgenstein's)—"the game of myth," Nietzsche would say, situated (but where?) as a problematic observer of Modernity. Through him, Modernity would become that culture that knows of myth and that, consequently, is also destined to incessantly recognize it within itself, thus practicing autophagy, self-disenchantment.

But anyone who knows of myth knows of its other as well—of everything that words necessarily forget and exclude (of the real, beyond any linguistic construction). One knows it and now, trained in memory, cannot forget it. "A question seems to lie heavily on our tongue and yet refuses to be uttered: whether one *could* consciously reside in untruth? Or, if one were *obliged* to, whether death would not be preferable?," Nietzsche writes in *Human, All Too Human*.[14] This reflection leads from the affirmative Nietzsche, who celebrates the human capacity to linguistically build its world, cancelling all transcendence, to the "negative" Nietzsche: the critical thinker as an insomniac in constant search for what has been forgotten—but which, be careful!, could no longer be a secret to be revealed—under the diurnal face of positivity.

The subject, placed at the peak of the metaphysics of Modernity, knows of myth and of its other and resents the untruth, the forgetfulness that its own words inevitably carry with them. Thus, dragged by the weight of questions that are heavy "as lead," it plunges into the abyss. Nietzschean *Genealogy* is the ensuing and relentless exercise of memory—a remembering of "the entire long hieroglyphic record, so hard to decipher, of the moral past of mankind,"[15] which ends up in the dissolution of the autonomous subject, now understood as the outcome of a cruel domestication, of a "capacity to forget" sedimented at the end in the very structure of language.

On the Genealogy of Morals (1887) fulfills the tendency of modern reason to enlighten itself, to direct its suspicion no longer to old myths, but rather to violence and interests, which are the conditions to which it would be submitted, and which work on it interiorly, from the shadows. The *Genealogy* is driven by the question about the "*value* of morality," that is, about the *value* of value. Value is the possibility of distinguishing, ordering, establishing a hierarchy and giving meaning to our experience. Value is equivalent to meaning. Nietzsche thus asks for the *meaning* of meaning. And the answer proposed by the Nietzschean genealogical knowledge is that the *meaning* of meaning is nothing but meaninglessness. Values do not hang from the sky. On the contrary, everything that presents itself as the result of a design, of an imperative inscribed in the very texture of the universe and of history, so to speak, is only the result of a slow sedimentation through which forgetfulness has been fulfilled—the erasure of its *human, all too human* origin, of the will to power, of self-affirmation, which works below the ground on that which is afterwards told to us as sacred history.[16] Facing a metaphysical thinking that gets lost in the blue of the sky, the genealogist opposes the gray of real history: "what is documented, what can actually be confirmed and has actually existed, in short, the entire long hieroglyphic record, so hard to decipher, of the moral past of mankind!"[17]

But in this way, Nietzschean genealogy only radicalizes the viewpoint of modern Reason. From this perspective, it is no coincidence that *On the Genealogy of Morals* begins with a reading of English "psychologists" (the empiricist and utilitarian thinkers). Indeed, Nietzsche draws radical implications from their gesture, which seeks to redirect all that is presented to us as extraordinary and unconditioned (the Good, Truth, Beauty) to the "bare ground" of everyday practices.[18] This gesture of modern Reason is already present in Galileo who, by leaving aside the question on the "what" (the essence) in order to focus on the "how" of phenomena, opens the door to the very fruitful mathematization of science, but at the same time, to the dissolution of the cosmos—the eminent order of the universe that medieval Christianity had inherited from Greece. The gesture is also present in Darwin. The novelty of and outrage at Darwinism do not stem from the fact that the human being descends from the ape but rather from the fact that humanity and Reason are the outcome of blind chance and not the outcome of a design. "The ancient covenant is in pieces; man knows at last that he is alone in the universe's unfeeling immensity, out of which he emerged only by chance": these are, as we already know, the eloquent and dismal words with which Monod once summarized the viewpoint of contemporary evolutionism.

But is a genealogical, nonmetaphysical knowledge possible? Nietzsche himself often seems to deny it. In fact, in several passages of his work, there is a tendency to *situate* himself in a kind of inverted metaphysics—one would also say a metabiology, considering the vitalism that impregnates Nietzsche's reflections on the "will to power"—from which history could be understood as the fall from an origin, understood as fullness, and to which we shall eventually return. The disquieting paradise of the "splendid blond beast" (which leaves behind "a disgusting procession of murder, arson, rape, and torture, exhilarated and undisturbed of soul, as if it were no more than a students' prank"),[19] depicted by Nietzsche in *On the Genealogy of Morals*; Nietzsche's nostalgic invocation of a Nature that is "pure, newly discovered, newly redeemed,"[20] in the paradoxical conclusion of a paragraph in *The Gay Science* containing an accurate critique of the anthropomorphization of nature: these are two examples that evidence this inversion.

Given both its repetition and its structure, the metaphysical *slip* by Nietzsche the genealogist is telling. Indeed, the genealogical enterprise can be globally understood as a critique of the metaphysical concept of history, which here, however, rises again. To this history, genealogy opposes the idea of an "effective history"—the history of an origin no longer understood as metaphysical *Ursprung*, waiting to unfold the possibilities that have been always lurking within it (such unfolding would be history, metaphysically told), but rather as *Herkunft* ("provenance," ordinary, gray, never venerable) and *Entstehung* ("emergence," singularity that sets in motion changes that, once sedimented, are metaphysically turned into the products of a design of which things themselves would be the carriers).[21]

But history is never "effective" (gray, ordinary) enough. It always presupposes a certain kind of narrative, a historiography without which "what is really verifiable, what has effectively taken place" (*Genealogy*, Prologue) slips through the genealogist's hands like sand (gray, ordinary sand). The narration—language—requires metaphysics, while simultaneously producing it, as that deep spring from which it sprouts. However, the essential form of any narrative logic (and thus of any metaphysics) is constituted by statements of the kind "S is P," which predicate something about a subject and to which Nietzsche refers in a key section of his *Genealogy*.[22] The issue there is the "morality of *ressentiment*," that is, the reactive, mediated character of moral judgments pertaining to the "man of *ressentiment*," who is opposed to the immediacy of self-affirmation that belongs to the "noble morality." And beyond the parables and the doubtful etymologies that Nietzsche presents (for example, the one that derives the German word *schlecht* ["bad"] from *schlicht* ["simple"]) in order to support his position (according to which moral judgments are just the sediment and the mask of the confrontation of wills to power), a careful reading reveals that what is at stake is the very structure of mediation and judgment—of which moral judgment is only a particular case. Nietzsche says:

> A quantum of force is equivalent to a quantum of drive, will, effect—more, it is nothing other than precisely this very driving, willing, effecting, and only owing to the seduction of language (and of the fundamental errors of reason that are petrified in it) which conceives and misconceives all effects as conditioned by something that causes effects, by a "subject," can it appear otherwise.[23]

This seduction of language produces a dissociation between the "subject" and its acting (the genealogist wants them identical, undifferentiated), in such a way that it becomes possible to insert the fiction of free will between them. Action is thus presented as a predicate that is added to a subject who, in its essence, would be free to act or not to act.

> So popular morality also separates strength from expressions of strength, as if there were a neutral substratum behind the strong man, which was *free* to express strength or not to do so.... [Thus] *the strong man is free* to be weak and the bird of prey to be a lamb—for thus they [the weak] gain the right to make the bird of prey *accountable* for being a bird of prey.... Just as if the weakness of the weak—that is to say, their *essence*, their effects, their sole ineluctable, irremovable reality—were a voluntary achievement, willed, chosen, a *deed*, a *meritorious* act.[24]

In the *Phenomenology of Spirit*, culture (*Bildung*, cultural education) is set in motion precisely at the moment in which the slave, who fears death (his "absolute master"), having renounced recognition by another consciousness and submitted to the power of the lord, "rids himself of his attachment to natural existence in every single detail; and gets rid of it by working on it."[25] By means of this cultural achievement, the slave leaves the lord behind. The lord, given that he is protected from natural existence by the slave, does not supersede it but remains submitted to it. One would say that Nietzsche in the *Genealogy* has found the essential form of work: the shadow-work of the concept, of metaphysics. The predicative structure "S is P" produces the subordination of facticity to possibility. Possibility is the guiding idea of metaphysics—a phantom that is more real than the real, of which facticity appears as the actualization or realization.[26]

Thus, with predicative language (with language in itself), the occupation of the "true" world by an "untrue" (possible) world begins, of which we cannot even know that it is untrue. In a peculiar way, this Nietzschean finding appears concealed within a praise to the figure of the bird of prey, of the lord. But who is this lord? Beyond the historical or philological proofs provided by Nietzsche's text, which are inevitably below philosophical speculation; beyond his antienlightened *pathos* that is part of the cultural context of romanticism, in which Nietzsche is inevitably and ambivalently immersed, it is possible to see behind this figure the search for shelter against the loss of speech, which threatens radical critiques of language—as we have seen with Barthes and Wittgenstein. Indeed, the language of the slave is seen in the *Genealogy*, again in an (anti)-Hegelian way, as marked by mediation (by *ressentiment!*), by contrast to the language of the lord, whose mark is immediacy.

> The lordly right of giving names extends so far that one should allow oneself to conceive the origin of language itself as an expression of power on the part of the rulers: they say "this *is* this and this," they seal everything and event with a sound and, as it were, take possession of it. . . . While every noble morality develops from a triumphant affirmation of itself, slave morality from the outset says No to what is "outside," what is "different," what is "not itself"; and *this* No is its creative deed. This inversion of the value-positing eye—this *need* to direct one's view outward instead of back to oneself—is of the essence of *ressentiment:* in order to exist, slave morality always first needs a hostile external world; it needs, physiologically speaking, external stimuli in order to act at all—its action is fundamentally reaction.
> The reverse is the case with the noble mode of valuation: it acts and grows spontaneously, it seeks its opposite only so as to affirm itself. . . . "we noble ones, we good, beautiful, happy ones!"[27]

For Nietzsche the perspectivist, cruel narrations, praises of force, and philological arguments could be nothing but myths. Therefore, it is not unexpected that in the passages in which these myths are presented most emphatically (Nietzsche himself performs this in the passages of *Genealogy* that I am commenting on), it should be possible to glimpse behind them the abysmal condition of possibility of each and every mythology: the language through which things speak by themselves, the one that human language and its mythical poiesis seek to leave behind; the one that, nonetheless, human language carries as its shadow. Thus, divested of its mythical envelopes, the Nietzschean lord is only the hypostasis of an original naming, that is, of a thesis on the "origin of language" (*Ursprung*, not *Herkunft* or *Entstehung*, is the suggestive word that Nietzsche the genealogist relies on in the passage quoted above). This is the positing of that extraordinary, impossible *Ursprache*, on which, as we already know, radical nominalism necessarily relies in order not to crystalize into the positivist extolling of the existing. Beyond this untruth, which weighs upon the diurnal word like lead, only "speaks true who speaks shadow" ("*Wahr spricht, wer Schatten spricht*": Paul Celan, "*Sprich auch du*").

Nietzsche presents his *Genealogy* as the reactivation of an "ancient fire,"[28] in which the aspirations of enlightened Reason will collapse. However, if what I have suggested is correct, the fire is not produced by the anarchic pyromaniac known as Friedrich Nietzsche but rather by modern Reason itself, at least in one of its faces. Against this Reason, which sets itself on fire, is there anything that can resist? In other words: is there some incombustible residue—the incombustible in Reason—that can withstand its own fire?

The answer may be in the question. The very subject that affirms with Nietzsche the interested and conditioned character of all truth, of all good and all beauty (and who says: "I do not speak: I am spoken by the conditioning elements—biological, socioeconomic, psychical, genealogical, even ontological—of my existence"), removes itself from its own holocaust, at the very instant that it affirms it. It is a lamb disguised as a wolf, as a bird of prey, which speaks beyond all conditionality, all context, all horizon. To speak about the impossibility of speaking, and only about that; to turn the fire, the desertification of oneself, into the abysmal condition for producing oneself: this is the constitutive paradox of Modernity that the Nietzschean *Genealogy* stages and through which the conditioned reveals its inherent incompletion, its abysmal opening toward the extraordinary.[29]

Chapter 6

The Truth Is That There Is No Truth

> Don't believe truth! Don't believe truth!
>
> —*Husbands*, by John Cassavetes

Truth, powerful concept. Truth is not only that which is sought for in the scientist's lab or the thinker's office. People kill for truth and die for truth. What is it that we call truth?

When we reflect upon truth, the first idea that comes to mind is that it must have something to do with a correspondence between our mental representations and exterior reality. In the philosophical tradition, this idea constitutes the so-called "theory of truth as correspondence," which has been the predominant way of considering the question of truth in our Western culture. The famous logician Alfred Tarski formulated this theory in the following way, not without hesitations: " 'Snow is white' if, and only if, snow is white," where the first term is a proposition, a linguistic expression of a mental representation, and the second term designates a state of affairs in the external world.

Difficulties soon come up, however. First, the definition seems to presuppose that we can compare our representations with reality "in a raw state," so to speak. Is such a thing possible? Can we, as one might say, look behind our representations, behind our language? Is it possible to signify the state of affairs "snow is white," without necessarily repeating the proposition " 'snow is white' "? Are not the quotation marks here a simple trick, which tries to avoid the uncomfortable feeling that the theory of truth as correspondence is only a simple play on words, an empty identity?

And also: How white and how snowy must snow be, so that the proposition "snow is white" be verified by experience? Examined closely, snow is not really white; it is rather gray. And it is continually dissolving and turning into something different, into nonsnow. Is the problem solved by introducing measurements? We might indeed agree to use the word "snow" only for water (H_2O) at a certain temperature and density. We might equally use the word "white" only for certain wave longitudes in the visual spectrum. Nevertheless, all measurement is an approximation, vague and without an end. The decision to end it and to establish a value (or to limit it to a certain degree of probability) is always just that: a decision.

These two simple observations aim at complicating the question of truth or rather to restore the complexity that the theory of truth as correspondence tends to keep hidden. The fact is that we are never just there, simply in front of things. The veil—the skin—of language is always in the middle, and it connects us with things but at the same time stands in the way between them and us. To say language is to say culture and history. Thus, truth turns out to be the outcome of a complex operation of social construction, crossed by the passions, emotions, and interests of human beings and by the glories and miseries of power.

How is truth produced in the time of the Internet? We live in an era where knowledges and discourses proliferate. In the middle of this "Babel tower," it is no longer possible to build an absolute order, a true catalogue. As in the famous parable that Borges imagined, the Internet can contain "not only thousands and thousands of false catalogues" but also "the demonstration of the fallacy of these catalogues, the demonstration of the fallacy of the true catalogue," and so on, until oblivion. On the other hand, how is it possible to distinguish a false catalogue from a true one, without presupposing that the problem of truth, which we wanted to examine, has been already solved?

The proliferation of knowledges and discourses is not of course only a contemporary phenomenon. Its origin might be traced back perhaps to the very dawn of human language, that is, to the newly acquired capacity to speak, not only of "that which is," but also of "that which is not." This is the capacity to speak of the possible, which is crucial to the human emancipation from nature, and to produce discourses that are not directly placed on the ground of things, but which have rather grown parasitically at the edge of other discourses. These parasitic discourses, which replicate other discourses, constitute our everyday speech. If we knew how to listen, we would perceive infinite and remote echoes in them.

With printing, science, technology, and communications, the capacity to replicate discourses becomes practically unlimited. General Stumm von Wordwehr ("mute dam of the word," if we pay heed to the German language) is one of the figures in *The Man without Qualities*. He is a sensitive man, well-intentioned, who, driven by the highest intentions (and with some stimulus from his War Ministry), decides to inquire into knowledge—"that" which the world of civilians values so much and that would be key to its superiority over the world of guns, a fact that Von Wordwehr does not question.

It is the years immediately prior to World War I, and the generals still have some free time. After a few failed attempts, Von Wordwehr goes to the Imperial Library, where the entire knowledge of his time is stored. There, he will very likely find someone who can guide him. However, he will be greatly surprised when he finds out that the library's *habitués* are specialists, who have abandoned all aspiration to totality. Only certain subjects that dwell in the depths of the library preserve some reference to the whole of knowledge. They are the authors of catalogues. But these predecessors of the authors of Google or other "search engines" for the Internet no longer read books—they restrict themselves to register the information displayed on the covers.[1] The Imperial Library's *sancta sanctorum* is taken by a robot, by an idiot.

The Babelic explosion of specialized languages is a response to the proliferation of knowledges and discourses. We often regret the incapacity of specialized subcultures to talk with one another. However, the incapacity of each subculture to talk with itself, with its origins, is even more perplexing. Indeed, a specialist is not someone who has direct knowledge of a "thing" (of greenhouse effect in the atmosphere or of the demographic trends in Central America) but rather someone who is firmly located in a tradition of knowledges, in a bibliography, in a "normal science" (Kuhn). Thus, for example, if one wants to research depression among cancer patients, the point of departure would not be the observation "with bare eyes" of the behavior of patients or of a sample population. It would rather be the bibliographic search that makes it possible to situate the knowledge to be produced within a horizon of preexisting discourses, either to confirm or to refute them and more generally to proceed with the production of further discourses.

With tools such as the Internet, handling quotations and references becomes the mark of professional and scientific excellence. There is nothing to object to this. On the contrary: by demanding that arguments be sustained by empirical evidence or by controllable documentations, modern societies guarantee the public character of knowledge, which is in principle open to anyone willing to make the effort. However, there is a high price to be paid, given that as time goes by (and does time not accelerate with the Internet?), the specialist, whether he wants it or not, ends up operating on a thick sediment of inherited knowledges, concepts, and practices. He is tied to a tradition to which his work cannot add more than a humble commentary, a footnote—otherwise he is subject to the accusation of lack of professionalism.

This sediment of interpretations (and of interpretations of interpretations, and so on to infinity) constitutes the wall that increasingly separates the specialist from the decisions based on estimations, approximations, or metaphysical considerations, often risky and tentative, and that were taken at some point by the founders of the field. How many scientists approach the original writings of Newton, Einstein, Bohr, or Heisenberg? How many revisit Galileo's concerns as he took the risky decision of considering mathematics the language in which the book of the universe is written—a Platonizing decision that went completely against the grain of the predominant Aristotelianism in the science of his time? When the Romans came into contact with the remains of Ancient Egypt, they found out with surprise that, in a few generations, the priests had lost the memory of hieroglyphic writing, whose inheritance they guarded with devotion. Something similar takes place in our time: we operate with languages whose true meaning we have forgotten. And to this forgetfulness, another, second-order forgetfulness is added: the forgetfulness of forgetfulness itself, the assumption by the specialist that he possesses a neutral knowledge, that he possesses truths that spring from the things themselves, aside from the complex production-apparatus of truth of which he is part.

As an antidote to cognitive stagnation, it seems sensible to somehow return to the origins, to a fluidity prior to the crystallization of knowledges. But it is difficult that the productivity requirements in the multiple fields of knowledge-production allow it. It would then be necessary to get used to live in a kind of mirror room, where discourses, which have somehow become independent of the subjects that once uttered them, reflect and refract one another indefinitely. At the end of the road, truth would be indistinguishable from rhetoric: what we call "true discourse" would be nothing but a particularly extended kind of rhetoric, which is influential and persuasive. There is no truth, there never was: that is the teaching that we have finally learned in the times of the Internet.

However, that in itself—that there is no truth—must be true in its turn. The skeptical paradox ("the truth is that there is no truth") is not a mere play on words—it points to something (some Thing?) which we also signify when we say "truth," and which must be above any rhetoric and any power game. "Sir, if it is indeed the case that you love me so much, how is it that you say it so well?," an innocent little shepherd from a seventeenth-century Spanish romance responds to an eloquent gentleman who tries to seduce her. But then it would be necessary to modify the prior diagnosis: life in the times of the Internet would consist rather in an incessant oscillation between two kinds of truth. On the one hand is public truth, which is institutionalized, and in which all discursive calculus and rhetorical sophistications are admissible. On the other hand is private truth, which is demanding, explosive, and plain, beyond all institution, protocol, and calculus. A truth that is not necessarily silent, but it is laconic—word from the margin, from the boundary, or from blank space; stuttering. Virginia Woolf anticipated it in *Orlando*:

> For it has come about, by the wise economy of nature, that our modern spirit can almost dispense with language; the commonest expressions do, since no expressions do; hence the most ordinary conversation is often the most poetic, and the most poetic is precisely that which cannot be written down. For which reasons we leave a great blank here, which must be taken to indicate that the space is filled to repletion.[2]

Chapter 7

The Endless Sacrifice

Art and the Production of the Extraordinary

Among the productions of the human being, works of art are distinguished by the ambition that they embody: the artist's ambition to be acknowledged as the producer of extraordinary objects, whose value is reduced neither to their utility nor to their exchange-value. Even if a painting by Rembrandt, as in the case of the inverted "ready-made" imagined by Marcel Duchamp, can be used as an ironing board (or as a mere decorative object); even if its circulation in the market can in fact mobilize millions, its peculiarity as a work of art would lie in its (supposed) difference from mere instruments, from mere commodities.

The modern disenchantment of the world is opposed to all forms of metaphysical "animism," to all attributions of extraordinary predicates—order, meaning, finality—to reality as such. This way, the stage has been set for the modern drama of alienation, which confronts an autonomous subject with a reality in which he cannot recognize himself. The idea of an immanent order of things, which is characteristic of the culture of traditional societies, has yielded to a "will to order" whose practice lacks any transcendental foundation. The good, the true, and the beautiful, deprived of support in being, have come to be (have they not always been?) mere constructs, masks for the very terrestrial wills to power, which struggle for hegemony. However, the very subject that asserts the interested and conditioned character of all truth, of all good and of all beauty (who says "I do not speak: I am spoken by the conditions—biological, socioeconomic, psychical, genealogical, even ontological—[1] of my existence) is subtracted, at the very moment of asserting it, from the maelstrom of interest: he speaks, beyond all conditionality, all context, and all horizon. *To speak about the impossibility of speaking and only about that*: here lies, as we have seen, the constitutive paradox of Modernity, through which the conditioned, the ordinary, would reveal its inherent incompletion, its abyssal opening to the extraordinary.

Along this line, the extraordinary constitutes Modernity's object of desire, both impossible and indispensable. It is a desire that, with all its paradoxical potential, becomes particularly evident in the realm of art, which exerts a sort of gravitational pull that modern thought can hardly eschew. Thus, since Kant's *Critique of Judgment*, metaphysics, ethics, and even epistemology seem destined to pursue in aesthetics the key to their most decisive truth. The reason is that, beyond the multiplicity of formats, technics, and traditions, modern art represents the stage on which productive strategies, oriented to pull their objects out of alienation by turning them, even if only briefly and problematically, into "auratic," extraordinary objects (Benjamin), unfold. And it is even conceivable that this multiplicity (and this can be considered as a defining trait of contemporary arts) should harbor the tendency to yield, precisely in favor of the highlighting of the gesture, of the operation of drawing the line between art and nonart. Thus, for example, starting with the Duchampian "ready-made," visual arts tend to depart from the tradition of "noble" technics and equipment (canvas, easel, oil) and to leave behind representation and image, in order to focus on the operation through which an ordinary object (a urinal, a scaffold, a beer can), placed in the sacred space of the museum or the gallery, is promoted to the extraordinary status of the work of art.

Alienation and its dialectical complement, the desire for the extraordinary, are the axes of the modern problem of art. Modernity has broken the narcissistic pact that secured the commensurability and the affinity between, on the one hand, language and human reason, and on the other, the universe.[2] From this point on, the disenchanted universe is a labyrinth—a "mirror of enigmas" (Borges, commenting on Leon Bloy) that returns not the soothing image of our own face, but the atrocious face of a monster.[3] Modern disenchantment guaranteed that, in the last instance, human works, no matter how humble and limited, would end up revealing their goodness, their correspondence with the immanent order of things. Once this horizon of redemption is removed, works are left to their own luck. Deprived of any metaphysical support, they enter into the constitutive drift of modern existence—drift of instrumentality, of means-ends chains, which have become planetary by virtue of globalization and the growing division of labor; drift of the market, in whose flux commodities are subtracted from their history; hermeneutical drift, finally, by virtue of which works, from interpretation to interpretation, lose their singularity and are integrated into the anonymous sphere of culture, of writings; the "literary space" of the library, we might also say in connection to Borges.[4]

By virtue of these circulation processes, works spread, following trajectories that are radically unpredictable—they become objects, things alienated from its producer and facing him like second nature.[5] At the same time, the very subject, ground (*sub-jectum*) of modern certainty, turns out to be contaminated, from its origin, with the virus of alienation and guilt. Works are indeed blood, guts, sweat, intellect, and energy of their producer: emanations of himself, in which he pursues recognition. However, where a perfect mirror was expected, we only find a mute, nonsignificant thing; it was meant to confirm our intimacy, but it represents rather its loss. The very subject that says "I think," that expects to find in the Cartesian *cogito* the primordial evidence of its identity with itself finds itself confronted with the irreducible experience of otherness. *Je est un autre* (Rimbaud); "To the other, to Borges, is whom things happen": it is in this kind of statement that the deep dialectic of Modernity is expressed, by virtue of which exteriorization, without which intimacy cannot be signified, immediately constitutes loss and alienation. Thus, the modern subject endlessly looks for its "lost" intimacy; a paradoxical intimacy it never possessed for its loss was already inscribed in its very origin.

The extraordinary is Modernity's object of desire, both impossible and indispensable—the supplement of "altitude" that the subject needs in the essentially unfinished operation of subjectifying itself and that constitutes its only substance, its only support in Being.[6] Modern art, on its part, is the staging of this aspiration, the dream of a perfect mirror, of a "true" work, somehow subtracted from the drift, from alienation and guilt. Thus, in Kant, disinterested pleasure—that is, pleasure uncontaminated by desires linked to the empirical existence of the object—which the "man of taste" experiences in the contemplation of the work of art, is the sign and at the same time the fulfillment of a commensurability that is strictly indemonstrable (its demonstration would have been the illusion of precritical metaphysics) but possible, and heuristically necessary, nevertheless, between empirical concepts (the entries of the *Encyclopedia* that somehow prefigure our experience of the world) and reality as such.[7] Although tainted now by nostalgia, this extraordinary demand presented to the work of art is still recognizable in some famous formulas—the work of art as marked by an "aura" (Benjamin) or as "the putting into work of truth" (Heidegger). It is with these formulas that the twentieth century eminently thought the topic of art. At the same time, only in facing this demand—facing the high tribunal that it establishes—empirical, factual works become uncertain, alienated, and guilty. Thus, the dialectic of Modernity is paradigmatically fulfilled in the realm of art.

Modern art can be understood as the attempt to preserve its privilege (the height of the work of art, which in the past testified to the "real" presence of the divinity in the world) under conditions in which the cultural substratum that sustained it has ceased to exist. Modern art is the attempt to create sacred, extraordinary objects in a world in which they are no longer possible. But in a world characterized by alienation, every work is *a priori* uncertain and therefore guilty. It follows that works of art, which still presume that they are glorious, are guilty in an eminent manner: guilty not only of their original guilt, but also of forgetting and hiding their guilt.

Let us note that this suspicion is by no means foreign to the (canonically modern) Kantian characterization of art. Indeed, like Kant, whoever makes disinterested, nonempirical pleasure the "mark" of art is automatically condemned to a distrustful self-observation regarding the highly interested pleasures (whose paradigm is sexuality) that might be engineering the aesthetic judgment behind the scenes. Here, as in other realms (ethics, for example), the obsession of the so-called "hermeneutics of suspicion" (Nietzsche, Marx, Freud) with material, empirical (ordinary) interests that condition thinking is not the opposite of Kant's philosophy (or of Reason or the Enlightenment, as it is sometimes believed) but rather the expression of a rigorously (post-)Kantian consciousness that, seeking the genuinely unconditioned, must thoroughly distinguish it from that which only pretends to be it.[8] This is an arduous and infinite task, insofar as, given its unconditioned, extraordinary nature, there is and there can be no empirical evidence linked to aesthetic pleasure (if there were, that pleasure would now be interested). Here the very structure of the extraordinary becomes evident (as we will see in detail later on, in connection to literary aesthetics in Borges's work): the extraordinary can only be reached by negation (in Borges, the aesthetic happening is "the imminence of a revelation that is not yet produced").[9] At the same time, this *via negationis* sets up the figure of the modern self-observer: the reflexive subject that is obsessively attentive to the signs coming from the invisible hand of the conditions operating within himself.[10] In Schopenhauer's "bad" reading of Kantian aesthetics (but is there a reading that is not "bad"?), this structure of the extraordinary becomes evident.[11]

Schopenhauer, as Nietzsche shows in his discussion of the "ascetic ideal," claims that aesthetic contemplation "counteracts *sexual* 'interestedness,' like lumpulin and camphor; he never wearied of glorifying *this* liberation from the 'will' as the great merit and utility of the aesthetic condition. . . . He, too, was pleased by the beautiful from an 'interested' viewpoint . . . , that of a tortured man who gains release from his torture?"[12] Earlier, Nietzsche mocked Kant's "disinterestedness" when contemplating statues of female nudes, and intentionally noted the difference between Schopenhauer's youth (he was twenty-six when he wrote *The World as Will and Representation*) and Kant's old age. Nietzsche the ironist can easily convince us, his post-Freudian readers, that the purported disinterestedness is nothing but the mask of (sexual) interest, which is invoked, sublimated, and/or repressed in it, in such a way that "sensuality is not overcome by the appearance of the aesthetic condition, as Schopenhauer believed, but only transfigured and no longer enters consciousness as sexual excitement."[13] But the subject is not only that mask. With Nietzsche, it is also the one who knows that it is that mask. And if that knowledge is in its turn a mask, it is worth asking about this new knowledge, and so to infinity. This escape into the infinite, whose engine is the performative contradiction of the one who says again and again "I do not speak," is the taking place of the production of the extraordinary.

The promised redemption, in sum, has turned out to be nothing but consummated alienation, and suspicion has remained at the very heart of art. This is how art ends up turning against its own "body"—against the entire apparatus of artistic representation, permeable to alienation—favoring the pure gesture of drawing the dividing line art/nonart, which I mentioned earlier. Contemporary art becomes conceptual ("the idea of the idea of art," as Joseph Kosuth says) and sacrificial (sacrifice is a paradox, an antinomial strategy of appropriation by destruction)[14]—it sacrifices everything that constituted the work of art's glory: the perfection of the craft, the expression of a distinguished subjectivity, the beauty of the images. By virtue of this negation, in a heroic and paradoxical turn, the work of art fleetingly recovers, at the edge of the abyss, its character of "auratic," extraordinary object, endowed with a transcendent value. Thus, contemporary art lives out of its own becoming-abyss, of the staging of its own impossibility. On the other hand, the suspicion mentioned above assigns to the artist the destiny of being his own observer, his own theorist. The modern dialectic of art leads the artist to imbue his work in theory: that is, to execute that erasure of the boundaries between theory and fiction (between metaphysics and fantastic literature) whose paradigmatic and self-conscious expression is Borges's work. This sacrificial and self-conscious scene would constitute the specific form of production of the extraordinary under conditions of modern alienation.

The impossibility of the auratic object, which Benjamin seeks to explain as a mere effect of the technologies of reproduction in *The Work of Art in the Age of Its Mechanical Reproduction*, is inscribed perhaps in the very structure of the work of art (for how might Modernity recognize an extraordinary object? How would Modernity recognize the Messiah?, one could also ask in a Kierkegaardian or Kafkian way). From there, via Marcel Duchamp and Andy Warhol, art becomes the vast sacrificial scene that it is today: the staging of the impossibility of the aura, reiterated once and again, by virtue of which the object fleetingly "recovers" it.

Let us continue this reflection on the contemporary work of art by commenting on the exhibition *Unidos en la gloria y en la muerte* (*United in Glory and in Death*), by visual artist Gonzalo Díaz, which took place in the National Arts Museum, in Santiago de Chile, at the beginning of 1998. Exemplar in its coherency and rigor, Díaz's exhibition provoked at the moment a series of commentaries: a textual density that the work itself, focusing on a text—a passage from a discourse written by Andrés Bello to present the Civic Code before the Chilean Parliament in 1855—seemed to solicit, and in which I am here intending to cut a path using the impulse provided by its friction.[15] Roberto Merino, Justo Pastor Mellado, and Pablo Oyarzún inserted their comments in the catalogue of the exhibition; Natalia Bavorovic and Carlos Pérez Villalobos did so in its presentation, after the inauguration of the work; last, but not least, Adriana Valdés and Alfredo Jocelyn-Holt published comments in the press.

The presence of installations or other abnormal objects in museums and galleries, among paintings and sculptures, has become familiar. It seems to be enough that an object legitimately crosses the doors of one of these buildings for the abnormal to adjust to the norm and be accepted by the enlightened audience. We say "legitimately": a beer can, brought into the museum by a visitor, would not be an art object. However, it would become one if an expert—a "curator"—approved it and if it were exhibited on a plinth, for example. This way, the reality of art seems to confirm the most certain, and also most disquieting, intuitions of the linguistic and hermeneutic constructivism of contemporary culture: all identity would be a linguistic construction. Consequently, that which confers an object its quality of "work of art," or any other thing, would be not an intrinsic characteristic of the object (in fact, no characteristic would be intrinsic, strictly speaking) but rather a performative statement (which produces a state of affairs rather than simply describing it) emitted by those who are socially authorized to do so. "A work of art is that which we say is a work of art," where "we" designates a community (a power group) conformed by academics and art critiques, artists, curators, museum and gallery managers, sponsors, and so on, whose distinctive trait is that they participate in the process by which art is socially constructed. This sociological evidence (tautology of power) seems to put a conclusion to any inquiry into art. From that point on, the task of critique would be reduced to producing a genealogy of the powers that be: a kind of glorified social life, a novel of habits in which what matters would be to determine who and under what circumstances he or she spoke, plotted, and established alliances or enmities with whom.

Gonzalo Díaz's work would seem to demand by itself that one question this tautology of power. Otherwise, it could hardly exert "the tenacious interrogation of power" that one of its commentators (Oyarzún) attributes to it. The attribution is accurate, insofar as what is "installed" (that is, uninstalled) in Díaz's installation seems to be the museum itself: the paradigmatic institution from which the tautology of power is announced in connection to art in the contemporary world. Thus, Díaz's work seems to demand a metasociological reflection on art: a reactivation of the question of the artistic in the work of art, even if the question were to lead us nowhere.

I say "metasociological" because it is not simply a matter of ignoring what the tautology of power tells us—ignoring it, by willfully and nostalgically trying to return the sacred halo to the work of art, is the distinctive mark of *kitsch*[16]—but rather of knowing if this wrapping, this absorption of art by power—a crucial episode in the politicization of art, which was once presented as a redemptive sign—leaves a gap somewhere. In fact, my contention is that the conception of the work of art as a sacred object, somehow subtracted from everydayness and mere instrumentality, and thus possessing an inherent value (beyond all usefulness or market value), was but a temporary moment in the becoming of Modernity. This moment, petrified in the famous formulas that we have recalled (the work of art as carrying a certain "aura" [Benjamin] or as "putting into work of truth" [Heidegger]),[17] would be superseded by the corrosive powers that modern critical reason sets loose in the world. From there, contemporary art (and Díaz's work in particular, given its exemplary character) constitutes a sort of vast sacrificial scene: sacrifice of what constitutes the work of art's glory—craft perfection, expression of a distinguished personality, beauty of the images. At the same time, by virtue of this sacrifice and in a heroic and paradoxical turn, the work fleetingly recovers, at the edge of the abyss, its character of "auratic" object, the carrier of transcendent value. Thus, as I have stated above, contemporary art would live out of its own becoming-abyss of the staging of its own impossibility.

In what follows, I will present a broad outline of what could be a sacrificial history of modern art. For pre-modern Christendom, the work of art has no special place in the economy of the universe. If it does, it is only by virtue of its adherence to an order: a transcendent order (a "super-order") that rules all things and that, in the case of human works, would be translated into a scale of values, a hierarchy of pious works within which art (sacred art) has a prominent place. The passage from an eminent order of being to the sphere of ethical-political, historical duties (from "being" to "ought-to-be," as philosophers often say) is not a trivial act. It presupposes that the order in question is not only transcendent (the product of a creation situated outside historical time), but also intelligible, suited to human reason. Therefore, the universe would be a sort of book, written in a complex "language," perhaps impossible to encompass in its totality but, at least in principle, intelligible to the human being. Creation, as premodern theologians usually argue, cannot emerge from the whim of a despotic and arbitrary God but from a rational order that the human being could in principle unravel.

The benefits of this worldview are evident. Human existence, with the pains and miseries that it entails, would not be the product of blind chance but rather of a design. Human beings would not be alone in the midst of a hostile universe. Guilt, which is an expression of the uncertainty of any human work—there is no way to completely foresee the outcomes of an action; it is always possible that there be unexpected effects, innocent victims—would be dissolved into the infinite goodness of creation. Evil—pain, misery—would lack a real existence: it would be but a lesser good, an appearance—a bad dream from which the happy ending of the story would allow us to wake up. Between the sacred and the profane, there would be a bridge for the believer to cross on his way to salvation. And pious works would secure this movement, safe from uncertainty and meaninglessness.

This happy world, however, always had its discontents. Can pain and misery be disregarded as mere appearance? The affirmation of meaning and goodness as the primordial truth of things—does it not constitute a kind of anesthesia, of easy consolation? Besides, the transit between the sacred and the profane not only has beneficial effects but also costs. Indeed, it is a movement in both directions, carrying not only the promise of sacralizing profane existence but also the threat of the radical profanation of the sacred. This ambiguity is concentrated in the pious work; expression of renunciation but also of arrogance; option for spirituality but at the same time pagan idol, a device through which the believer attempts to fulfill a sort of bribe to the divinity. Last but not least, to accept the possibility of deciphering the code of creation implies, in practice, enshrining the social power of an institution (ecclesiastic institution, state) whose legitimacy is based on its self-conferred privilege of fulfilling such deciphering, translating the transcendent order of things into ethical and political imperatives (acts, works to be performed or avoided) that are imposed upon subjects. Paganism, even if it is the residual paganism present in the idea of salvation through works, legitimizes this tyranny.

Works are fragments of identity scattered throughout the world. In Modernity's demagnified world, free subjects no longer recognize authorities above the authority of their own conscience. Their works, detached from the invisible web that gave them meaning and at the same time imprisoned them, spread around the world according to radically unpredictable trajectories. This alienation makes us eternally guilty. "Limiting man's possibility to useful works, what [Calvin] offered man as a means of glorifying God was the negation of his own glory."[18] From then on, the path to salvation—that is, to a certain recovery of one's own interiority from objectification—necessarily presupposes the sacrificial paradox to which we are calling attention. Sacrifice is salvation by negation, by annihilation. In a desacralized world, to sacrifice an object (also a subject) is the only way to save it from the all-encompassing sphere of utility, restoring its identity, its unity, its glory, for a fleeting moment. The sacrificing subject knows that no work can be sacred: to assume that it is sacred would be a mere trick to increase its utility, its market value, further burying it under the profane world. A sole path remains open: destruction. However, the destruction of works (including self-destruction) grants prestige and power to the one who performs it— another trick, another work gone astray, and consequently guilty. Poets who are excessively damned, prophets whose death is excessively beautiful, are destined to be inexorably transformed by this logic into market products, to see their portrayal printed in countless t-shirts. Sacrifice, by its own logic, is nullified each time that it crystalizes into a work. Then, in order to avoid crystallization, it must constantly sacrifice itself, becoming movement. The inner life of modern subjects could be understood as this ceaseless movement, as a spiral that, in each step, crosses once again the stages of Guilt,

Sacrifice, Absolution, and Doubt. Evidently, the modern man on the street is neither Rimbaud nor Che Guevara—nor a humanist, an artist, or a philosopher, concerned with the ultimate meaning of things. Nevertheless, if the logic that I have shown is accurate, this spiral will drag him each time that he asks, even if in a disorderly manner, about the meaning—the glory—of his acts or that he has the experience of feeling guilty. Glory and death will appear to him as inexorably intertwined, as in the title of Rebeca Matte's sculpture in front of the National Arts Museum, which Gonzalo Díaz cunningly installed in neon letters at the top of the museum's facade.

Luther's and Calvin's strong critiques of the entire device of pious works, of the entire premodern arithmetic of salvation, have to be placed in this context. Luther's well-known commotion in the face of the wealth of the Roman Catholic Church did not stem from ascetic scruples, but rather from the aspiration to glory associated with it. In fact, the Reformation will make possible the emergence of a world (the capitalist market) in which—except for the phenomenon of commodity fetishism, the insidious return of paganism denounced by Marx—objects, deprived of all transcendent meaning, are confronted to one another in their nudity, as values that can be exchanged. Salvation is not a matter of works anymore, but rather of predestination, of an inexplicable grace granted by an unknown God with whom it is only possible to establish communion in the intimacy of individual conscience, eroded at the same time by uncertainty. From this viewpoint, contemporary atheism can be seen as the legitimate child of the Reformation: not as the product of the Nietzschean, excessive "death of God" but rather as a kind of purely monotheistic religiosity. This is a relationship with a God that does not create by emanation—for then the universe would participate in his glory and would crush the human being—but rather by absence. This God retracts, leaving a void, a nothingness in which the human being's life and freedom are possible. Thus, Modernity would not entail the renunciation of the idea of transcendence but rather the purification of its animist residues.

In the premodern hierarchy of works, cathedrals and other works of art certainly have a privileged place—but not by virtue of their beauty and greatness, that is, of an aura, understood as a quality that is somehow associated with an object. It is rather the opposite: art testifies to the real presence and effectivity of the divinity in the world. Its privilege, which predicates like "greatness" and "beauty" seek to describe, proceeds from there. The first stage of modern art can be understood, from this viewpoint, as the attempt to preserve this privilege—the height of the work of art—but under conditions in which the cultural context that sustained it no longer exists. Thus, the privilege in question must be necessarily understood as the outcome of a quality inherent to the work of art itself—or rather, in a movement that prefigures the following stage, as an emanation of the distinguished personality of the artist, the creator. Art is the attempt to create sacred objects in a world in which they are no longer possible: a solipsistic religion, of which the artist is prophet, priest, and sole believer, engaged at the same time in an arduous struggle against modern nation-states. In essence, this is a religious war between rivals who compete for filling up the void of meaning created by Modernity; the romantic topic of the Artist struggling against Power unfolds on its basis.

The *pathos* of modern art, the psychic *pathos* of the artist, torn between delusions of grandeur and the evidence of his own abjection—between the joyful solitude of the modern subject and the melancholic mourning for the community of believers—can be explained on the basis of this syndrome of individual religion.[19] But the logic of the Reformation does not stop there: the twentieth century sees its irruption in the field of art. If works are inherently guilty, then works of art, which still want to be glorious, are guilty in an eminent manner: guilty not only of their original guilt but also of arrogance, forgetfulness, and concealment of their own guilt. The work of the Reformation in the realm of art is expressed by the demystifying labor of the Antipoet. Against the heroic aspirations of the Poet and his purported capacity, as a "small God," to restore or to Adamically bestow meaning to things, the Antipoet is the one who observes with a skeptical and plebeian gaze the joys (and miseries) of such a distinguished man. The Antipoet is the simple man infiltrated in the *sancta sanctorum* of Art in order to unveil the penultimate mystery: the Artist is a mortal like anyone else; he suffers from humiliating illnesses, he defecates, he counts money in the bank, he flirts with wealthy ladies, and he tries to give a good impression in circles of power. We now know this, thanks to the Antipoet. And we know that we know it: we will never be able to forget it.

After this overview, we are ready to visit Gonzalo Díaz's installation. We will do it like a wanderer (perhaps like a lady) who had inadvertently entered the Arts Museum in December 1997 or January 1998. The figure of the lady, introduced by Justo Pastor Mellado at the end of his text *La faena del texto [The toil of text]*, included in Díaz's catalogue, is an invention that is not trivial. "The Revolution is not a ladies' stroll," Mellado writes, quoting Lenin, whose presence in this context is symptomatic. Indeed, the Revolution has competed with Art in the radical attempt to fill in Modernity's void of meaning; to accept its benefits, while trying to ignore its costs. Failing in this attempt, both have ended up yielding to the spirit of the Reformation. Therefore, the lady can now continue her stroll in peace. Let us follow her.

Given that it is a building that holds the sign "Museum" at its front, our lady would have the reasonable expectation to find works of art inside.[20] And starting with Rebeca Matte's sculpture, which provides the name for Díaz's installation, *Unidos en la gloria y en la muerte*, followed by the other sculptures and paintings, this expectation would not have been disappointed. The descent into the underground room named Matta, by contrast, would have been a kind of expulsion from this paradise: the descent into a Calvinist space, utterly deprived of images, end-of-the-century in its clean and minimalist display of elements, proceeding from the profane world of technics (neon lights; metallic scaffolding, following the technical terms that Díaz skillfully deploys), and lacking the mystery, the aura that is still associated with fabrics, paintbrushes, inks, and other "noble materials." Images have been replaced in *Unidos en la gloria y en la muerte* by a text in neon (Andrés Bello's quotation), which runs through the four walls of the room, as well as through the crowbars that interrupt and put distance to the reading, and that seem to parody an engineer's work—a work that would be necessary if the building eventually dents, as some predict. The technological invention event translates into minimal gestures. The work is not "by" Gonzalo Díaz, but the name of the author appears floating in the void, as a kind of fabrication mark; the technical information of the materials is detailed with an obsessive precision; the technicians who contributed to the work receive the same treatment as in the credits of a film or a piece of software.

The lack of images recalls the biblical prohibition that weighs upon them and that was retaken by the Reformation. The image is the element that is seductive in itself. It is at the core of the ambivalent commerce between the sacred and the profane, which is the seed of paganism and of the possibility of enslaving human beings. Therefore, they must be handled with distrust and sublimated into the word. Hegel, a conscious Lutheran, writes in the *Encyclopedia* developed for his students at Nuremberg: "[T]he image is annihilated, and the word replaces the image. . . . Language is the supreme power among men. . . . Language is the annihilation of the sensuous world in its immediate existence." But images never finish dying. They are left adrift, like remainders of a gigantic shipwreck, available for the mass media to produce consolation artifacts with them, which we all at some point demand. Suggestively, the passage by Bello chosen by Gonzalo Díaz can be understood as a reference to the moment, full of mystical resonances, in which the kingdom of the image—the original kingdom of the father in which the restriction of the instant satisfaction of the son's desire is still merely contingent,[21] explicitly violent, and thus paradoxically fragile—abdicates its powers and leaves the scene in favor of the Law. Pablo Oyarzún comments: "What is said in this passage marks the limit of the force of the law"—the limit of force: that point at which the rationality of the law vanishes into the atavistic powers expressed in the authority of the father. But maybe this is a test of its efficacy: the Law replaces the Father or, if we follow Freud, it is the outcome of his assassination. Read somehow "sideways," Bello's assertion can be understood as encouraging parricide, which makes possible that the Law, agreement among brothers and equals, exists.[22] This way, the scene assembled by Díaz could be read as the scene of a crime. But is it a crime? Or is it a trivial event, like the falling of a stone? It is impossible to know: as Wittgenstein shows in his *Conference on Ethics* (which might as well be titled *Conference on Aesthetics*, because the issue, in either case, is absolute value-judgments), for a culture that has desacralized the world, soberly choosing to "write the book of the world"—instead of seeking to decipher the book of creation—"murder would be at the same level of any other occurrence, such as the fall of a stone."

The phantasmagorical brightness of neon could still recall a mystery, an opening to a beyond. But the technical specifications send us back to reality: anyone with access to the technical know-how and the corresponding materials (12 mm ⌀ glass, argon gas, electrical components) can reproduce the effect. "There shall be neither mystery nor any desire to reveal mystery": this is how Horkheimer and Adorno characterize Modernity in their *Dialectic of Enlightenment*.[23] Facing Art's eminent guilt, which I have mentioned above, as the outcome of the Artist's resistance to abandoning his old privileges, Díaz responds with sacrifice—the sacrifice of the images, as we have seen, and of everything that sustained the glory of the work of art. This is a renunciation to artistic representation that, along the way, as Pablo Oyarzún points out, opens the path for its replacement by "the most profound, dynamic, and decisive stratum in which the operations unfold." The logic of sacrifice, however, exceeds any work in which one would intend to express it (given that such a work should be sacrificed in its turn, and so on). Brought into the realm of art, this dynamic of sacrifice suggests that, beyond the will of the artist, there would be a kind of unavoidable ruse of representations, a kind of inertia that would lead Oyarzún's operations to be again, in their deliberate unfolding, a sort of second-order representation. From this viewpoint, the distance between an installation like the one by

Díaz and the work of a visual artist attached to the tradition of representation does not disappear, but it decreases and acquires a different character.

By the way, our lady—let us go back to her—does not need to know about all this. What lies in front of her is a set of elements foreign to the tradition of the arts—specifically, a metallic scaffolding that pretends to support the museum ("pretends," because otherwise the museum would be closed to the public: a lady reasons this way). Of course, it is possible that she is being fooled, but the lady will surely not think that way. She will leave the museum perplexed, but calm, for it is a serious museum after all, which cannot but contain works of art. This perplexity, the lady thinks, must be the effect that the artist intended, an expression of the depth of his vision. Thus, in her naiveté, the lady has come across a crucial question, which we have anticipated: through the sacrifice—the renunciation of auratic art—staged in the sacred space of the museum or the gallery, contemporary art fleetingly recovers, like an agonic spasm, its aura. However, this strategy (of profanation) presupposes the sacredness of what it seeks to desecrate: the sacredness of the museum, which is given to it by power, and whose legitimacy remains in place. In this sense, Díaz strains to go beyond: he turns the museum into the very object of his installation, and in this way, he makes manifest its arbitrariness, its lack of ground—for which the crowbars, an expression of the power of technics, ironically seem to compensate—its dependence on the tautology of power. But again, is this an interrogation posed to power or a ruse of power itself? Power is perhaps strengthened by exhibiting its plasticity, its aptitude for absorbing all questioning, the same way that representation returns absolutely each time that one seeks to negate it. Perhaps power lives and is nourished by being interrogated.

Reflecting on the passage between the sacred and the profane, the sacralization of life that, for the Christian tradition, is exemplarily expressed by the coming of the Son of God into the world, Kierkegaard concluded that this event could only take place in a paradoxical manner, on condition that no one would ever find out that it happened. A theological parable of Modernity, conceived in the manner of Kierkegaard or Kafka, would then say that the Messiah, Savior of the moderns, could only be an unknown individual whose life goes by in anonymity—a subject who should even renounce renunciation itself, renounce his *pathos*, in such a way that the Wittgensteinian book of the world would contain no sign of his existence. Therefore, it is possible that somewhere, at this very moment, the exemplary Work of Art of the modern world is being produced. But, in the same way as that "uncertain Quevedian translation (which I do not intend to publish) of Browne's *Urn Burial*," with which Borges concludes his *Tlön, Uqbar, Orbis Tertius*, such a Work should be destined to be never seen (not even by its author: he is blind!).

In the middle of this reflection, I went back to the Matta Room. It was a Sunday morning in the summer of 1998, and I was alone in the building, among the neon lights and the crowbars. For an instant, it was as if some Thing, an Absence?, addressed me with its silent word. But Doubt immediately entered the scene: Did I feel it, or did I only believe that I had felt it? Did I believe it, or did I only believe that I believed it?

Was there a murder? Or was it just a stone that had fallen?

Postscript: The Origin of the World

Bergamme is a malformed dwarf who is obsessed both with theology and with stealing famous paintings. He executes this last obsession aided by his small height and by the blindness that, he says, takes hold of the multitudes when they wander "museumly" in a quasihypnotic state through exhibition rooms. Once the works are in his power, Bergamme strives to bring them back to life, "unfinishing" them until they are unrecognizable. It is the year 2020, and soon all works will have been cloned. Thus—*definitive de-unification*—the very idea of an original will have become meaningless. Bergamme knows that the countdown has begun. Before its unicity vanishes forever—but note: since over a century ago, restoration technics have been transforming "masterpieces" into imitations of their photographic reproductions—Bergamme must hurry to recover the work that, in his erudite and obsessive delirium, he considers the alpha and omega of the entire history of painting. It is *The Origin of the World*, by Gustave Courbet (1886): a close-up, zoom-in of feminine genitals presented by a faceless body, which, after the death of its last owner, belongs to the *Grand Musée*, where it is exhibited to the multitude. In order to achieve his goal (the *sub-traction* of *The Origin of the World*, whose *incompletion* and unicity he seeks to preserve), Bergamme will develop a friendship with Gerbraun or Ger Braun, chief of the museum, and with his assistants, Quevedo and Elise; with the hygrometrist Alf Le Crapaud (Alfred the Toad) and his assistant, the very beautiful Josette Goldsmiche; and with Roberte, the museum's top restorer, who is in charge of the final *de-unification*.

Interrogated by Gerbraun about the episode that unleashed his obsession, Bergamme says:

It was in London, when there was an exhibition by an American anartist whose name I will not reveal. She sold not only her artworks in galleries, but also her body. "As long as the audience has not penetrated me—she wrote in a catalogue that included her prices—it will not be able to feel my art." Well, behind so much arrogance there was a hidden truth that only a male artist can experience, given that the secret of every painting is a tension toward this origin of the world, painted too exactly by your Gustave Coubert. In her engulfing ambition, Bergamme continued, this American anartist, who sold her body as a "work," had ended up taking herself as *The Origin of the World*. Or, if you prefer, as a presentational rather than representational work, into which it was necessary to penetrate in order to feel correctly. Thus, she took herself to be an "installation."

–And tell me, hehe!, this "installation . . . ," have you visited it?

–Let me keep my answer in reserve.[24]

This is the dialogue between Gerbraun and Bergamme. With these ingredients, visual artist and writer Serge Rezvani (Jewish, Russian-Iranian, living in France) develops the narration *L'origine du monde. Pour une ultime histoire de l'art à propos du "cas Bergamme."* In the style of the great enlightened novels (Diderot, Sade), the text skillfully combines episodes, some of them tricky and some of them erotic, with subtle reflections around the state of art in the contemporary world and erudite references that invite deciphering. We know, for instance, that *The Origin of the World* was part of the patrimony of psychoanalyst Jacques Lacan, who had the work in his country house, always discreetly covered by a sliding wood panel. Since his death, the work has been exhibited at the Musée d'Orsay (also at www.lacan.com/courbert.htm, with Lacan's sliding wood panel). Now, psychoanalysis (Freud, Lacan) has something to say about the old biblical interdiction of images—about its paradoxical character, given that, psychoanalytically speaking, there is no desire without Law. This is the interdiction that the *museumsy* exhibition of *The Origin of the World*, now with no sliding panel, radically transgresses.

On the other hand, already since its first epigraph, the novel mentions *The Unknown Masterpiece*, the famous text by Balzac originally published in 1831, which deals precisely with the *incompletion*, with the chaos that would haunt the work seeking to present the real without remainder. There, Balzac narrates the experience of Frenhofer, an old metaphysical painter, who for over a decade has strived to produce a pictorial work, the nude of a beautiful woman, whose perfection should make her indistinguishable from a real woman. Frenhofer is not looking for mere empirical semblance, but rather for Form: "The Form," he says, referring to his admired Raphael, "is in his figures what it is in reality: an interpreter so that ideas and sensations can be communicated, a vast poetry." Nevertheless, Frenhofer is a modern artist, which means that he lacks a metaphysics that, by securing his yearning *a priori*, would exempt him from its factual fulfillment (in this, he is close to Joyce or, rather, to Joyce read by Borges as embodying "the splendid agony of a genre," in "From Allegories to Novels"). Consequently, he can only rely on his technical skills, fatally limited, in order to pictorially cope with a reality that exceeds him by definition. In fact, facing the inquisitive gaze of Porbus and Poussin, Frenhofer's colleagues in front of whom, finally, "the unknown masterpiece" is revealed, the work appears as a "chaos of colors, tones, imprecise subtleties, a kind of formless fog." Only a naked foot—"a delicious foot, a living foot"—like "among the rubble of a city that was burnt down," has survived Frenhofer's fury, his uncontrollable appetite for reality.

Thus, paradoxically, perfection and *incompletion* turn out to be synonymous. But the topic of the *de-unification* of works is also connected to Walter Benjamin's famous essay on the technical reproducibility and the "loss of aura" (of the unicity and artisticity) of the works of art, a process that would go back to lithography and would reach its peak with photographic reproduction and film (of course, Benjamin did not get to know of digital technology or cloning). It is less known that for Benjamin himself (*Theses on the Philosophy of History*, I), behind the sober materialist face of Modernity, would lie the delirious theology: it would be no more and no less than its secret double, its unmoved mover. But theology, "as we know, is wizened"—Benjamin says—"and has to keep out of sight."[25]

Chapter 8

Outline for an Ethics of Immortality

> If a man could write a book on Ethics which really was a book on Ethics, this book would, with an explosion, destroy all the other books in the world.
>
> —Ludwig Wittgenstein, "Lecture on Ethics"

1. In his epilogue to his celebrated collection of stories *The Aleph*, dated May 3, 1949, in Buenos Aires, the year in which the book was published, Borges describes the narration "The Immortal" contained in it as an "outline for an ethics of immortality."[1] This chapter seeks to elucidate the enigma presented by this phrase.

2. "The Immortal" can be read as a parable on writing, on the relationship between the "literary space" (as described by Blanchot) and the figure of the author, which has become problematic and evanescent.[2] For the Borgesian reader—that observer of literature, that "reader" that Borges exemplarily personifies—this space seems to be the condition of possibility of the literary fact. This fact—the work that is situated, dated, and signed—is nothing but the actualizing of that condition of possibility. In order to happen, literature must be there, like a reserve, a memory, an unconscious from which the work necessarily nourishes itself, beyond the author's intentions.

Borges pays more attention to the literary space than to the works that actualize it, which explains his predilection for quotation and commentary; his preference for writing "notes on *imaginary* books" over "a laborious madness and an impoverishing one . . . of composing vast books."[3] It also explains the Borgesian deconstruction of the figure of the author and its replacement by an intertextual game that operates at the margin of any subjective intentionality and of any temporality; the erasure of the boundaries between literary genres. These boundaries are replaced, we would say, by the all-encompassing category of "writing," which extends even to the traditional privilege of theory over fiction.[4]

Temporality is the possibility of inscribing the new (that which bursts in: the event, singularity) within a history, within a world—of inscribing the new in a world's horizon, thus divesting it of its destructuring potential. In Borges, by contrast, literary temporality (the history of literature) has been replaced by a spatial configuration. It is the library (the Library of Babel), of which all diachrony has been expelled ("from any hexagon one can see the floors above and below—one after another, endlessly," we are informed by the narrator in Borges's famous allegory)[5] and which brings about a desolating and absolute presence and availability ("the Library is total"). This replacement (a true "refutation of time") legitimates the use of the concept of "literary space" in connection to Borges's writing strategy. Only on the basis of its fulfillment (and only then) will it be possible to turn novelty into a modality of oblivion, as in the passage by Francis Bacon with which Borges begins "The Immortal" ("that all novelty is but oblivion").[6]

The refutation of time implicit in the idea of literary space, and expressed in the allegory of the Library of Babel, can be seen as an ideal projection of the synchronic atmosphere in the libraries that Borges so frequently visited. With the contemporary "museumification" of culture and the proliferation of technological tools for the quotation, the *pastiche*, or the *remake*, this atmosphere escapes, so I speculate, its secular confinement within enclosed facilities. We should add to this the progressive appearance of the modern character of the "man of letters," whom Borges himself discerns in writers like Flaubert, Mallarmé, and Valéry, and the very invention of literature as a specific activity, removed from the enslavement to the old administrators of historical temporality: religion and the State.

Nothing prevents us from expanding this overview from the refutation of literary temporality to the refutation of historical temporality, taking nominalism (a fundamental determination of Borges's thought) into account.

Indeed, for Borges, nominalism constitutes a kind of insurmountable horizon of modern culture. Its ubiquity is such that it has become invisible:

> Nominalism, which was formerly the novelty of the few, encompasses everyone today; its victory is so vast and fundamental that its name is unnecessary. No one says that he is a nominalist, because nobody is anything else.[7]

Borges writes this in "From Allegories to Novels," where he traces such victory. Nominalism and realism would be the names of the contenders who have been confronting each other once and again throughout the history of philosophy (which is not, he warns, "a vain museum of distractions and verbal games"). Borges adds: "[F]or realism universals were primordial . . . , for nominalism, individuals." And it is the epochal triumph of the latter that explains the passage from the allegory, "fable of abstractions," to the "fable of individuals," the novel, an event for which Borges offers an ideal date: that day in 1382

> [i]n which Geoffrey Chaucer, who perhaps did not think of himself as a nominalist, wanted to translate into English Boccaccio's verse "*E con gliocculti ferri l Tradimenti* (And with hidden irons the Treasons), and repeated it this way: "The smyler with the knyf under the cloke."[8]

What is at stake in this fundamental philosophical dispute? No more and no less than our relationship with historical temporality. Under the appearance of an ontological thesis (universals as the ultimate elements of the real), realism posits an essential correspondence between being and thinking, between language and reality. Now, many of our words—nouns, in which the sedating "substantiality" of the world is realized and finds expression— are abstract, universal: this simple fact suffices to make language a device that produces the forgetting of differences, universalization. It follows that, in order for language to exhaust the real, universality should be inscribed within the ultimate texture of things. Therefore, either manifest or reluctant, all realism is Platonism. Nominalism, by contrast, would want to keep open the gap between words and things. This is why the real appears to it like the boiling of an irreducible singularity, of an infinite complexity, which the universality of language could never grasp.

The dialectic of the "fable of individuals," the novel inaugurated by Chaucer's insignificant translation, may depict this impossibility. Indeed, the novel intends at first to inscribe individual reality in the medium of language. Insofar as it succeeds, it becomes "realist novel": fable of universalized individuals (let us note the oxymoron, which anticipates the outcome), in Borgesian terminology. But this success is at the same time its failure: the individuals that the novel has integrated into the horizon of language are no longer individuals but rather abstractions. Thus, the powers of language are unequally measured against a slippery reality. As in the Eleatic paradoxes, in which Borges was so interested, each time these powers seem to have reached their goal, the goal has been displaced and awaits them farther away. And the reason is that it is a transcendent goal, whose transcendency is however no longer the "white" transcendency, commensurable with the word and therefore reassuring for realism, but rather an opaque transcendency, before which the word can only fail.

Bouvard and Pécuchet ("the man who forged the classic novel with *Madame Bovary* was also the first to break it," Borges says, referring to its author); Hofmannsthal's *Lord Chandos Letter*, for whom "everything dissolves in fragments," and who, lacking a perfect language (in which "mute things speak"), chose silence; Joyce's *Ulysses* ("with its planes, times and precisions, the magnificent agony of a genre"): these are some of the milestones of this failure, whose fulfillment is turned into fiction by Borges himself in "Funes el memorioso." As we know, this is the story of a country worker called Ireneo Funes, who having lost the capacity to forget due to an accident, lies still on his sickbed. Confronting the infinite singularity of experience, which approaches him like a landslide of waste ("my memory, sir, is like a garbage heap," the narrator says at one point, during a long night without sleep),[9] Funes both despises and resents the universality of words. He cannot sleep nor think, the narrator concludes: "[T]o think is to forget differences, generalize, make abstractions."[10] "Funes el memorioso" (is it a Borgesian miniature of *Bouvard and Pécuchet*?) would be, from this perspective, the final stop in the road started by Chaucer: the parable of a wretched nominalism, which experiences the universality of language as an estrangement of the real, as an exile.

But who is right? Do being and thinking correspond to one another or not? It is an undecidable question, insofar as it would require a thinking of thinking, which would confront the same question. It is an unavoidable question, however, in which historical being and its limits are at stake. Indeed, in immediate experience, "being" and "thinking" are not equivalent. Hegel could proclaim that "everything real is rational, and everything rational is real," but nothing in everyday experience supports this (which is why philosophy is necessary). In the brief and often painful human life, rarely do moral accounts balance out, as reason would demand: rarely is the good rewarded or evil punished. For that to happen, a time extension is necessary, and this extension is history. History is always sacred history: either openly as a history oriented toward salvation, or undercover, as the secularized history of progress. History is the therapeutic device that legitimates suffering and that, as a temporality that goes beyond the duration of individual life, makes political life possible. History has been the supreme political technology, through which men of power, the "athletes of the State" obsessed with "great things," have managed to articulate great amounts of human energy around their megaprojects.[11]

For realism, the universe is a book written in characters that are legible to the human being. Certainly, they are not legible to all human beings, but only to the chosen ones to whom the keyword has been given, making it possible to read the book and to translate it into ethical-political norms, which tell their peers how to live in order to obtain salvation. Realism is the fundamental factor in the legitimation of historical powers. Nominalism, by contrast, whose time is made of synchronic and spatialized instants, is hostile to history and to the powers instituted by it. Located within the gap between being and thinking—this gap that is always open and bleeding—nominalism seeks to extract from this distance the symbolic energies to judge history as a block, disavowing all identity between ethics and politics.

The nominalist refutation of historical temporality has its basis in the Modern Age, after the Reformation launched the nominalism developed in the convents of the late Middle Ages into the public sphere. The nominalist idea adopted by Luther and Calvin of a God whose designs, by virtue of their divinity, are to be impenetrable to human reason, radically undermines the grounds of the terrestrial power of the church. Some central characteristics of Modernity derive from there, such as the primacy of individual consciousness, turned into the only contact point between the human being and an uncertain transcendence, as well as the legitimation and later development of systemic forms of action (which are a-valoric, and therefore unhistorical: they do not alter the balance of the savings account of salvation), power, and social articulation, such as techno-science and the market. For better or worse, and even if modern consciousness is to remain divided between history and space for a long time, the temporality of history has been undermined at its base, refuted.

And yet, and yet. . . . When concluding his *A New Refutation of Time*, Borges ("Borges"), split into a reader of his own text, denounces the vanity of such an enterprise: "Denying temporal succession, denying the self, denying the astronomic universe, are apparent desperations and secret consolations," he claims, in the face of a destiny that is "irreversible and iron-clad," which he often expresses through brusque figures, like the river, the tiger, or the fire.[12] "Time is the substance I am made of," he also says. And he concludes: "The world, unfortunately, is real; I, unfortunately, am Borges."[13] But pay attention: only in the face of a nominalist consciousness, subtracted from history and thrown into a space without consolation or salvation, can the real appear as that iron destiny. The medicine (the secret consolation) coincides here with the illness itself.[14] Nevertheless, the new (the real that exceeds all anticipation, all possibility) has not been canceled. On the contrary, it now becomes present as a radical alterity, as the exteriority that refracts all inscription in a temporal horizon; as the "messianic event" (Benjamin), the longed-for and feared catastrophe (so is death in Borges's work) of mystical traditions that, I speculate relying partly on Borges himself, work underground upon Modernity's consciousness.[15]

> 3. "The immortal" is presented as the relationship of a manuscript found in a version of Pope's *Iliad*, acquired in 1929 by the princess of Lucinges from someone called Joseph Cartaphilus, a mysterious antiquarian from Izmir who died shortly after. The manuscript tells the story of Flaminio Rufo, a Roman tribune dwelling in front of the Red Sea who, disappointed by having "barely seen the face of Mars," embarks on a search for a river whose water grants immortality and of which he knew through a dying horseman. After crossing inhospitable territories, Flaminio Rufo finds himself, wounded and exhausted, at the side of a mountain inhabited by troglodytes who carry a subhuman, almost mineral existence. From that side, one can see, on the other shore of an impure creek, a fabulous city, which Flaminio Rufo identifies as the City of the Immortals. However, the city is empty, and its architecture is monstrous. Flaminio Rufo, disappointed by his search, assimilates to the monotonous and elementary life of the troglodytes, with whom he tries in vain to establish communication, particularly with one whom he has named Argos (recalling Ulysses's dog).

However, after unexpected rain over the desert, truth is revealed to him: the troglodytes are the immortals, and their miserable condition is the result of the indifference that is inherent to eternity. The creek by which they live is the longed-for river. The monstrous city has been built by them as a monument to chaos. Argos turns out to be Homer; more than eleven hundred years have passed since he composed the work that, with Flaminio Rufo, has encountered him once again. Finally, the immortals will leave aside their indolence, going out to look for the river that, they speculate, will restore mortality. This finding is given to Flaminio Rufo, now split into the *homme de lèttres* Joseph Cartaphilius. It is possible to deduce that the manuscript that narrates these events was written shortly before his death.

Once the narration of these astonishing events is over, we witness a new split: the narrator *in fabula* Joseph Cartaphilus, now duplicated in a reader of his own text, gives us information that is even more astonishing, if this is possible: "*The story I have narrated seems unreal because in it are mixed the events of two different men,*" he says.[16] The second man would be Homer, whose literary habits can be intuited under the original surface of the text. A new comment, this time by the main narrator of the story ("Borges"), completes this information. This comment refers in its turn to a comment on Cartaphilus's manuscript, produced by "the most tenacious pen of Doctor Nahum Cordovero."[17] In this manuscript, which "is biblically entitled *A Coat of Many Colors*," Cordovero multiplies with erudition the quotations that would weave Cartaphilus's text: he sees in it a patchwork of references that go from Pliny to Bernard Shaw.[18] Finally, he concludes that the document is apocryphal. "Borges," for his part, denies the conclusion, without rejecting Cordovero's erudition. He does so with the following, suggestive words, with which the narration ends: "'When the end draws near,' wrote Cartaphilus, 'there no longer remain any remembered images; only words remain.' Words, displaced and mutilated words, words of others, were the poor pittance left him by the hours and the centuries."[19]

These "words of others" constitute precisely the unconscious, the literary space that has been working from the shadow upon Cartaphilus's text, to the point of making its authorship diffuse and anonymous. "I have been Homer; shortly, I shall be No One, like Ulysses; shortly, I shall be all men; I shall be dead," Cartaphilus has also said, anticipating his death.[20] The originality and the novelty in Cartaphilus's writing (in any writing) are therefore nothing but an appearance, an oblivion that is cleared away by the proximity of the end. The literary space, like the language on which it is constructed, erases the differences that constitute the illusory individuality and places the man of letters in an eternity that is not fullness but rather indifference. Death plays here a polyvalent role. On the one hand, its inexorable character, which resists dissolution within language (each and every refutation: "and yet, and yet . . ."), determines that, for the subject that has undergone the experience of immortality (of the word, of writing), death is the only happening of its difference. Therefore (this is a constant topic in Borges), the subject can only recognize itself and fully exist in the fleeting imminence of death. As Cartaphilus notes,

> death (or its allusion) makes men previous and pathetic. They are moving because of their phantom condition; every act they execute may be their last; there is not a face that is not on the verge of dissolving like a face in a dream. Everything among the mortals has the value of the irretrievable and the perilous.[21]

This acknowledgment is peculiar for it consists in a negation. Death is the instant in which that fleeting subjectivity knows itself to be illusory; in which, however, and by virtue of that very knowledge, it seems to admit an irrefutable reality. Existence, in its turn, would be only postponement, resistance to the pull of the primordial ocean of the word. A theory of modern subjectivity could begin here. Indeed, the modern idea of the subject has the notion of *autonomy* (Kant) at its core: the subject is that space subtracted from all heteronomous legislation, from all determination that does not proceed from its own reason. Nevertheless, everything in Modernity proclaims heteronomy: the subject is successively dissolved in the causal legislation of physics (the mechanics rooted in Newton); of political economy (Marx); in domestication, discipline, and punishment (Nietzsche, Foucault); in the drives of the unconscious (Freud); and (last but not least) in language ("language speaks," Heidegger). But only a subject could proclaim the dissolution of the subject. The subject is the one who says "I do not exist"; who, by saying it—affirming once again its quality of "man without qualities" (Musil), its sinking—withdraws fleetingly and paradoxically from all determination and fleetingly conquests its autonomy. Sacrifice is that strategy of affirmation by annihilation, always at the verge of the abyss. Modern subjectivity would have a sacrificial structure—"I think, therefore I do not exist, therefore I exist . . ." This, we speculate, is a sort of unfolding version of the experience of the Cartesian *cogito* and its truth.

On the other hand, it is impossible not to see in Cartaphilus, as a reader, the literary transposition of Borges himself. This is a reader at the verge of the abyss, capable of detecting in any text the return of a tradition; a *memorious* reader who, in "The Immortal" and other stories, would have fictionalized the foundational myth of his own literature. Myth is a performative discourse, which makes possible the leap from being to ought to be (from the corroboration that something is the case, to ethics) and which, consequently, confers on those who enunciate it a transvalued, normative legitimacy.[22] In the same way, Borges, through this foundational myth, seems to offer his writing as a normative model: as that ethic for immortals or men of letters (which emanates from Borges's work while at the same time investing it with its normative power) whose content we still ignore, but which would make possible to judge the artistry, the more or less accomplished character of literary works. This normative character would also account for the hegemonic role of the literary practices associated with Borges's name in the global culture of memory in the second half of the twentieth century.[23]

4. The literary unconscious that, from the shadows, weaves Cartaphilus's manuscript (and this is one of the main tenets of "The Immortal") has a name: Homer—someone of whom, like of Shakespeare, we conveniently know nothing or almost nothing.[24] Homer's privative circumstance consists, Borges has said, in the "difficult category of knowing what pertains to the poet and what pertains to the language";[25] it is therefore an empty name, through which language and the literary tradition of the West would speak without interference. This tradition, represented by its paradigmatic texts, would constitute a genuine *Scripture*, to which Western culture would inexorably return; a sort of symbolic capital of finite dimensions—"Four are the stories. During the time we still have we will continue to tell them, transformed," Borges says in "The Four Cycles"[26]—around which singular, empirical *scripts* would inevitably orbit.

5. The literary space, as we have seen, is the condition of possibility for empirical scripts. This trait, called "transcendental" in philosophical language, defines it. Now, the idea of possibility constitutes precisely the resting point on which Kant relies in order to transfer the normative content of premodern metaphysics into the nominalist culture of Modernity, thus

founding the project of a Modernity not lacking ethical content. Possibility is indeed a sort of ghost, a metaphysical aura that is added to phenomena, a ghost that nevertheless possesses an ontological consistency that phenomena lack in their contingency.[27] Indeed, the observation of phenomena makes possible only to infer statistical regularities, which are expressed in general statements. The structure that "makes them possible," by contrast, brings about universal, necessary statements. But a universal statement transcends mere empirical existence as an equally empirical observer might experience it. Even at the level of physical phenomena, universal statements convey an "ought to be," a norm to which facts, whether they are actually observed or not, must necessarily adjust if they are to be considered observable.

Kant's interest in Newton's and Galileo's science (expressed in his sentence: "to put philosophy on the secure path of science") is meaningful in the context of his bold philosophical enterprise: the search for some trace of normativity, for a resting point as the condition of possibility for an ethics within the horizon of Modernity. Modern science is the radical empiricist wing of Modernity. However, Modernity claims the right to speak of phenomena by means of universal and necessary statements, valid on Earth as well as in the galaxies farthest away. Kant asks himself: How are these statements (judgments) possible? How is it possible that there are universal statements that, however, are not deprived of empirical content, are not empty like the statements of formal logic? The answer lies in the question. The "possibility," which precedes phenomenal reality, is the key to universality. The idea of possibility provides the minimal metaphysics (the zero degree of metaphysics) required by the passage from empirical being to norm in modern conditions. The same happens (cannot but happen) with the Borgesian "ethics for immortals." This is why the "outline" of such an ethics is given to us in a text that mythically founds the idea of literary space, as the condition of possibility of literary phenomena, of singular literary works.

Possibility claims to anticipate and prefigure the experience weaved within it. Or rather, through the concept of possibility, a certain phenomenal or literary experience, historically and culturally situated, is imaginarily invested with normative power, as if it were the product, not of the uncertain human history, but of a design written in the heaven of essences. At the same time, it is in in the dialectical essence of modern reason that its corrosive powers (the diverse "hermeneutics of suspicion")[28] should be deployed against the metaphysical remainder present in transcendental thought, disclosing its profane history, its genealogy, and driving it to the complex of contingent circumstances and experiences that would constitute its human, all too human origin. However, this exercise of critical reason presupposes again a norm, a *surplus* of signification from which history might be observed and judged. In this manner, at an upper level in the spiral of critical thought, possibility and norm become once again awkwardly present. Finally, the idea of possibility (as in, for example, Adorno's *Minima Moralia*, his "melancholic science") is reduced to a virtual point, to an impossible but indispensable "perspective of redemption," a sort of spatial and visual hypostasis of an endless questioning.[29]

The literary space, transposition into the literary realm of that minimal metaphysics that ethics calls for, cannot but experience a parallel process of purification of positive contents, a mythical askesis. Above, I have identified that space with the literary tradition, with a Scripture, an Absolute Book that empirical writings would only repeat.[30] Until that point, it was possible to understand (the names of Homer and Shakespeare, and the idea of the four recurrent stories, seem to indicate this) that this Writing could indeed possess a positive content, that it could constitute a sort of literary canon like the one proposed by Harold Bloom in *The Western Canon*, and to which, with the "anxiety of influence" in the middle, all good literature should refer.[31] But what is a Writing, an Absolute Book? What is the relationship between this Scripture and the scripts that repeat and interpret it?

An Absolute Book can be understood in principle as the source of an equally absolute authority (religious, political, cultural). This is how the institutions of the great monotheistic religions have tended to read the book that contains their revelation. Nevertheless, this interpretation is fragile: sooner or later the purported positive content falls prey to some Dr. Nahum Cordovero (some cultural critique, possessing the tools of history and the sciences of language), who will have no difficulty in interpreting the book as a patchwork, a mixture of texts whose purported sacred character would be but the sacralization of a will to power.

Religious authority and religious critique coincide here in giving the book a positive content and differ only in the question of its origin. Certain mystical interpretations, however, deny that any such content can be associated with the absolute. In these interpretations, Scripture withdraws to a virtual point: a pretext lacking a positive content, on the basis of which an infinite interpretation is unleashed. Jewish mysticism, which is rich in reflections upon the relationship between the absolute and writing (the absolute as Scripture), expresses this tendency in an extremely plastic and concentrated manner. This mysticism focuses on the relationship between Revelation, the "written *Torah*," and the "oral *Torah*," the profuse set of commentaries, and of commentaries of the commentaries, which the former would have brought about. Now, according to the bold image proposed by the nineteenth-century Hasidic mystic Rabbi Mendel Torum of Rymanow, the "written *Torah*" (the divine, absolute word actually present in the texts that are considered sacred) is reduced to the letter *aleph*, the beginning of the Hebrew word "I" (*anoji*) with which Adonai starts his speech to Moses at the Sinai. Everything else would be human writing, oral *Torah*. But *aleph* is a mute letter, the sole opening of the glottis before it starts vocalizing. It is therefore a pretext, empty but unavoidable, which projects a culture of reading, of interpretation.[32]

It is possible to recognize in this mystical strand the antiauthoritarian, and therefore nominalist, spirit of Modernity. Indeed, in order to preserve the ethical tension associated with transcendency while preventing it from playing on the side of power, it is necessary that the true name of the divinity be "Nothing" and that its word, Scripture, contract into a mute letter. Analogously, the reference to an empty signifier, to a hollowed-out pretext, is the only way in which the categorical imperative of an "ethics of immortality," as the criteria of the artisticity of literary works, can be performed in a nominalist culture. But a referentless reference is a pure act of referring: an interrogation, thrown into the void, of the artisticity of the artist's own work. Thus, literary (ethical, artistic, extraordinary) work would be those (and only those) that thematize themselves and include in their plot the obsessive question about literature and about their own literary artisticity: works turned toward themselves, self-referentially, whose prototype can be found in Borges's works. These works endlessly seek to reach themselves, endlessly plot the theory of their own literary practice.

> 6. On the other hand, self-reference is the paradoxical fulfillment of the vocation of realism in literature. This is not, however, the realism of a reality simultaneously apprehended and constructed in language, but rather the realism of the Real as the object of repulsion and desire, beyond all inscription. The classical place in Borges's literature where this question unfolds is the essay *Partial Magic in the Quixote*. Borges

reviews there a series of occurrences in the literary procedure which, after a text by André Gide, is often designated with a term taken from heraldry: putting-in-abyss, *mise en abyme*, by virtue of which the work, symbolic artifact that belongs to the world of the author and the reader, breaks into its own interior in the ideal plane of fiction. Examples of this resource, whose effect is an infinite regress (Borges says about Scheherazade: "that the queen may persist and the motionless king hear forever the truncated story of the *Thousand and One Nights*, now infinite and circular"), are *Quixote*, whose characters are surprisingly readers of the book who know its author; *Hamlet*, whose plot includes a sort of miniature of the work itself; and the night 602 in *One Thousand and One Nights*, in which Scheherazade begins a narration that closely resembles the text that contains her as a character.[33] Reflecting on the anxiety that these artifices produce, Borges concludes: "[T]hese inventions suggest that if the characters of a fictional work can be readers or spectators, we, its readers and spectators, can be fictitious."[34]

Self-reference ("we can be fictitious") makes manifest that the resources with which we draw the limits of what we call "world" are not fundamentally different from the limits drawn by literature in order to build its fictions. In other words, the world is a symbolic construction, a horizon drawn in the medium of language. And once we have crossed the threshold of the world, there is no going back. It is not possible to look behind language to have access to the Real: it has been left behind as an object of desire, both longed for and impossible ("At that very instant: / Oh, what I would not give for the joy / of being at your side in Iceland. . . . / At that very instant / the man was at her side in Iceland," Borges writes in a poem with a suggestive title: "Nostalgia for the Present").[35]

It is one thing to be confined to language as if it were a prison (this is Wittgenstein's figure); it is another one to know of this confinement. This requires a point of observation, a certain elevation, which is granted precisely by self-reference. Self-reference is the source of strange paradoxes, like that of the liar ("I lie," etc.), and also of fantastic inventions like that of the perfect map, which by virtue of its perfection must contain itself, thus throwing us into an infinite regress. Such figures disturb us, not by virtue of their irrationality but because they emerge from logic, from the very heart of rationality. Thus, they constitute a kind of linguistic equivalent of the Lacanian anamorphosis: cracks through which the disquieting glint of the Real can be obliquely glimpsed; traces of the absence, of the lack that constitutes us, which have been left within the deep grammar of language and reason. This is the key of the Borgesian fantastic, whose relationship with the "ethics of immortality" I would like to make manifest.

Conventional fantastic literature presents to the reader strange facts that are difficult to explain and throws him into a hesitation between a natural explanation (it was actually a dream, a hallucination, or an effect of laws still unknown, but natural) and a supernatural explanation. The hesitation, which is often incarnated by one of the characters, must be experienced by the reader; there lies the specificity of the genre.[36] However, at this point, the strangeness does not yet surpass the form of legality: in one or the other pole, whether it is a natural or a supernatural, a physical or a metaphysical explanation, the legality of experience has not yet been put into question. One could even say, in the manner of the Kantian "experience of the sublime" (in which the subject, facing for example the spectacle of an unleashed nature, undergoes the experience of his quasi-annihilation), that the hesitation induced by the fantastic story constitutes a sort of initiation ritual, at the end of which the sovereignty of reason turns out to be dramatically and triumphantly confirmed.

> This is not the case with the Borgesian putting-in-abyss, a device that seeks to open a path for a more primordial disruption of experience. The narrator in "Tlön, Uqbar, Orbis Tertius" is aware of this effect when, early in the story, he stops at the following circumstance:
>
> We became lengthily engaged in a vast polemic concerning the composition of a novel in the first person, whose narrator would omit or disfigure the facts and indulge in various contradictions which would permit a few readers—very few readers—to perceive an atrocious or banal reality.[37]

The Real, behind all its banality and atrocity, awaits behind these specular games. And the polemic at stake, suggestively developed in the proximity of a mirror ("from the remote depths of the corridor, the mirror spied on us," the narrator notes), leads to an astonishing narration that presents a world invaded by the encyclopedia of an imaginary planet, Tlön, in which one can glimpse (certain clues lead to this) an allegory of the linguisticized world, the world constructed and deconstructed in language—a world that is increasingly our world.[38]

By means of self-referentiality and its abysmal effect, we have come across a link between the paradoxical "ethics of immorality" and the call for the Real. It could not be otherwise. Ethics demands the abandonment of the "magic circle of existence"—there where the real and the rational, history and truth, converge—in order to access an Other Truth, from whose point of observation history itself can be judged. The transcendence of the divine, matter extraneous to conceptualization in the form of a radical material, the Kantian idea of the unconditioned—all of these have successively supported this demand. To us, however, devoted functionaries of the book of the world, it is given to experience it in the form of the return, of the discreet explosion of the Real.

Chapter 9

Politics of Space and of the Gaze

> Long live the murderer, so that he sees our victory standing.
>
> —Graffiti on the corner of Lord Cochrane
> and Tarapacá, December 1998.

> Every evil, the sight of which edifies a god, is justified.
>
> —Friedrich Nietzsche, *On the Genealogy
> of Morals*, Second Essay, § 7

Introduction: To Suffer for the City

In a passage of his essay on "hyperpolitics," Peter Sloterdijk asks: "How should we call those who, once they have taken responsibility for great things, never abandon them?"[1] In other to answer this question accurately, Sloterdijk suggests, these subjects must be distinguished from mere megalomaniacs: the latter, "in order to achieve something," get themselves into issues that are too big for them and leave them waiting. By contrast, Greek philosophy and its equivalents in India and China would have been characterized by purifying the concern with great things (*ta megala*) from maniac elements: "Their concern is precisely to remove the maniac factor from the old practices of wisdom, in order to be dispassionate in the school of what is big, which is what gives something to think about."[2]

Sloterdijk suggests that we use the word "megalopaths" for these "citizens of the cosmos" (*kosmopolites*, according to the originally humoristic expression of the exiled Diogenes of Sinope). Alexander the Great still practiced a maniac politics, "driven by the drunkenness of the abstract quantity." His tutor Aristotle, by contrast, "was among the first to think beyond mania . . . and to organize the great within scientific disciplines, by means of cold conceptual routines." Sloterdijk adds, referring to Aristotle:

> Therefore, only after him can it be said that philosophy, as the exercise of the soul and as a style of knowledge, really established itself in the *polis*. Since then, throughout two millennia, it has been gaining validation as a megalopathic theory of a megalopathic praxis, as a cult or therapy for great patients—that is, citizens of the polis, functionaries, theologians, and statemen, who are the ones that get to perceive the new magnitude of the world.[3]

Thus, philosophy is primarily a therapy for select patients (Sloterdijk also calls them "athletes of the State"), who recognize one another through a new type of psychic bond ("friends are men focused on walking through the heights and the abysses of the great"), and whom one must protect, by means of an ethics of the "golden mean" prefigured by Aristotle, from vertigo and the mania that abysses and heights usually produce.

Despite its upright origin, philosophy was destined to transcend the walls of the palace and to overflow toward the *polis*, now the field of the megalopathic exercises of the elites. Indeed, given that "for many people, to live in the city is the same as to suffer for the city. [Thus] the reflection on the coexistence in the city must generate *eo ipso* a theory that explains and justifies—ontologically, cosmologically, and eschatologically—the suffering for the great."[4] This way, not only does philosophy descend to the city, but its tasks are decisively expanded: not only palatial *phronesis*, but also ontology, cosmology, and eschatology—the theory of being, of the ordering of the universe, and of its finality—are originally and inherently associated to the explanation and justification of the "suffering for the great." Sloterdijk adds in a note:

> This is why, together with friendship, which represents in a way the diurnal image of the relationships between successful men in the great world, compassion comes to the fore, benevolent love (*caritas*) as a new way to regulate the participation in the destinies of the losers, and to shape environments in the "dark zone" of the empire.[5]

An adequate organization of interior environments would have sufficed for the development of a friendship between successful human beings—not, however, for the political justification of the suffering for the great. Ontology, cosmology, eschatology, that is, philosophy altogether, if they are to effectively fulfil their political destiny, must provide their services not within the limited scale of the interactions between individuals (*eros, paideia*), but rather by means of devices that amplify their effects at the level of the *polis*. In order to be effective, the megalopathic therapy must be inscribed in the space of the city. Consequently (this is the thesis that, relying on Nietzsche and Foucault, I will be sketching here), the architectonic organization of that space (with its monuments, landmarks, and perspectives, and the optical game of transparencies and opacities that they institute) might be understood as a sort of philosophical palliative-dispensing apparatus. Before becoming flesh, before descending on the human bodies in order to mold them according to the requirements of the city, metaphysics should become wall, stone. In a primordial sense, architecture would be a petrified metaphysics.

Device I: The Spectacle

Among the most powerful symbolic resources available to the faction of the megalopathic therapists, the positing of a universal order that would rule all things (and that a healthy *polis*, like the Republic imagined by Plato, should somehow reproduce) excels. The passage from this eminent order (*kosmos*) to the sphere of the individual's obligations in the city presupposes that the order in question is not only transcendent, safe of bothersome empirical interferences, but also intelligible, commensurable with human reason. The task of the philosopher consists in securing that the universe responds in effect to a rational order, which human beings—more precisely, those trained in the megalophatic arts—might in principle unravel and translate into political concepts, whose legitimacy would then be sheltered from dispute.

The benefits of this interpretation, first developed by the Greek megalophatic therapists and later on adapted and refined by the Christian West, are unquestionable. Human existence, with its pains and miseries, would not be the product of mere hazard but part of an order in which these pains and miseries would find justification. By contrast to the uncomfortable suspicion of pre-Socratic thinkers (Heraclitus, §53: "War is the father of all and the king of all": no coherence could be expected from this lineage) and of Christian Gnostics, human beings would not be thrown in the midst of a hostile and absurd universe. Tragic guilt, as the expression of the uncertainty inherent to human existence—there is no way to wholly foresee the outcomes of an action: Oedipus, the enlightened hero, the redeemer of Thebes, has nonetheless murdered his father and fornicated with his mother—would vanish in the infinite goodness of creation. Evil (the pain of those who suffer for what is great) would lack actual existence: it would be nothing but a lesser good, an appearance, a bad dream from which we wake up at the just and happy end of history. Between the sacred and the profane, a bridge would lie for the believer to traverse in his quest for salvation. And the performance of pious works, weighted on the scale of good and evil operated by the megalophatic elite, would secure this passage, beyond uncertainty and meaninglessness.

Nevertheless, in order for this comforting interpretation to be an effective antidote against the world's absurdity, a thorough accounting of the evils to be justified—*adjusted*, attuned somehow with justice—is required. According to Nietzsche, this would have been the task of the gods—a task that his Foucauldian posterity might well call *panoptic*:

> So as to abolish hidden, undetected, unwitnessed suffering from the world and honestly to deny it, one was in the past virtually compelled to invent gods and genii of all the heights and depths, in short something that roams even in secret, hidden places, sees even in the dark, and will not easily let an interesting painful spectacle pass unnoticed. . . . "Every evil the sight of which edifies a god is justified": thus spoke the primitive logic of feeling—and was it, indeed, only primitive?[6]

For the healing of the world, the most remote suffering must be made visible: it must have an observer. But once the divine observers have been placed in their elevated points of observation, it becomes necessary to provide them once and again with new spectacles that keep their interest alive. In other words, for the megalopathic therapy to be effective, the profane history of the gods must be repressed and forgotten. In its place, the megalopathic therapists will erect their transcendent divinities. Evil finds its origin and simultaneous justification in these divinities, as an episode of a sacred history.

The concept of a divinity that not only creates evil but also enjoys it—that creates it *for* its enjoyment!—is a paradox, a theological scandal. But it did not seem to bother the Greeks so much. Rather, as Nietzsche points out, they made wars and war songs so that the gods (and their representatives, the poets and the philosophers) would not lack entertainment:

> With what eyes do you think Homer made his gods look down upon the destinies of men? What was at bottom the ultimate meaning of the Trojan Wars and other such tragic terrors? There can be no doubt whatever: they were intended as *festival plays* for the gods; and, insofar as the poet is in these matters of a more "godlike" disposition than other men, no doubt also as festival plays for the poets.
> It was in the same way that the moral philosophers of Greece later imagined the eyes of God looking down upon the moral struggle, upon the heroism and self-torture of the virtuous: the "Herakles of duty" was on a stage and knew himself to be; virtue without a witness was something unthinkable for this nation of actors.[7]

Visibility, which in the well-distributed economy of the cosmos legitimates the suffering for the city, is to have an expression in it. Only the subjects that experience daily this visibility can indeed accept pain and behave like mature citizens. Visibility was inherent to the Greek agora, with its horizontality and lack of structure, a tendency to *isegoria* ("equality in the agora") and to an unrestricted freedom of expression (*parrhesia*): both make difficult the attribution of responsibilities to individuals.[8] The rigorous visibility imposed by the architecture of the theater is opposed to the architectonic horizontality of Greek democracy in its stage of irresponsible, childish latency: the theater (*theatron*) is in its origin a "place to see." Richard Sennett says:

> The theater fan . . . is a tight design, organizing a crowd in vertical rows, magnifying the lone voice below, exposing the speaker to all, his every gesture visible. It is an architecture of individual exposure.[9]

It is important to note that these theatrical spaces, with the visibility they impose, have an explicitly political function. After the fifth century BC, the *ekklesia*, the assembly of all the citizens, would convene almost weekly at the theater on the hill of Pnyx, ten minutes away from the agora. Unlike at the agora, where bodies were often standing up straight (*orthos*) and moved among a whirlwind of other bodies, at the theater, bodies remained seated, unmoving and identifiable. In Greek culture, however, to sit in this manner had a connotation of submission. Thus, Sennett says, "a young girl came to the house of her new husband and signified her submission to his rule in a ritual which made her sit for the first time by his hearth."[10] The sitting position was also associated with *pathos*, with affliction, "an unnatural state . . . when [the human body] falls farthest from its ideal of strength and integrity."[11]

Pathos is opposed to *orthos*. In this sense, the spectacle, the megalopathic therapy that underlies Greek democracy, will determine that the rectitude of the citizens—their vertical posture in the middle of the agora's horizontality—yields to a new organization of space. In this organization, verticality has been transferred from subjects to architecture, to stone; meanwhile, bodies have become passive. The city leaves behind its childish state of latency and becomes virile, phallic in its choice of verticality.

Megalopathic therapies, in sum, have the aim of explaining and justifying the "suffering for the great," which, for many, as we know, is inseparable from political life. Theology and metaphysics fulfill precisely this function: to make sure that, despite "appearances," at the end of history, humanity's ethical accounts will be in perfect equilibrium. The gods are the required observers for the accounts to be done thoroughly. On the other hand, in order for this therapeutic knowledge to imbue the life of the city, it is necessary that its discourse be amplified by means of architectonic devices. An example of this is the theater, whose vertical orientation favors visibility and makes possible the invention of the "animal with the right to make promises" (Nietzsche), the responsible subject. Indeed, although the gods see everything, their representatives on Earth, the "athletes of the State," can only aspire, if they act with justice, to optimize their optic perception of the ordinary men under their watch—to make this perception as similar as possible to that of the gods, whose cosmic dispositions, on the other hand, they must translate into ethical-political precepts. The megalopathic therapist legitimates its role by calling himself a representative, a "soldier of the cosmos."[12] Of course, there is also the error, the inaccuracy inherent to all representation; but for that we have the inexhaustible account of the gods, which makes up for any nonexplained difference in the accounts.

Christianity will not modify this megalopathic device in any significant way. The plurality of pagan gods and the Greek ambivalence regarding the very idea of creation had prevented Antiquity from assuming the paradox, pointed out earlier, of a world created by a good God—a God whose creation is intelligible to the human kind, which then can guide its actions on the basis of its intellection—and the awkward presence of the evil, pain, and misery of those who suffer and are oppressed by the city. The Greek gods could be "conceived of as friends of cruel spectacles" (Nietzsche) without trouble. To the Christians, by contrast, this possibility had to be eliminated. A possible alternative, supported by some, is Gnosis. To put it simply, Gnostics proposed to write evil (including in it the pagan political institutions, and the Greek cosmos, which legitimates and harbors it) into the account of a perverse demiurge fighting against the true god, whose uncontaminated kingdom is yet to come; but this alternative, an-archic and a-political in a primordial sense, is not viable in the long run. The long run is precisely the temporality of those whose eschatological hopes—justice now!—have been frustrated: a temporality in which, consequently, it is not possible to do without megalopathic therapies, metaphysics, and politics.

The long run had already retaken its rights in the fourth century CE, when Augustine, after giving up the Manicheism that he had professed until then, takes once again the path of metaphysics, the same that the first Christians had violently recused. Indeed, utilizing the metaphysical distinction between essence and appearance, Augustine deprives evil of substantiality. Thus, evil would not exist in reality (in the hyperreality of essences): it would be but a lesser good, an appearance, a derivative of a substantial good, that is, human freedom. Only this freedom would introduce evil in a creation that, in an essential sense, would be exonerated from it. Freedom, and not evil, is what the spectacle of the universe would ultimately offer to the divinity—the only God—who would thus be exonerated from the charge of perversely enjoying pain.[13]

Thus, the Greek megalopathic device is both preserved and perfected, and with it is the tendency to verticality that constitutes its amplification at the urban level. The high towers, the domes and cathedrals of the city in Medieval Christianity are the vanishing points that lead the profane gaze toward the heights. They are also the tangible proof that a wisdom, Revelation, flows to them from heaven and makes possible the decipherment of the Book of the Universe and its translation into a scale of pious works, which provide the believer with a guarantee of his salvation. And under their roofs, the ceremonies, the rituals of individuation and obedience, take place; those rituals that turn the believer into a person, whose signature will be imprinted in his works, making sure that they will be noted and credited to his personal account of salvation.

Device II: The Panoptic

There are multiple factors that, by increasingly disturbing the medieval order, give rise to the Modern Age. The incipient bourgeoisie, the urban classes interested in productively investing economic surplus, will struggle against an order that relies on the dilapidation of a significant fraction of it, using it for unproductive consumption by the class of megalopathic therapists, the nobility and the clergy. On the other hand, the nominalist theology of the late Middle Ages, and the Reformation later on, will subject the intellectual grounds of the classical megalopathic device to a radical critique. The idea of the universe as an intelligible order was indeed the hinge that made possible the passage between the profane and the sacred, sacralizing everyday life by safeguarding it from uncertainty and meaninglessness. However, as the critiques of this happy world would acutely perceive, the passage also takes place in the opposite direction, favoring the profanation of the sacred. In fact, the idea of creation as an intelligible order makes God into a being at the level of human reason: a sort of idol, an anthropomorphic creation like the one that Feuerbach will still consider with suspicion in his nineteenth-century critique of religion. The class of megalopathic therapists has done nothing but produce a divinity in its own image; nothing, thus, but divinized itself to legitimize its dominion. Therefore, in order to undermine it, it is necessary, if not to kill God, at least to confine him to the realm of private beliefs, releasing him from his megalopathic functions in the city. The void that opens up with this absence of God coincides with the freedom of the moderns, a freedom that is synonymous with the autonomy of a subject that has the courage to make use of his own reason, as in Kant's famous claim.[14] At the same time, only the void left by God's retreat will make possible the unfolding of practices that, like technoscience and market economy, demand a desacralized, disenchanted world, in which—and only in which—things can be seen as tools or commodities, deprived of any intrinsic value or meaning.

It is possible to see in the plague an additional element in the decomposition of the Medieval order. Michel Foucault calls attention to this in *Discipline and Punish*.[15] Unlike leprosy, which can be controlled by means of a merely exclusionary, binary power (the lepers there, the healthy here), the plague is a phenomenon that transgresses boundaries and exceeds the megalopathic strategies for containing anxiety on the face of meaninglessness. It is a contagious and inexplicable evil, which arrives without warning, decimates entire populations, and submits the virtuous and the sinners to the same atrocious suffering. The plague "mingles," as Foucault says. Therefore, it summons an imaginary of the carnival: "suspended laws, lifted prohibitions, the frenzy of passing time, bodies mingling together without respect, individuals unmasked, abandoning their statutory identity."[16] The plague, beyond its physical effects, is a political and metaphysical event. It is the chaos that threatens the earthly city, infiltrates and contaminates the very core of the classical megalopathic device, which is constituted by the notion of order, as we already know.

However, as the plague itself makes manifest, the loss of confidence in the transcendent meaning of things does not result in giving oneself up, in letting oneself go to the carnival and its indifferentiation, but in the unfolding of an iron *will to order*, whose highest expression is the techno-scientific enterprise, its disciplines and technologies. Indeed, facing the plague and its festive imaginary, Foucault says that a political dream emerges "which was exactly its reverse":

> Not the collective festival, but strict divisions; not laws transgressed, but the penetration of regulation into even the smallest details of everyday life through the mediation of the complete hierarchy that assured the capillary functioning of power; not masks that were put on and taken off, but the assignment to each individual of his "true" name, hit "true" place, his "true" body, his "true" disease. The plague as a form, at once real and imaginary, of disorder had as its medical and political correlative discipline. . . . The plague-stricken town, traversed throughout with hierarchy, surveillance, observation, writing; the town immobilized by the functioning of an extensive power that bears in a distinct way over all individual bodies—this is the utopia of the perfectly governed city.[17]

Disciplines and technologies occupy the void left by the classical megalopathic device that Christianity had inherited from Greece, and they are only thinkable on the basis of that void. Given that the gods have retreated (they have ceased to fulfill the role of spectators: they are blind), it is necessary for the human gaze to stand in for them, as in the episodes of the plague during which, Foucault says, "the gaze is alert everywhere."[18] The panoptic, an architectonic device developed by English utilitarian philosopher and social reformer Jeremy Bentham, is the artifact that makes possible the maximization of vigilance. "We know the principles," Foucault says:

> At the periphery, an annular building; at the center, a tower; this tower is pierced with wide windows that open onto the inner side of the ring; the peripheric building is divided into cells, each of which extends the whole width of the building; they have two windows, one on the inside, corresponding to the windows of the tower; the other, on the outside, allows the light to cross the cell from one end to the other. All that is needed, then, is to place a supervisor in a central tower and to shut up in each cell a madman, a patient, a condemned man, a worker or a schoolboy. By the effect of backlighting, one can observe from the tower, standing out precisely against the light, the small captive shadows in the cells of the periphery. They are like so many cages, so many small theaters, in which each actor is alone, perfectly individualized and constantly visible. . . . Visibility is a trap.[19]

By means of the panoptic, a reduced number of guards can control a multitude of inmates. However, reducing the megalopathic effects of the panoptic to a mere arithmetic of visibility would be to misunderstand its radical novelty (an event in the "history of the human mind," as it was called by a certain Julius, a few years after Bentham).[20] The panoptic accomplishes the perfect dissociation between watching and being watched. On one side, at the central ring, nothing but observers, reduced to a pure gazing eye; on another side, in the body of the building, subjects who are perfectly and constantly visible. But pay attention!: not effectively "watched," but "visible." The visual asymmetry makes it impossible to verify the actual presence of the watchman. Thus, the vigilance-effect goes on even if the central tower is empty. The major effect of the panoptic is then

> [t]o induce in the inmate a state of conscious and permanent visibility that assures the automatic functioning of power. So to arrange things that the surveillance is permanent in its effects, even if it is discontinuous in its action; that the perfection of power should tend to render its actual exercise unnecessary . . . ; in short, that the inmates should be caught up in a power situation of which they are themselves the bearers.[21]

> He who is subjected to a field of visibility, and who knows it, assumes responsibility for the constrains of power; he makes them play spontaneously upon himself, he inscribes in himself

the power relation in which he simultaneously plays both roles; he becomes the principle of his own subjection.[22]

The old gods, and the very god of Hellenized Christianity, were already—or they are for us, their historians and mourners—the names given to a condition of thorough and constant visibility, capable of giving meaning to hidden pain; or of securing its recycling, its transformation into the good, either by means of the cruel and joyful spectacle offered to the gods, or by means of its conversion into beneficial freedom. And even though God is dead (or he has retreated, or he is blind), this condition is still necessary for the production of responsible subjects, capable of absorbing the suffering associated with life in the city.[23] But now visibility must be *technologically produced*. The efficacy of the panoptic does not consist, as I have already pointed out, in a merely arithmetical effect. I can now clarify this remark: what is primordial is the production of panopticized subjects, who have internalized the devices of their own vigilance. If physical panoptics (prisons, hospitals, schools, streets and public places covered by TV cameras) would seek the actual vigilance of subjects, their failure would be spectacular. As in Borges's cartographic fables, the behavioral map cannot represent the territory, for it would lead to hypertrophy or to an infinite regress. Rather, as it happened sometime with confessional practices (Foucault), they are large-scale learning games, through which a thorough and tireless self-observer is installed and preserved within subjectivity; an effective "interior bureaucrat" (Sloterdijk), who does not weight upon the State budget nor is it menaced by strikes, because it works with the very energy of the subject that it seeks to watch.

Taking distance from a literal reading of Foucault, we might surmise that the physical panoptic is just a sort of threshold leading to the metaphysical panoptic, being at once its imperfect realization. In fact, the devices of contemporary power rarely have the shape of the ring with a central observation tower, proposed by Bentham and analyzed by Foucault. Rather, they tend to work like so-called black boxes, inhabited by panopticized subjects.

Device III: The Black Box and the Coffin

The concept of "black box" is crucial for the functioning of the modern world. The market of technologically complex products (cars, phones, home appliances, computers) bases its constant expansion on designing "friendly" interfaces, which isolate the "user" from any aspect that is irrelevant for the operation of a given artifact. In order to drive a car, for example, it is not necessary to know about mechanics; similarly, an internet user has no need to be aware of the complex transactions (between local phone companies, satellites, computers of all sizes and brands) that take place behind his back. As long as there are no failures, the interfaces situate the user in front of a black box, safeguarded from complexity.[24] The same happens with specialists at different levels: in order to write computer software, it is not necessary to know about hardware, but only to master the programming language.

Current organizations (corporations, institutions) tend to operate on the basis of this same principle. They are hierarchical organizations, whose units translate into partial goals the global aims. And as long as these goals are being fulfilled, each unit is a black box exempted from sending information toward the outside; information and control are transferred to the upper levels only in exceptional cases. Thus, while the global goals of the corporation are being met, no one should care whether the accounting section is using either computers or pencils. This question will become visible to the management only if, for example, the billing is not ready on time or the information necessary to make decisions is missing.[25]

Organizational black boxes constitute metaphysical panoptics where, except for rare situations, individuals take charge of their own vigilance, where the bureaucrat, the inner megalopath, takes the burden and exonerates the central power.[26] Now, there is a political and existential statement about black boxes for which Viennese architect Adolf Loos is well known.[27] Other trends in modern architecture seek to reconcile the private with the public. Loos, by contrast, is suspicious: in this promised reconciliation, he sees a sort of ornamental artifice through which the hard truth of the modern world, which consists in fragmentation, is whisked away. By exposing it to the public gaze, that false reconciliation betrays the last stronghold in which individuals can still preserve their intimacy. Loosian architecture, by contrast, is characterized by the intention of preserving the space of intimacy at all costs. According to Loos,

> The exterior need not reflect the public realm, nor express the private realm. It is a mere dividing line between the public and the private, which transmits nothing to the interior life except light; it is a wall and a mask that, not representing anything, falsifies nothing. It does not unite, but rather splits apart.[28]

The distinction between exterior and interior, public and private, runs parallel in Loos to the distinction between architecture and art: "The work of art," he says, "is the artist's private issue. Not so the house. The work of art is accountable to no one; the house, to everyone. . . . The work of art is revolutionary and the house is conservative."[29] If architecture is exposed to gazes and is responsible to everyone, it is precisely in order to preserve a realm that is refractory to gazes and to their correlate, responsibility. Architecture's task is to build a "defensive perimeter of privacy." But privacy is not here a mere abstraction: the interior of the Loosian house—a house in the Vienna of Musil, of Kokoschka, of Schönberg, of Wittgenstein and Freud, to mention just a few names—is defined by harboring works of art, either actually or potentially. But then it should be possible to approach Loos from the inside to the outside; not from architecture, but from art, whose possibility the former would only preserve. Loosian interiority is constituted in frontal opposition to the panoptic of the modern world: an opposition that, however, having decisively internalized the principle of what it wants to reject, throws the unfortunate Loosian inhabitant to an inward flight—from interior to interior, from black box to black box—whose only possible points of arrival are the uterus and the coffin.

In a world that lacks certainty—and even with more of a reason, in a world that knows itself to be uncertain: our world, Loos's world—every work, either humble or glorious, constitutes a sort of fragment of one's own identity thrown into a drift that is beyond our control. By means of works, the human subject expresses itself, exteriorizes its being; but it immediately loses itself: the work, pulled by circulation—circulation of commodities, in the last instance—moves away and becomes unrecognizable: here we have the modern problem of alienation, in a few words. Sacred works, by contrast, were characterized by being true, by being bestowed with an inherent value that safeguarded them from any profane drift. In this modern world that, for good or bad reasons, is intent to recognize only profane objects, art seeks to preserve for itself the old prerogatives of sacred works. It seeks to produce "auratic" objects, whose value is irreducible to instrumentality and market exchange. From there, the essential tension that defines this art emerges, and that, as I have said elsewhere, tends to make a vast sacrificial scene out of it. Contemporary art is characterized by staging once and again its own impossibility and by attempting, in this manner, to recover its aura fleetingly and abysmally.

Sacrifice is a radical strategy for pulling things out of the all-encompassing sphere of instrumentality and market exchange. It is a form of redemption by annihilation. Nevertheless, there would be another path for art, more basic, and perhaps more lucid and desperate as well. In order for the work not to be betrayed by circulation, one could simply subtract it from circulation, masking it and confining it within a black box, isolating it through a defensive perimeter of privacy. However, the Loosian dweller is already a panopticized subject. The black box that harbors him, finally free from indiscrete, disturbing external gazes, is the right place to foster panoptic exercises in the shadows.[30]

The panoptic, according to Foucault, produces "so many small theaters, in which each actor is alone, perfectly individualized and constantly visible."[31] We may also say that they are facilities especially adapted to the viewing of images—in the manner of the "camera obscura," the device that seems to have been a model for Descartes's concept of subjectivity[32]—in which the subject, turned toward himself, is both actor and privileged spectator of the theater of his own subjectivity. But is this not an adequate description of his psyche? And what is psychoanalysis—another Viennese invention—if not an interiorization of the old megalopathic spectacle, with all its paraphernalia of cruel myths, of heroes and gods?

The principle of metaphysical panopticism has been fulfilled in the Loosian subject. This subject, becoming invisible to others, has become eminently visible to himself. As Foucault announced in connection to the physical panoptic, he can constantly experience visibility as imprisonment. Nevertheless, the contradiction of the subject that, attempting to protect himself from representation, rather fulfills its principle, brings about a dialectic, a movement. The subject—this the very lesson of psychoanalysis—can build protective capsules for himself, temporary shelters against himself, against the threat of himself, which will soon be invaded again by the interiorized vigilance, and so on, and on, and on.

In the classic megalopathic device, verticality, spectacle, exhibition, masculinity, and the phallus prevailed. Now the opposite is the case: inhibition, hiding, folding; in sum, feminization, with the uterus as the point of arrival. Uterus? Yes. But also—why not?—coffin, grave. Facing the grave, indeed, the Loosian prohibition against the impure mingling of art and architecture is lifted: architecture as art begins and ends in the monument and the grave. In the grave, we could say, the flight to the inside of the inside has stopped. The subject who, as Wittgenstein (another tormented Viennese) claimed it, "does not belong to the world,"[33] has finally recovered his truth, his intimacy, now indeed safe from every gaze. The grave is the black box in its completion, in its fullness.

Postscript: I'm a Loos-er

In the preceding text, the mark of the genealogical knowledge inaugurated by Nietzsche and practiced by Foucault, among others, is evident. Like science, whose point of view (the principle of objectivity) it radicalizes, genealogy is fully modern: it knows that any invocation of an extraordinary value (Truth, the Good, Beauty) is but a power scheme, which legitimates itself by pretending to have a sort of direct line of communication with the transcendent order of things. Modernity knows this and can no longer forget it.

To metaphysics—which links each and every historical occurrence to a full and substantive origin in which that occurrence would have been already present as possibility; which therefore understands history as a fall and as a promise of redemption—genealogy opposes an obsessive attention to ordinary events, insignificant and forgotten events that, by sedimentation, have brought about that which, *ex post*, seems to be the product of a design forever written in the heaven of essences. "Genealogy is gray, meticulous, and patiently documentary."[34]

A careful reader will notice, however, that a paradox is hidden here. The genealogical deconstruction of metaphysical truth (its public exhibition as non-truth) is often understood as an exercise of critique of power, which, as we know, uses such truth to legitimate the suffering of the many. But how is one to avoid the suspicion that the critique of power might be power itself, its (pen)ultimate and most clever strategy? Indeed, as, we have *seen*, visibility (which "is a conviction") constitutes the core of every power device. Thus, enlightenment, performed over this very fact, would be its paradoxical fulfillment.

Does this labyrinth have an exit? Or is the genealogist of morals the perfect Loosian inhabitant, as the one sentenced for life to perform panoptic exercises over himself? And if this is the case, why worry so much? Why so much passion for truth, why so many arduous texts? Why not a sober acceptance of facticity and live thereafter as "happy positivists" (Foucault himself once proposed this ironically), who already know that there is only nontruth and power?

The genealogist resembles some of Kafka's characters, who, instead of erecting the Tower, dig the "pit of Babel." They do so because they do not ignore (they are modern, no melancholic knowledge escapes from them) that "invocation of the sun is idolatry" (Adorno).[35] But digging is tiresome. Then, again, why bother, unless one believes that the pit—the grave—can be a sort of trampoline. Then it would indeed be a matter of descending, of descending to the bottommost place, in order to be then catapulted to a realm in which, for an instant, visibility is not, and has never been, a sentence. "Invocation of the sun is idolatry," Adorno writes. And he concludes: "Only the spectacle of the tree withered in its heat gives a presentiment of the majesty of the day which will not scorch the world on which it shines."[36]

Without forgetting any detail, incriminating itself without mercy, metaphysics is a game—perhaps not the only one—in which one wins by losing.

Chapter 10

Notes on the Spectrality of Objects

> How easy it would be not to think of a tiger!
> —Borges, "The Zahir," *Labyrinths* (159)

"Bonadea, Kakania; systems of happiness and balance." This is the title of one of the chapters in *The Man without Qualities*, which examines the structural discontent in the soul of the citizens of the Musilian Kakania.

This Central European culture lacks the faith in history displayed by the modern avant-garde. In the finite and limited human life, rarely do moral accounts balance out: goodness is rarely rewarded, evil is rarely punished, and the innocent victims of power's megalomania accumulate beyond all justification. Thus, the settling of moral accounts, as the precondition for individuals who are unequal in wealth and power to accept the suffering for the great, demands a postponement. *We call this postponement (or credit) history.* History (even the one that latches on the secular ideal of progress) is thus always sacred history (theodicy, "justice of God," following the accurate expression coined by Leibniz): the promise that the pains of today will be nothing but an illusion, a kind of dramatic device that stresses the intrinsic rationality and goodness of the world, which at the end (always at the end) shall come to presence in all its majesty and splendor.

In its different forms, history is always a saving and uplifting metanarrative. And if, following Jean-François Lyotard, post- or late Modernity is understood as the crisis of metanarratives that provide meaning, we might recognize in the Kakanians—whom God, according to Musil, cut out their "production credit"—the very forerunners of our skeptical age. But pay attention: the essential elements of such crisis were already contained in the once-and-again-staged primeval scene of Modernity. This scene, which turns Modernity into a paradoxical successor of itself has, as we already know, its prototype in the Reformation of Luther and Calvin. In its most radical moment, the Reformation explodes the bridge between the sacred and the profane, whose most concrete expression in medieval society had been "pious works." Pious works, from acts of charity to the building of cathedrals, constituted a sort of stairway to heaven that the believer, aided by the ecclesiastical institution, could walk through without uncertainty regarding his own salvation. This bridge thus made it possible to sacralize——historicize——profane life, giving it direction and meaning. However, it also constituted (the Reformation put its critical emphasis here) a sort of profanation of the sacred: the legitimation of the power of a very worldly institution (the medieval church, whose head, the pope, is also the pontiff, the maker of bridges), which claims for itself the right to "read" the book of the universe, and to translate it in terms of ethical-political norms whose validity is thus beyond discussion.

Against this sacralization of power, the Reformation wielded the critical arguments developed by medieval nominalism, whose idea of creation consists in an intelligible order, commensurable to human reason. Medieval Christianity "imported" this idea from Greece, turning God into an idol, a concoction at a human scale. An omnipotent God, however, should not be limited by anything, not even by logic. Any predicate that limits him would betray this divine potency. He must then be an unknown, absent God, whose true name would be "Nothing"—as in some mystic traditions at the margins of the great monotheistic religions. From this perspective, pious works are seen as grotesque attempts to bribe the divinity. From now on, salvation can only come from the grace bestowed by a will that is as enigmatic as it is omnipotent.

The essential elements that constitute the social and cultural landscape of Modernity become possible—that is, legitimate—by virtue of the void left by a dying or retreating God. First among these elements is the sovereignty of the subject, whose conscience, hunted by doubt, now constitutes the only and problematic contact point with an opaque transcendence. Next is techno-science, as an expression of the will to order, to the humanization of a hostile universe ("man knows at last that he is alone in the universe's unfeeling immensity, out of which he emerged only by chance," biologist Jacques Monod will write in his well-known summary of twentieth-century evolutionism, *Chance and Necessity*).[1] Finally, we have instrumental action and market economy, as supposedly a-valoric and a-historic forms (they neither add to nor subtract from the personal account of salvation) of the social coordination of action.

From this perspective, the defining feature of the Kakanian culture seems to be the reactivation and strengthening of the modern nominalist and Calvinist distrust toward the consolations of meaning and history. In fact, this reactivation had already been taking place in thinkers like Kierkegaard or Nietzsche, whose writings the Musilian Viennese citizens had read attentively. Thus, to the salvational history of the philosophers, Nietzsche had opposed the idea of *genealogy* or *effective history*. Genealogy, as Michel Foucault wrote, "deals with events in terms of their most unique characteristics, their most acute manifestations," for in it, "the forces operating in history are not controlled by destiny or regulative mechanisms but respond to haphazard conflicts."[2]

Dealing with events in terms of this uniqueness, however, calls for a memory capable of prying into the insignificant leftovers, the wastelands of meaningful history and language; of the whole apparatus of culture through which the infinite complexity of experience is silenced, forgotten, sacrificed for the benefit and glory of meaning and the dramatic progression of the historical narrative. It is necessary to pry even beyond, into the waste of the waste, until plunging into madness and silence. For a consciousness in constant vigilance, such as that of Musil and his contemporaries, the "great style,"[3] which, so to speak, polishes the corners of the real, has ceased to be a possibility. This is the case, for example, of von Hofmannsthal's *Lord Chandos Letter*, the fictionalized lament of a consciousness that has become memorious and that deplores the amnesia associated with words. The story, which is presented as a letter by Lord Chandos, "the younger son of the Earl of Bath,"[4] to his mentor and friend Francis Bacon, describes the effects of a devastating spiritual crisis suffered by the addressor. The crisis consists in the transition from a condition in which "all of existence [is] one great unity" (and the subject is located at the center of the world, and nothing is mere appearance), to the experience of an unlimited fragmentation and decentering:

> My mind forced me to see everything that came up in these conversations as terrifyingly close to me. Once I saw through a magnifying glass that an area of skin on my little finger looked like an open field with furrows and hollows. That was how it was for me now with people and their affairs. I could no longer

grasp them with the simplifying gaze of habit. Everything came to pieces, the pieces broke into more pieces, and nothing could be encompassed by one idea.[5]

The gaze of Chandos-Hofmannsthal, behind which we can perceive the radical empiricism of the great Viennese scientists (Mach, Hertz, Boltzmann), is akin to the gaze of the Angelus Novus, the "angel of history," the main character of a stunning allegory written by Walter Benjamin at the end of the 1930s. Where others see progress (the reassuring succession of causes and effects), the implacable gaze of the angel sees "one single catastrophe which keeps piling wreckage upon wreckage and hurls it in front of his feet."[6] For both Hofsmannsthal and Benjamin, the only possible redemption would consist in an unthinkable yet indispensable reestablishment of the original bond between words and things at the vanishing point of human historical existence. In fact, Chandos-Hofmannsthal's narration ends with the invocation of a linguistic utopia "[i]n which I might have been granted the opportunity not only to write but also to think in not Latin or English, or Italian, or Spanish, but a language of which I know not one word, a language in which mute things speak to me and in which I will perhaps have something to say for myself someday when I am dead and standing before an unknown judge."[7]

This is the environment in which Musil writes his *Man without Qualities*. As the title of these reflections suggests, I shall turn to one of the chapters of the book, which is a source of knowledge on the spectralization of objects. In this chapter ("Bonadea, Kakania: Systems of Happiness and Balance"), Musil leads us, as in the best voyeuristic literary tradition, into Bonadea's intimacy. Bonadea, the "good goddess," is the heartbroken lover of Ulrich, the man "without qualities"—a mere aggregate of sensations: such is the subject, genealogically observed—that leads the story. In the scene, Bonadea, who has a "compulsive love of clothes and adornments,"[8] is in front of a mirror, covered only by a corset. She is devoted to finding distractions from her emotional widowhood through a complicated *toilette*. Suddenly, however, the narrator forces us to leave this friendly place and to follow him into a reflection upon the halo, the sacred aura that emerges from words and also from objects. This is the quotation, which I reproduce *in extenso*:

> Clothes, when abstracted from the flow of present time and their transmogrifying function on the human body, and seen as

forms in themselves, are strange tubes and excrescences worthy of being classed with such facial decorations as the ring through the nose or the lip-stretching disk. But how enchanting they become when seen together with the qualities they bestow on their wearer! What happens then is no less than the infusion into some tangled lines on a piece of paper, of the meaning of a great word. Imagine a man's invisible kindness and moral excellence suddenly looming as a halo the size of the full moon and golden as an egg yolk right over his head, the way it does in old religious paintings, as he happens to be strolling down the avenue or heaping little tea sandwiches on his plate—what an overwhelming, shattering sensation it would be! And just such a power to make the invisible, and even the nonexistent, *visible* is what a well-made outfit demonstrates every day of the week. Such things are like debtors who repay our investment in them with fantastic interest, and in that sense all things are indebted to us. For it is not only clothes that have such power, but also convictions, prejudices, theories, hopes, faith in something or other, ideas, even thoughtlessness insofar as it is its quality of self-reflexiveness that gives it a sense of its own rightness. All these, by endowing us with the properties we lend them, serve the aim of presenting the world in a light that emanates from ourselves, and this is basically the task for which everyone has a method of his own. With great and varied skills, we create a delusion that enables us to coexist serenely with the most monstrous things, simply because we recognize these frozen grimaces of the universe as a table or a chair, a shout or an outstretched arm, a speed or a roast chicken. We are capable of living between one open chasm of sky above our heads and another, slightly camouflaged chasm of sky beneath our feet, feeling as untroubled on earth as if we were in a room with the door closed. We know that our life is ebbing away both outward in the inhuman distances of cosmic space and downward into the inhuman distances of cosmic space and downward into the inhuman microspace of the atom, while we go on dealing with the middle stratum, the things that make up our world, without troubling ourselves at all over the fact that this proves only a preference for impressions received in the middle distance, as it were.[9]

Indeed, in their familiarity, the beings that populate the universe (chairs, tables, clothes, speeds, roast or raw chickens) make themselves present signaled by a halo. This is the halo of substantiality. For old metaphysics, substance designates the ultimate subject, the one that is not an attribute of any other. Modernity, however, hardly grants substantiality to the world. The world appears to Modernity not as an order (the systematic catalogue of a museum or the series of chapters in a natural history book), but rather as the inhuman chaos of interstellar distances and subatomic abysses, which Musil's text recalls. From this perspective, which is the one of modern science, the "dazzling appearance" of things, of the objects and forms that we recognize in the world, is the product of an arduous shadow work at the margins of conscious life—the sediment of the repeated interaction of human beings with their surroundings, which has been progressively placed in the conceptual and linguistic distinctions by means of which we observe and catalogue the world.

Another famous Kakanian, namely Ludwig Wittgenstein, used to observe that language contains an entire metaphysics. The work that humanity has inverted and forgotten in the production of the significant totality that we call our world returns to it under the alienated mask of things. Things make up the familiar furniture of the world. Their presence preserves, however precariously, the comforting illusion of a hospitable world, created in a human scale that, nonetheless, the nominalist and Calvinist Modernity strives once and again to dispel. Nevertheless, in its comfortable familiarity, this world is full of specters. The same supernatural halo that makes up the signature of objects must be the remainder, the trace of the colossal expenditure of human energy demanded by the production of a reality in which the same halo is subsumed and forgotten. "If all those leaps of attention, flexing of eye muscles, fluctuations of the psyche . . . could be measured," Ulrich-Musil observes in another part of his novel that "the grand total would surely dwarf the energy needed by Atlas to hold up the world."[10] This is the energy that is confined to an underground, spectral existence, from which it emerges—return of the repressed—in the halo of objects or, as shown by psychoanalysis, another Kakanian invention, in the nocturnal and strange aspects of psychic life.

The twentieth century witnessed how the dissolving, anamnesic energies of Modernity have striven to remind us of the forgetfulness that makes up our world. We already know the relationship between reification and forgetfulness established by the so-called "critical theory."[11] The other important trends of contemporary thought are situated in the same perspective. With their specific nuances, psychoanalysis, semiology, deconstruction, and phenomenology, to name a few, coincide in disclosing the linguistic constructive work behind the solidness of things. Thus, as in Marx's famous claim in the *Manifesto of the Communist Party*, all that is solid has melted in the air, in the gentle breath of words. However, we still feel a strange satisfaction when we go shopping. Despite all the cognitive transformations that we have experienced, commodities (clothes, in Musil's allegory) keep their halo. Commodities are our pious works: the world can very well be an opaque, chaotic abyss, but it recovers its familiarity as soon as we shop.

We are confronted here by the phenomenon of "commodity fetishism," to which Marx devoted a famous section of *Capital*:

> The mysterious character of the commodity-form consists . . . simply in the fact that the commodity reflects the social characteristics of men's own labour as objective characteristics of the products of labour themselves, as the socio-natural properties of these things. Hence it also reflects the social relation of the producers to the sum total of labour as a social relation between objects, a relation which exists apart from and outside the producers.[12]

Marx also asserts that commodities are physically metaphysical objects. Commodity fetishism is a paradigmatic form of the forgetfulness of the complex human interactions that give rise to objects, forgetfulness for the sake of an abstract piece of information, the exchange value, which appears however as a material quality of these same objects (for example, as the result of a balance between abundance and scarcity). When they enter market circulation, commodities forget their humble origin, the concrete labor, the very material expenditure of human energy and pain—muscle and blood, bone and nerve—invested in its production. These pants and this shirt were maybe produced in China, with fabric coming from India, following an Italian design. Its arrival in Chile was made possible by a distributing company located in New York, funded by a London bank, transported by a ship with a Liberian flag, whose crew comes mostly from the Philippines, and finally unloaded by Peruvian dockers. We pay no attention to any of this when we buy. In the last instance, the only trait that distinguishes commodities from one another is an abstract piece of information: their exchange value, their price. Thus, the market embodies an efficient abstraction device, a device for oblivion. Through it, the complexity of the social is visibly diminished. Economic agents can abstract from all the hidden complexity of the objects they have in front of them and limit themselves considering a mere, abstract piece of information. This simplification, by the way, explains the operational success of market economies. On the other hand, it makes possible the existence of the very science of economics, such as we know it.

But where stories existed, their ghosts remain. The ghost is the nocturnal face of abstraction, its spectral double. Excesses of abstraction and forgetfulness are always paid with a proliferation of specters. Therefore, psychic health requires a mediation, a careful search for a middle term, for the form that redeems specters from their estrangement by offering them a place in the world. This mediation is precisely design. The function of industrial design, according to the Ulmian Tomás Maldonado, is "to mediate dialectically between needs and objects, between production and consumption."[13] One might say then that design provides stories: stories that substitute, that somehow make up for those that were suppressed. Indeed, objects appear in the market not only possessing their price, but also displaying a materiality, a form that has a history. The producer of a bottle of wine, for example, wants the product to stand out from its competitor not only by its price—to that aim, he orders a pleasant bottle and a label that conveys a story, quite literally in many cases ("this wine has been produced with fine grapes from the area of . . .").

This way, design seems to be at the service of what we could call the "irrational part" of the market. This is a complement required by its abstract rationality, for the sake not only of the differentiation of products but also, if we have followed the previous development, of the neutralization of anxiety in the face of a strange world. There is, I speculate, a trend in design that takes up the task of invoking the modern *horror vacui* without hesitation, providing that prosthesis of history—prosthesis of materiality—that human beings, thrown into the modern drift, do not cease to require in order to maintain a certain psychic equilibrium. This trend, I speculate further, has paradigmatic representatives, such as William Morris and the "styling" school after the Great Depression of 1929. As Carl Schorske shows in a suggestive comparison between Morris and Wagner, Morris's path, from the ardent Catholicism of his youth to the socialist utopianism of his later years, is characterized by the nostalgia of a familiar world that, essentially, would have been the medieval world.[14] This is a world in a human scale—but was it really?—of which we would have been unjustly expelled, and to which we might eventually return. This conception transpires, for example, in Morris's distinction between art and design. According to Morris, the greatness of art consists in exposing us directly to the real: the real without filters, which through art would unfold its entire disturbing potential.[15] Design, by contrast (Morris's expression is "the lesser arts"), situates us in an environment that is "quiet, peaceful, calm, and comfortable," in Anna Calvera's words.[16] Ultimately, Morris seems to posit a primordial agreement, which should in truth be characterized as Catholic, between human beings and their world. This agreement is health. In fact, in 1881, in a sort of anticipated response to the prohibition of ornaments that after 1908 will be associated with the name of architect Alfred Loos (*Ornament and Crime*), Morris resorts to the idea of health. His aim is to refute those who choose to live between white walls or who, "when asked with what manner of books they will furnish their room, would answer, 'With none.' "[17] Morris's response is based precisely on a concept of health: "I think you will agree with me in thinking that both these sets of people would be in an unhealthy state of mind, and probably of body also; in which case we need not trouble ourselves about their whims, since it is with healthy & sane people only that art has dealings."[18]

There is, however, another trend in design. It is a Calvinist, unsatisfied trend, which chooses rather to appeal to that component of the human condition that, following Morris's image, we might call "sick" and that is never comfortably at home in its environment. To conclude, I would like to point out that the critique of ornamentation identified with Alfred Loos, and then with rationalism, Bauhaus, and its successors, can only be understood in the context of what we might call Modernity's Calvinist, anamnetic, iconoclast fury. The absence of ornamentation, as we know, becomes itself an ornament. On the other hand, there is nothing in the circle, the quadrilateral, or the triangle that makes them more "rational" than a sinusoid, a fractal, or any random line—just like there is nothing "primary" about primary colors, beyond the linguistic superstition that designates them that way. The real issue is neither rationality, nor the excess or lack of ornamentation. Alfred Loos's exteriors, according to Massimo Cacciari, "are organized in the direction and in the dimension of money. They must be *pure* money, *perfect* money, so as to function without stridency in the universe of circulation and exchange."[19] Like the geometrical shapes of rationalism, money is abstract, simple. Consequently, what really seems to be at stake here is a purposeful search for the simplest shapes, for the poorest and the most dispossessed—as if design really wanted to whisper to us the secret of the vacuity and the poverty of the world.

Postscript: How Easy It Would Be Not to Think of a Tiger!

Modernity is crossed by the question of memory, which includes material culture, objects. Now, in his story "The Zahir," Borges presents the parable of an unforgettable object: "*Zahir* in Arabir means 'notorious,' 'visible . . . ,' the people (in Muslim territories) use it to signify 'beings or things that possess the terrible property of being unforgettable, and whose image finally drives one mad.' "[20] However, the Zahir is an interchangeable, insignificant object. Borges says:

> In Buenos Aires the Zahir is an ordinary coin worth twenty centavos. The letters N T and the number 2 are scratched as if with a razor-blade or penknife; 1929 is the date on the obverse. (In Guzerat, towards the end of the eighteenth century, the Zahir was a tiger; in Java, a blind man from the Mosque of Surakarta whom the Faithful pelted with stones; in Persia, an astrolabe which Nadir Shan caused to be sunk to the bottom of the sea; in the Mahdi's prisons, along about 1892, it was a little compass which Rudolf Carl von Slatin touched, tucked into the fold of a turban; in the Mosque of Cordova, according to Zotenberg, it was a vein in the marble of one of the twelve-hundred pillars; in the Tetuán ghetto, it was the bottom of a well.)[21]

"How easy it would be not to think of a tiger!," Borges also says, in the assertion that serves as an epigraph for this chapter. But, how different it would be if the tiger were at the same time a blind man, an astrolabe, a compass, a marble vein, the bottom of a well! In this case, we would be facing a universal equivalent: a Zahir, an abstract, unforgettable object. Indeed, if the forms, the qualities of objects stem from oblivion, then an entity without qualities—a sort of zero degree of being—is doomed to be unforgettable.

This object is, for us, currency, money. Money, as universal equivalent, is the terminal obsession of our spirit. In the same story, Borges describes a dream in which he says: "I was the coins guarded by a griffon."[22]

Chapter 11

Psychoanalysis

The Future of an Illusion

Psychoanalysis provides a privileged point of view from which to glimpse the mythical core of Modernity. As an interpretative science, psychoanalysis is capable of reinterpreting and even rejecting any empirical evidence that, for example, would attempt to falsify its basic claims. Freud's abandonment, in the dawn of psychoanalysis, of the "theory of seduction" (a crucial event in its history that still today raises passionate discussions), represents a good example of this interpretative nature. Facing a patient that claims that he has been sexually abused in his childhood, the analyst can always defuse such claim, interpreting it as an illusion, a construction mediated by the Oedipus complex and the unconscious, those theoretical acquisitions of psychoanalysis (obtained, so to speak, at the expense of a literal listening of the narratives provided by patients). Karl Popper's critique of psychoanalysis (and also of Marxism) is based precisely on this interpretative aspect: by resorting to "the unconscious" and to "class consciousness," respectively, both disciplines would grant themselves an unlimited reserve of interpretation; a capacity to reject or reinterpret any empirical evidence provided by the interlocutor, reducing it to false consciousness, ideology, and symptom.

This debate underlies Popper's attempt, in his *The Logic of Scientific Discovery*, to draw a "criterion of demarcation" capable of distinguishing between scientific and metaphysical disciplines. And that criterion would be given by "falsification": only those disciplines inherently open to refutation by some possible evidence, and thus, not all-encompassing, would deserve to be honored as rational and scientific. This honor is then undeserved by psychoanalysis (also by Marxism); in fact, the very nature of the Freudian unconscious (its declared definition in terms of "technical methods of filling up the gaps in the phenomena of our consciousness")[1] determines its inherent unworthiness. In the sober and axiomatic *An Outline of Psychoanalysis*, written shortly before his death, Freud explains:

> We have discovered technical methods of filling up the gaps in the phenomena of our consciousness, and we make use of those methods just as a physicist makes use of experiment. In this manner we infer a number of processes which are in themselves "unknowable" and interpolate them in those that are conscious to us. And if, for instance, we say: "At this point an unconscious memory intervened," what that means is: "At this point something occurred of which we are totally unable to form a conception, but which, if it had entered our consciousness, could only have been described in such and such a way."[2]

As developed in the *Critique of Pure Reason*, Kant shows that there are two ways in which our representations can correspond to their objects. Either the representations are formed by means of empirical induction (and then they cannot seek more than mere generality); or the objects are to be somehow constituted by our representations. This latter way, as we know, is the transcendental strategy, through which Kant seeks to inject into Modernity that minimal metaphysics without which it would be deprived of all normative content. However, in Freud's time (and in Popper's, another Viennese, though from a later generation), the Kantian strategy had already expired. In fact, the most lucid attempt to reconstruct a transcendental philosophy in the conditions of the twentieth century (Wittgenstein's *Tractatus*) is the precise manifestation of its crisis. In the *Tractatus*, Kant's material logic (the entire representational framework including space, time, causality, and the remaining categories that made it possible to conceive of a synthesis between the universality demanded by reason and empirical experience) has vanished. As in the situation of anarchy—"this rule [of metaphysics] gradually degenerated . . . into complete **anarchy**"[3]—that Kant envisages in the prologue to the first edition of the *Critique of Pure Reason*, those two sources of knowledge have split apart. Thus, in the *Tractatus*, the sole universality and necessity still standing correspond to logical propositions; these, however, are empirically empty. At the same time, the truth of science relies exclusively on fragile induction, on mere probability. Thus, ethics, aesthetics, each and every discourse claiming access to a sphere of normativity (including philosophy, and the very *Tractatus*) retreat into silence, as the paradoxical price to pay for their elevated dignity.

This is bad news, as it were, for a politics that would still want to find inspiration in Kant's legacy. Popper's political thought is structured around this problem: the possibility of an "open society" that, on the one hand, would not be ruled by an "anything goes"; that should be well stocked on the normative side, while knowing at the same time that normative content is given neither by mere empirical generalizations and statistical replicas of what is, nor by the totalizing and (for Popper) totalitarian universality of metaphysics. Popper's science, which is open and falsifiable, seems capable of filling the gap. However, the criterion of demarcation is inherently aporetic, and through this aporetic weakness, metaphysics infiltrates and contaminates Popper's "open society"—because we might turn the criterion of demarcation unto itself, and ask: is it falsifiable? If it is not, it would be just another name for metaphysics. And if it is, then there must be at least one theory that is not falsifiable, but that is not outside the horizon of scientific reason. In either case, the unwanted metaphysics has forced its way into the sacred sphere of science. And it could not be otherwise. Metaphysics is the rationalized myth that translates its fabulous and personalized powers in terms of nature, necessity, and universality. Myth, as we already know, performs the passage from "being" to "ought"—in the last instance, myth expresses *that* with regard to which, in each and every social formation, there is no "freedom to err" (nominalism itself, in the case of Modernity), as I have said above. From this viewpoint, psychoanalysis is no more and no less mythical, metaphysical, and prescriptive than the Popperian "demarcation criterion." The former, with the unconscious as a method "of filling up the gaps in the phenomena of our consciousness," prefigures and gives expression to the psychic life of modern subjects; the latter seeks to institute a norm for legitimate discourses within an "open society."

I intend to treat psychoanalysis as the partially self-conscious expression of the foundational myth of Modernity's nominalism—of the performative core that prescribes the peculiar amalgam of memory and forgetfulness, which those who are modern are destined to recognize in our concepts and in our words. And, from this point of view, the deep truth of psychoanalysis—its "historical-experiential truth," symptomatic truth, to use Freud's own terminology–would be rooted, not in the inductive generalization of clinical experience, as is often assumed with blatant epistemological naiveté, but in its capacity to give voice to this myth. And this would be the secret of its power, and of the inexhaustible fascination that it has been exerting over modern consciousness ever since its development more than a century ago.

Perhaps the most convincing evidence of this mythical fascination comes from its detractors. Regardless of its positive aspects, of the somewhat empirically verifiable theses that follow from any doctrine and in which its supporters tend to remain captive, the detractors are often acutely sensitive to its background conceptual and vital options, the ones that give life to it and constitute its core of meaning. In the case of psychoanalysis, to make a list of these sensitive subjects would be a challenging task. Let us again recall Wittgenstein, who was an erudite, distinguished, and paradigmatic detractor of Freud, of whom he was a contemporary (as was also that other famous detractor, Karl Krauss). Freud's writings had already attracted Wittgenstein's attention around 1919. During the 1940s, he had conversations on the topic with his friend and disciple Rush Rhees, whose many notes have been published. We are especially interested in what Wittgenstein said about myth—the illusion that, surprisingly, would dwell at the very core of that effective machinery of disenchantment and enlightenment: psychoanalysis. Wittgenstein says:

> Freud refers to various ancient myths . . . and claims that his researches have now explained how it came about that anybody should think or propound a myth of that sort.
>
> Whereas in fact Freud has done something different. He has not given a scientific explanation of the ancient myth. What he has done is to propound a new myth. The attractiveness of the suggestion, for instance, that all anxiety is a repetition of the anxiety of the birth trauma, is just the attractiveness of a mythology. "It is all the outcome of something that happened long ago." Almost like referring to a totem.
>
> Much the same could be said of the notion of an "Urszene" [primal scene]. This often has the attractiveness of giving a sort of tragic pattern to one's life. It is all the repetition of the same pattern which was settled long ago. Like a tragic figure carrying out the decrees under which the fates had placed him at birth. . . . It may then be an immense relief if it can be shown that one's life has the pattern rather of a tragedy—the tragic working out and repetition of a pattern which was determined by the primal scene.[4]

It is a "powerful mythology," Wittgenstein concludes.[5] In what follows, I intend to approach precisely this "mythology." In order to do so, I will use as my guiding thread the reading of a text by Freud which is usually considered minor and marginal (if not eccentric and even senile: its writing concluded in London in 1938, when the author entered the terminal stage of the difficult illness that would lead to his death a little over a year later). The text is *Moses and Monotheism*, a work whose first two parts had been previously published in *Imago* (1937), the theoretical organon of the Viennese psychoanalytic community, and whose last part, much more extensive and substantial than the previous ones, had been developed by Freud in 1934, as evidenced in his correspondence with Arnold Zweig and Lou Andreas-Salomé.[6] On grounds of political prudence, which are also registered in his correspondence, Freud did not publish the manuscript from 1934. The idea was not to compromise, with a work that partly repeats the findings of *Totem and Taboo* (1912), the precarious tolerance that the conservative Catholic authority in the Viennese government implemented toward psychoanalysis, in a Central Europe that was threatened by Nazism (a threat that obviously concerned Freud, a Jew). But this political difficulty associated with *Moses and Monotheism*, considered in an isolated way, is still external to psychoanalysis. There are others, which we will identify later, that emerge from its own nature and that do not go unnoticed by its author. Nevertheless, the work (and this circumstance could not be indifferent for its understanding) apparently *had* to be written, and indeed it had been written, despite the uncertainty and the risks linked to its publication. How are we to understand this compulsion?

In psychoanalytic terms, one would say that the danger that loomed over Freud the man (*der Mann Freud*), over his knowledge, and over his people—total danger, "final solution"—could not but hasten the "return of the repressed": the reactivation of the *Urszene* of psychoanalysis itself, of those disputed questions that make up its core and its most decisive truth, but that in its "normal" practice (I am referring here again to Kuhn's "normal science") psychoanalysis must necessarily repress, forget. The explicit plot of *Moses and Monotheism* shows us a Freud determined to answer the question regarding the essence of Judaism (and of Anti-Semitism); regarding its strange persistence even under the strict conditions of the Enlightenment and in the intellectual life of that radical *Aufklärer*, Sigmund Schlomo Freud and, why not, in his scientific invention, psychoanalysis. The questions regarding monotheism (a reiteration, a quarter of a century later, of the knowledge acquired in *Totem and Taboo*), Judaism, and Christianity, as well as the self-reflection on psychoanalysis, are closely linked to one another in *Moses and Monotheism*.[7]

What are Freud's fundamental theses in *Moses and Monotheism* that make it possible to ground this link? The core of the book is the claim that, for completely accidental reasons, an obscure Semitic tribe located in Egypt at the time (which would later be the Jewish people) was set to perform a spectacular "return of the repressed." Freud says, repeating the findings of *Totem and Taboo*: "[M]en have always known . . . that once upon a time they had a primaeval father and killed him."[8] However:

> The great deed and misdeed of primaeval times, the murder of the Father, was brought home to the Jews, for fate decreed that they should repeat it on the person of Moses, an eminent father substitute. It was a case of acting instead of remembering, something which often happens during analytic work with neurotics.[9]

The murder of the father as a foundational event of culture is the ethnological hypothesis that Freud, based on ideas from Atkinson, Darwin, and above all William Robertson Smith, had formulated in *Totem and Taboo*. The origin of culture, of morality, and also of religion, would lie in the archaic murder, repeated again and again, of the protofather, who in prehistorical times would have ruled despotically over the horde, the inchoate form of any ulterior sociability. His murder (or rather, the elaboration of this traumatic even in the collective psyche) would be at the basis of cultural achievements as important as morality (the Law, a sort of sublimated form of the father's despotism, stemming from the renunciation of violence by the brothers who kill him and take his place, with an equilibrium of terror in the middle), exogamy, and the incest taboo (a similar renunciation of the possession of women, mothers, and sisters in the horde). At the same time, religion would be a form of "return of the repressed," a sort of psychosocial analogue of the neurosis that affects the individual psyche, by means of which the original trauma would reclaim its rights, but would be at the same time tempered, deformed, and culturally sublimated.

Freud adds to this ethnological hypothesis some circumstantial traits. First, he adds the hypothesis, supported by philological and interpretative arguments whose fragility he does not cease to point out, that Moses, considered as a historical figure (a quality that Freud rarely grants to biblical heroes), would have been not of Hebrew origin, but rather Egyptian. On the other hand, Jewish monotheism would be the outcome of the import, performed by Moses, of an Egyptian religious innovation. Pharaoh Amenhotep IV would have established monotheism as the State religion, under the form of an exclusive worship of solar power, Aton, and acquired the name Akehnaten from that point on. The religion of Aton was characterized by the belief in a single God; by the rejection of anthropomorphism, magic, and sorcery; and by the absolute denial of any ulterior life. After Akehnaten's death, however, this great heresy would have been quickly reversed, and the Egyptians would have returned to their ancient gods. Moses, for his part, would have been an Egyptian priest or nobleman and a fervent monotheist. In order to prevent the religion of Aton from disappearing, he would have become the leader of an oppressed Semite tribe that dwelled in Egypt at the time, pulling it out of subjection and creating a new nation. He would have given them a version of monotheism that was even more spiritualized and lacking images, and in order to distinguish them, he would have introduced among them the Egyptian custom of circumcision.

Freud's "conjectural history" (*Historie*) does not stop there. Relying on the historian Ernst Sellin, who would have found signs of this in the prophets (mostly in Hosea), he posits that the Jews would have murdered Moses. Indeed, the primitive mass of ancient slaves would not have tolerated the libidinal renunciations associated with the new faith. In a great uprising, Moses would have been murdered. The memory of this murder (the magnicide of the true creator of the Jewish people: a deicide) would have been buried deep in the unconscious. Afterwards, in the oasis of Meribat Qadesh, the Hebrews would have established an alliance with other Semitic tribes, whose ferocious volcanic divinity, called Yahweh, became their national god. Or rather, Moses's god merged with Yahweh, and Moses's great deeds were attributed to a Midianite priest of the same name. However, throughout a period of centuries, the buried tradition would have regained strength until it was reaffirmed and emerged victorious. After that, Yahweh was given the spiritual and universal qualities of the mosaic god. Nevertheless, the memory of Moses's murder would have remained repressed among the Jews, reemerging only with Christianity, though in a deformed way.[10]

By turning Moses into an Egyptian, Freud forecloses the possibility that the story he is telling be reduced to a Jewish national affair. It is Moses's murder that is specifically Jewish. This way, and following a process well known to psychoanalysis, a spectacular "return of the repressed" is triggered: the buried memory of the primordial, traumatic episodes of human prehistory described in *Totem and Taboo* begins to resonate, so to speak, with a psychic energy proceeding from the crime that is once again represented.[11] Thus, the psychic traits linked to this *Urszene*, described earlier, are reactivated: eclosion of guilt, sublimation in the form of worship of a God-Father, establishment of the Law.

"Early trauma-Defense-Latency-Outbreak of the Neurosis-Partial return of the repressed material" is the psychoanalytic schema of the development of neurosis, already applied to "mass psychology" in *Totem and Taboo*.[12] Freud returns to it once more in order to interpret the irresistible reemergence of Mosaic monotheism, after the period of forgetfulness and latency marked by the episode of Meribat-Qadesh.[13] One of the most salient cultural implications of this monotheism, according to Freud, is the interdiction of images. Freud says:

> Among the precepts of Mosaic religion is one that has more significance than is at first obvious. It is the prohibition against making an image of God, which means the compulsion to worship an invisible God. I surmise that in this point Moses had surpassed the Aton religion in strictness. Perhaps he meant to be consistent; his God was to have neither a name nor a countenance. The prohibition was perhaps a fresh precaution against magic malpractices. If this prohibition was accepted, however, it was bound to exercise a profound influence. For it signified subordinating sense perception to an abstract idea; it was a triumph of spirituality over the senses; more precisely an instinctual renunciation accompanied by its psychologically necessary consequence.[14]

Beyond the invocation of a hypothetical replacement of matriarchy by patriarchy, which would have unleashed a preference for reasoning over sensorial evidence (the means by which paternity and maternity are established, respectively), Freud's explanation of the prohibition of images emphasizes animism, the cultural expression of a fundamental narcissism, whose development would tend to spiritualize (desensorialize) God—to give priority to its abstract representation over its sensorial image. And indeed, from the viewpoint of psychoanalysis, it is possible to understand narcissism (the tendency to turn the world into a mirror of the I) as the primordial drive of culture and animism (which affirms a primordial commensurability between thinking and being, between human reason and world) as its most developed expression. But it is possible to go even further. Within this sort of narcissistic invariant of culture, monotheism is a turning point, in a way: a spiritualized God is still a God in the image and likeness of man, that is, an idol. By virtue of its own dynamics, the interdiction of images cannot stop at spiritualization and the devaluation of sensorial representations, as Freud seems to understand in the paragraph quoted above. As in the paradigmatic, and also Jewish, prohibition on the name of God, the interdiction must extend itself into anti-animism, or rather into that sort of shattered animism, critically turned upon itself, that will reappear with Modernity's nominalism.

In any case, strict monotheism and the prohibition of images, which are characteristic of the Jewish religion, have unleashed the cultural achievement that Freud calls *der Fortschritt in der Geistigkeit*, "the progress in spirituality." And it is here that the fate of psychoanalysis and of Judaism (but also of Christianity) converge. The preface to the Hebrew edition of *Totem and Taboo*, which I have quoted in a footnote above and quote again here, contained a promise:

> No reader of this book will find it easy to put himself in the emotional position of an author who is ignorant of the language of holy writ, who is completely estranged from the religion of his fathers—as well as from every other religion—and who cannot take a share in nationalist ideals, but who has yet never repudiated his people, who feels that he is in his essential nature a Jew and who has no desire to alter that nature. If the question were put to him: "Since you have abandoned all these common characteristics of your countrymen, what is there left to you that is Jewish?" he would reply: 'A very great deal, and probably its very essence.' He could not now express that essence clearly in words; but some day, no doubt, it will become accessible to the scientific mind.[15]

The promise that the "scientific mind"—psychoanalysis—should fulfill is to "explain . . . clearly in words" the essence of Judaism: a Judaism that (with the prohibition of images in its midst) would contain the driving force of secularization, and whose fate would then merge with the fate of Modernity and with the peak of its self-consciousness—psychoanalysis itself.[16]

The suspicion that accompanied the history of psychoanalysis—that it is a "Jewish science"—is thus strangely validated.[17] However, the emphasis should be placed on *science*: psychoanalysis. Freud, indeed, is the one who has succeeded in articulating the secret—the murder of the father, of God—buried deeply within the Jewish unconscious. This articulation fulfills, at least in part, the therapeutic goal of psychoanalysis: the trauma emerges out of its unconscious confinement, and the compulsive power that is exerted upon the psyche is neutralized. Thus, Freud is the therapist, the healer of the Jewish collective neurosis. In this sense, and notwithstanding Freud's admiration for the moral heroes of Jewish history (Moses, the prophets, Rabbi Jochanaan ben Sakkai), his role resembles rather the one of that other Romanized (universalized) Jew, "Saul of Tarsus, who as a Roman citizen was called Paul," in whose spirit perception dawned. "It is because we killed God the Father that we are so unhappy."[18]

For the Freud of *Moses and Monotheism*, the relationship between Judaism and Christianity is complicated. On the one hand, Christianity (for example, in its acceptance of images) would constitute a kind of pagan, "Egyptian" regression, by contrast to the Jewish monotheist purity.[19] At the same time, however, Christianity would have overcome Judaism insofar as, by turning Jesus into the sacrificed "son of God," it would have acknowledged (even if in a deformed and indirect way) the murder of the God-Father (for only the sacrifice of a son could compensate for the criminal affront done to the father). By contrast, "the poor Jewish people, who with its usual stiff-necked obduracy continued to deny the murder of their 'father,' has dearly expiated this in the course of centuries."[20] Consequently, Christianity would have been liberated to some extent from guilt and the return of the repressed, which would make up the heavy burden of the Jewish culture. This liberation would be the key of its enormous display of historic energy: "Christianity marked a progress in the history of religion: that is to say, in regard to the return of the repressed. From now on Jewish religion was, so to speak, a fossil."[21] However, being "originally a Father religion, Christianity became a Son religion. The fate of having to displace the Father it could not escape."[22]

"He was a man with a gift for religion, in the truest sense of the phrase. Dark traces of the past lay in his soul, ready to break through into the regions of consciousness."[23] These are the words Freud used to describe Paul. However, they could perfectly be applied to himself. *Freud, just like Paul, knows that at the beginning there was a murder*. The question at which we finally arrive, taking up our inquiry into the character of psychoanalysis, which we could call "mythical-poetic," is: How does he know?

Earlier, as I summarized the argument of *Moses and Monotheism*, I pointed out the essential role of Freud's "ethnological hypothesis," which he had developed in *Totem and Taboo*, published in 1912, following ideas developed by Atkinson, Darwin, and Smith. However, more than a quarter of a century later, Freud must acknowledge that this ethnological knowledge has been declared obsolete by the scientific community. He does so with the following words:

> I have often been vehemently reproached for not changing my opinions in later editions of my book, since more recent ethnologists have without exception discarded Robertson Smith's theories and have in part replaced them by others which differ extensively. I would reply that these alleged advances in science are well known to me. Yet I have not been convinced either of their correctness or of Robertson Smith's errors. Contradiction is not always refutation; a new theory does not necessarily denote progress. Above all, however, I am not an ethnologist, but a psychoanalyst. It was my good right to select from ethnological data what would serve me for my analytic work. The writings of the highly gifted Robertson Smith provided me with valuable points of contact with the psychological material of analysis and suggestions for the use of it. I cannot say the same of the work of his opponents.[24]

"I am not an ethnologist, but a psychoanalyst." The burden of proof, Freud seems to be saying, would belong to psychoanalysis, whose theoretical frame would be solid enough to reject or to keep in suspense—"contradiction is not always refutation"—any "new theory" coming from ethnology. Indeed, against what could be maintained from an empiricism or a naïve theory of falsification, this is precisely what scientific theories do. No theory is left aside for being contradicted by any random fact. Rather, the power of scientific theories is measured by their capacity for denial, that is, the capacity for rejection/reinterpretation of facts. In this case, however, a crucial fact is at stake, and not only for a theory of culture inspired by psychoanalysis, which could be considered as its periphery. For psychoanalysis is but a theory of culture and of the emergences of individual consciousness within it. In fact, there are several passages in which Freud explicitly invokes the questionable "archaic inheritance" in order to explain phenomena from the realm of the individual psyche. In *Moses and Monotheism*, for example, he says:

> In studying reactions to early traumata we often find to our surprise that they do not keep strictly to what the individual himself has experienced, but deviate from this in a way that

would accord much better with their being reactions to genetic events and in general can be explained only through the influence of such. The behaviour of a neurotic child to his parents when under the influence of an Oedipus and castration complex is very rich in such reactions which seem unreasonable in the individual and can only be understood phylogenetically, in relation to the experiences of earlier generations.[25]

Freud seems to invoke psychoanalysis, which is devoted to the study of the individual psyche, to legitimate an interpretation of culture whose center is the murder of the protofather (and the preservation and transmission of "archaic memory," in the manner of a phylogenetic event). However, the psychoanalytic explanation of the phenomena of the subject's psychic life requires at the same time, and circularly, that interpretation. For its part, the concept of an archaic inheritance, phylogenetically preserved and transmitted, lacks a biological ground—as Freud also acknowledges in *Moses and Monotheism*. Beyond all evidence, then, at the margin of and even against all scientificity, Freudian psychoanalysis shows that it is under the compulsion to assert that the murder was at the origin. We are not facing an empirical fact, a valid notation in the book of the universe, but rather a myth, a constitutive illusion.

"A tradition based only on oral communication could not produce the obsessive character which appertains to religious phenomena. It would be listened to, weighed and perhaps rejected, just like any other news from outside; it would never achieve the privilege of being freed from the coercion of logical thinking."[26] Assessed by its own standards, the Freudian story of the murder of the protofather and the archaic inheritance—which cannot be rejected "just like any other news from outside"—has a compulsive character. Freud has not been able to free himself from the religious (neurotic) compulsion of his own imagery. From this perspective, the therapeutic-cultural work of psychoanalysis (the therapy of Judaism and, by means of it, of Christianity and of Modernity itself) has been left unfinished. We, however, readers of Freud to whom this imagery has been communicated, can continue on his path (the one of *der Fortschritt in der Geistigkeit*, the progress of spirituality).

At the beginning, there was murder. We, Freud's readers, now free of his Paulist imagery, can wonder what in this problematic memory of the origin still exerts its compulsive power upon us. And well, we are modern, we are practical nominalists. Even without the flowery Freudian ethnological imagery, we find compelling stories that place a trauma at the beginning. "At the beginning, there was trauma": Walter Benjamin's interpretation of Modernity might be summarized in this formula.[27] Indeed, in its Freudian meaning, the traumatic event is not simply a forgotten event, which returns obsessively to consciousness after a period of latency. Rather, its very obsessive character, the "compulsion to repeat" that it can trigger, shows that it is an event whose forgetting is part of its very definition, so to speak.

> The historical power of the trauma is not just that the experience is repeated after its forgetting, but that it is only in and through its inherent forgetting that it is first experienced at all. . . . For history to be a history of trauma means that it is referential precisely to the extent that it is not fully perceived as it occurs; or to put it somewhat differently, that a history can be grasped only in the very inaccessibility of its occurrence.[28]

Trauma is an ineradicable web of memory and forgetfulness, only apprehensible "in the very inaccessibility of its occurrence." The same happens with language, as nominalist Modernity asserts: language is fatally marked by alienation, by forgetfulness. *Therefore, for us, the origin is bound to come to presence as trauma.* By means of a reflection on the crisis of lyric poetry—a crisis that Baudelaire would have internalized and staged in his own work ("traumatic poetry")[29]—Benjamin arrives at the idea of trauma as the concentrated expression, not of an archaic memory, but of the very contemporary experience of Modernity. The crisis would be the outcome of the modern impossibility to give meaning to one's "experience" (*Erfahrung*) by integrating it within an order, a narration, a language. Tradition, within which this integration took place, has become intransmissible. The attempts to recover it (for example, as erudite knowledge) do nothing but confirm its essential dislocation.

Benjamin traces this modern dislocation in two directions: on the one hand, in its theoretical and literary registers; on the other hand, in its experiential register. In the former, Benjamin moves through Dilthey and Bergson, until he arrives at Proust and his concept of "involuntary memory." Beyond all intentional consciousness, this memory is activated by the impact of a random stimulus (for example, the flavor of a madeleine, which triggers the lost memory of the city of Combray, in the first volume of *In Search of Lost Time*). Benjamin quotes Proust:

> It is the same with our own past. In vain we try to conjure it up again; the efforts of our intellect are futile. . . . [The past is] somewhere beyond the reach of the intellect, and unmistakably present in some material object (or in the sensation which such an object arouses in us), though we have no idea which one it is. As for that object, it depends entirely on chance whether we come upon it before we die or whether we never encounter it.[30]

Benjamin finds in Freud (in *Beyond the Pleasure Principle*) a theoretical framework that allows him to expand Proust's literary intuition, identifying consciousness with primordial oblivion. Benjamin writes: "Freud's fundamental thought, on which these remarks are based, is formulated by the assumption that 'consciousness comes into being at the site of memory trace. . . .' Therefore, 'it would be the special characteristic of consciousness that, unlike what happens in all other psychical systems, the excitatory process does not leave behind a permanent change in its elements, but expires, as it were, in the phenomenon of becoming conscious.' "[31] He adds that "the basic formula of this hypothesis is that 'becoming conscious and leaving behind a memory trace are processes incompatible with each other within one and the same system. Rather, memory fragments are 'often most powerful and most enduring when the incident which left them behind was one that never entered consciousness.' "[32]

Beyond the scientific language (neuro-physiological, thermodynamic) in which Freud formulates this hypothesis, Benjamin identifies in it the key to modern experience, in which consciousness, as in Borges's Ireneo Funes, is always at the verge of being overflown by the fatal, traumatic landslide of memory. Also in *Beyond the Pleasure Principle*, Freud says that "we describe as 'traumatic' any excitations from outside which are powerful enough to break through the protective shield."[33] The protective shield, as we know, is consciousness. But what comes to break through it this time is not the return of a mythical past, but rather the very reality of modern life. This reality is that of the media ("the replacement of the older narration by information, of information by sensation, reflects the increasing atrophy of experience");[34] of photography ("a touch of the finger . . . gave the moment a posthumous shock, as it were");[35] of the alienated experience of the worker in the machine (and of the player of a game of chance); also of cinema, whose images, in the manner of a Dadaist *collage*, are a montage of images out of context, and therefore traumatic.[36] Primordially, however, the accident that has fallen upon modern life is the reality of urban life, with its anonymous, uprooted, and errant multitudes.[37] Within this uprootedness, even erotic experience has been disjoined. "The delight of the urban poet is love—not at first sight, but at last sight. It is a farewell forever which coincides in the poem with the moment of enchantment. . . . But the nature of the poet's emotions has been affected as well."[38] The poem Benjamin mentions is Baudelaire's sonnet "À une passante" (*"une écailr . . . puis la nuit! Fugitive beauté / Dont le regard m'a fait soudainement renaitre, / Ne te verrai-je plus que dans l'éternité . . . // O toi que j'eusse aimée, ô toi qui le savais"*).[39]

This way, relying on Benjamin and leaving aside the heavy burden of the Freudian "archaic inheritance," it is possible to maintain that psychoanalysis—knowledge of trauma—would essentially express, in a condensed and paradigmatic manner, the experience of Modernity. However, at this very moment (yes, this one), a multitude of academic experts write and unwrite the most varied theses on Baudelaire, on Benjamin, on Proust, and on Freud. Consequently, and by means of the very critical imperative (the Freudian "compulsion of logical thinking") that characterizes modern nominalism, whatever enchanting and compulsive element was still there in the demystified, Benjaminian version of the nominalist myth of psychoanalysis is itself subject to the erosion of disenchantment—until it becomes nothing but "another novelty coming from outside." That way, however, nominalism loses its compulsive character. Freed from mythical imaginary, it retreats into its purest expression. This purified nominalism, I believe, is the version of psychoanalysis associated with Jacques Lacan.

For Lacanian nominalism, of which I can only present an outline here, the cultural gain provided by language (by the symbolic sphere) has its counterpart in the loss of a prelinguistic, archaic immersion in the Real (I capitalize the word following a Lacanian custom): a sort of expulsion from Eden (but pay attention, an Eden that we never really inhabited), whose referent would be the relationship between child and mother, and that unstable self-identification that is produced by the "mirror stage" (in which the child experiences his identity—the mirror returns his own image—but also its loss: that "I," thus reflected, is already Other). Lacan writes:

> For the real does not wait [*attend*], especially not for the subject, since it expects [*attend*] nothing from speech. But it is there, identical to his existence, a noise in which one can hear anything and everything, ready to submerge with its roar what the "reality principle" constructs there that goes by the name of the "outside world."[40]

Lacanian thought is by no means unaware of the nominalist paradox. By virtue of this paradox, the nominalist, who asserts the radical unknowability of the Real (its primordial alterity in connection to our language), knows, however, of the Real—precisely as something unknowable, as other. In other words, nominalism seeks to exclude the projection of the forms of reason into the Real and thus to ban, once and for all, the passage between being and thought. But insofar as its unknowability is in itself an unverifiable postulate (for in order to verify it, a sort of "thinking of thinking" would be necessary, which would face again the same problem), it can be nothing but a projection. Thus, once again in its Lacanian version, the nominalist postulate is violated at the very instant that it is asserted. However, nominalism, as well as the modern world instituted by it, are not "refuted" by this paradox. Rather, the paradox is the source of energy that keeps modern reason working. It is the key to the discontent, but also to the constant self-reflective pirouette that characterizes it. In fact, Lacanian thought has internalized the nominalist paradox, in such a way that it is at the basis of its most basic notions. Thus, according to it, the Real is not a "place" (an Eden: remember the admonition above) from which we would have been unjustly expelled, and to which we might return. The immediate fusion with being (enjoyment, Lacanian *jouissance*, to be distinguished from desire) is not a "state" to be sought, but rather death, the catastrophe of human life. As the divinity in Angelus Silesius (the possibility of the impossible, of the more than impossible: "*das über-unmöglichste ist möglich*"), like death in *Being and Time* ("the possibility of the absolute impossibility of Dasein," §50), the Real only acquires existence paradoxically, in its very impossibility.

Given this impossibility, Lacanian psychoanalysis rejects (or rather, reinterprets as necessary fantasies) each and every narration that contrives to explain the loss of original *jouissance* as the outcome of a prohibition that would have been instituted by the Law.[41] In rigor, there is no such loss, but rather the outcome of an impossibility which the very emergence of the symbolic order nonetheless presents, postfactum, as the outcome of a prohibition:

> The paradox (and perhaps the very function of the prohibition as such) consists of course in the fact that, as soon as it is conceived as prohibited, the real-impossible changes into something *possible*, i.e., into something that cannot be reached, not because of its inherent impossibility but simply because access to it is hindered by the external barrier of a prohibition. Therein lies,

after all, the logic of the most fundamental of all prohibitions, that of incest: incest is inherently impossible (even if a man "really" sleeps with his mother, "this is not *that*"; the incestuous object is by definition lacking), and the symbolic prohibition is nothing but an attempt to resolve this deadlock by a transmutation of impossibility into prohibition. *There is One* which is the prohibited object of incest (mother), and its prohibition renders accessible all other objects.[42]

The prohibition, which makes all other objects accessible, is enforced by the Law. Paradoxically, the Law is not opposed to desire, nor does it suppress it. On the contrary, it institutes desire; it is its condition of possibility.[43] The desire for the mother is identical to the function of the law—the same law that bans her as an object of possession makes her an object of desire. By itself, except for this law-produced inaccessibility, there is nothing in the mother that might turn her into such a desirable object:

> If the paths to *jouissance* have something in them that dies out, that tends to make them impassable, prohibition, if I may say so, becomes its all-terrain vehicle, its half-track truck, that gets it out of the circuitous routes that lead man back in a roundabout way toward the rut of a short and well-trodden satisfaction.[44]

No mythical narration could therefore explain the institution of the Law, its prehistory. By virtue of this now consummated disenchantment device (as we pay attention to Lacan's interest in linguistic and even topological formalization), they all become mere fictions, as, again, "another novelty coming from outside." The Law, however, the impossibility inherent to language, still stands. But, of this mythical, prescriptive, performative core, it is no longer possible to speak. At most, in the absence of the myth of the murder of the primordial father, his presence has withdrawn into a name, a sort of cultural and linguistic black hole, as infinitely ponderous as it is devoid of content: the Name-of-the-Father:

> The Oedipus complex means that the imaginary, in itself an incestuous and conflictual relation, is doomed to conflict and ruin. In order for the human being to be able to establish the most natural of relations, that between male and female, a third party has to intervene, one that is the image of something

successful, the model of some harmony. This does not go far enough—there has to be a law, a chain, a symbolic order, the intervention of the order of speech, that is, of the father. Not the natural father, but what is called the father. The order that prevents the collision and explosion of the situation as a whole is founded on the existence of this name of the father.[45]

Modernity's fate, in sum, is fulfilled in this withdrawal of myth into an empty signifier. As I proposed earlier, the Reformation, which turned the late-medieval nominalist theology into a religion for the masses, reactivated the Jewish prohibition of images. Indeed, the image is the *medium* through which the sacred becomes present in the sensuous world, the bridge that sacralizes the world but that, at the same time, makes possible the instrumentalization of the sacred. But the instrumentalization of the sacred is total instrumentalization; total seizure by a power, thus become tyrannical, of each and every sanctuary from which a judgment upon history still might be passed. For its part, a mature humanity, qualified to drag history as such before the Law, ought instead—in a process that prefigures the ontogenesis of the individual subject in Lacan, with its overcoming of the imaginary in the symbolic—to be capable of abandoning this childish state of *jouissance*. In other words, it ought to renounce the happiness of the image in order to enter the strict world of ethical duty. But this renunciation should also, and eminently, encompass the very imagery of duty, whose unfolding we have traced in Freud. Without imagery, however, duty becomes both imperative and ungrounded: this is the paradox of Modernity, which would find its most developed, self-conscious expression, I have suggested, in Lacanian psychoanalysis. Prohibition, however, institutes desire. Therefore, the desire for the forbidden image would be a constitutive element of the modern psyche, endowing it with its very specific tension and outward energy. Nonetheless, in our contemporary society, with its endless and pervasive proliferation of images (deepening, with the very dissolution of the Law's imaginary foundation, its Max-Weberian *Entzauberung*[46]), the source of this tension and energy is depleted, spent in a generalized, perverse *jouissance*; vanishing into the technologically mediated supply and demand of images, whose libidinal charge is inversely proportional to its availability, to its proliferating abundance.

The Name-of-the-Father: empty signifier; name of a name; initial iteration of an infinite process of naming and contraction. Mystical traditions know of this process of contraction, refuge, withdrawal. In fact, the

Lurianic Kabbalah knows of a God who creates, not by expansion, but by withdrawal, and that by virtue of this process opens the space within which life and human freedom are possible, a God whose (pen-)ultimate name is Nothing, No-one. To quote a psalm that, once upon a time, Paul Celan composed: "No one kneads us again out of earth and clay, / No one incants our dust. / No one. // Blessed art thou, No One."[47]

Notes

Preface to the English Edition

1. "Nominalismo" was also dropped. For English readers, "nominalism" is mainly a philosophical trend within late-medieval scholastics. However, in my book, "nominalism" designates an all-encompassing component of the modern spirit, to the point of becoming invisible. As Jorge Luis Borges writes: "Nominalism, once the novelty of a few, today encompasses everyone; its victory is so vast and fundamental that its name is useless. No one declares himself a nominalist because no one is anything else." Jorge Luis Borges, *Borges: Selected Non-Fictions*, ed. Eliot Weinberger, trans. Esther Allen and Suzanne Jill Levine (Penguin: Penguin, 2000), 339.

2. For an at-length exposition of the issues I am discussing here, see Eduardo Sabrovsky, "Philosophy in Latin America: Some Introductory Remarks," *Journal of the British Society for Phenomenology* 45, no. 1 (January 2, 2014): 1–11, https://doi.org/10.1080/00071773.2014.915646.

3. "The Argentine Writer and Tradition," *Labyrinths* (London, 1970), p. 216.

4. The expression has been coined by the Argentinian thinker and literary critic Beatriz Sarlo, *Borges, a Writer on the Edge* (London: Verso, 1993).

5. "The Argentine Writer and Tradition," p. 218.

6. Bauman, Zygmunt. 1987. *Legislators and Interpreters: On Modernity, Post-Modernity and Intellectuals* (Cambridge: Polity Press).

Preface to the Spanish Edition

1. Ludwig Wittgenstein, *Philosophical Investigations*, trans. G. E. M. Anscombe, P. M. S. Hacker, and Joachim Schulte (Malden, MA: Wiley-Blackwell, 2009), 49, §97.

2. Immanuel Kant, *Idea for a Universal History with a Cosmopolitan Aim*, in *Anthropology, History, and Education*, eds. Günter Zöller and Robert B. Louden, trans. Allen W. Wood (Cambridge: Cambridge University Press, 2007), 118.

3. Ibid.
4. Ibid., 120.
5. My generation: those who were around twenty years old at the time of Chile's Unidad Popular and the Military Coup; those who were more or less capable of anticipating the failure of the rightly called "real socialisms" and, as full adults, of seeing these nefarious anticipations fulfilled. The previous generation also had its part: metaphysical nationalism, that is, German nationalism, reduced to National-Socialism—to the chimneys of the crematorium, to the city crushed by bombings.
6. I tend to put history under the sign of the tragicomic. However, until now, I have focused mostly on the tragic. The comic emerges, as we know, from the attempt at repetition: "the first time as tragedy, the second time as farce," Marx writes, paraphrasing Hegel, in *The Eighteenth Brumaire of Louis Bonaparte*. This farcical repetition is the one perpetrated, from their comfortable globalized podiums, by the contemporary proponents of the now-called (pay attention to the words!) "communist *hypothesis*." One of its most salient representatives is philosopher Slavoj Žižek, who has published a book with precisely that title (*First as Tragedy, Then as Farce* [London: Verso, 2009]), in which, from the first paragraph, he defensively attempts to persuade us that, even for reasons of IQ ("The title of this book is intended as an elementary IQ test for the reader," reads the first line of the book), we should link Marx's sentence not only to him and his fellow travelers (in the sense of an air trip, with awarded miles) but with "the attacks of September 11, 2001 and the financial meltdown of 2008" (p. 1). Žižek defends the idea of a "Stalinist humanism" and of the "partial" character of truth ("for truth is partial, accessible only when one takes sides, and is no less universal for this reason," p. 6). However, this very aggressive side taking culminates in a very moderate position: the task, he adds, is "not . . . a direct climatic confrontation, but to undermine those in power with patient ideologico-critical work" (p. 7). Thus, "the most dangerous philosopher in the West"—this is the funny quotation that Verso placed on the cover of the book, symptomatizing the farcical scene to which it belongs—turns out to be one more among us: a patient citizen, an academic who is distinguished from the herd only by his histrionic excesses. I engage with Žižek in more detail in my book *Chile, tiempos interesantes: A 40 años del Golpe Militar* (Sangiago: Ediciones UDP, 2013). There, I examine contemporary local (Chilean) and global politics, going back to its historical antecedents.
7. Robert Musil, *The Man without Qualities*, trans. Sophie Wilkins (New York: Vintage, 1995), 327.
8. Ibid.
9. Continuing with the "discovery" that underlies this book, I must say that, just like the notion of *the extraordinary* struck me while reflecting on the candid conference on "ordinary language philosophy," I arrived at nominalism as a metaphysics that grounds the modern age, by contrast to the medieval realism, through the work of Jorge Luis Borges. In "From Allegories to Novels," Borges writes

that "nominalism, which was formerly the novelty of a few, encompasses everyone today; its victory is so vast and fundamental that its name is unnecessary. No one says that he is a nominalist, because nobody is anything else" (*Other Inquisitions: 1937–1952*, trans. Ruth L. C. Simms [Austin: University of Texas Press, 1964], 157). This observation, both brief and blunt, does not imply that no one holds realist convictions. But they would be just that: convictions which, as in the "ethics of conviction" that Max Weber opposes to an "ethics of responsibility" (the calculable anticipation of the outcome of action) in *Politics as Vocation*, are confined to the interiority of each person. In other words (mine, not Borges's): whether we want it or not, we are practical nominalists each time we make use of techno-scientific gadgets, each time we act with an expectation of success in politics, or each time we simply (simply?) go to the grocery shop, the bank, or the supermarket.

10. Ludwig Wittgenstein, "A Lecture on Ethics," *The Philosophical Review* 74, no. 5.

11. Ibid., 6–7.

12. Ibid., 11.

13. Ibid., 7.

14. "Sovereign is he who decides on the exception" (Carl Schmitt, *Political Theology: Four Chapters on the Concept of Sovereignty*, trans. George Schwab [Cambridge, MA: MIT Press, 1985], 5). "The exception in jurisprudence is analogous to the miracle in theology" (ibid., 36).

15. Lukács's text, originally written in Hungarian, is titled "Bolshevism as a Moral Problem." *Chile, tiempos interesantes* includes my translation into Spanish from the English version of 1977.

16. Walter Benjamin, "Theses on the Philosophy of History, in *Illuminations: Essays and Reflections*, ed. Hannah Arendt, trans. Harry Zohn (New York: Schocken, 1969), 257.

17. Ibid., 257–58.

18. Henri Atlan, *Entre le cristal et la fumée: Essai sur l'organisation du vivant* (Pairs: Seuil, 1979), 29.

19. Beyond any idealized "tiger's leap into the past" (Benjamin, "Theses on the Philosophy of History," 261).

20. Carl Schmitt, *The Concept of the Political*, trans. George Schwab (Chicago: University of Chicago Press, 2007), 71.

21. Benjamin, "Theses on the Philosophy of History," 264. The sentence comes from the Gospels (Matthew 7.13:14). However, Benjamin attributes it to "the Jews." In any case, as Joyce writes in *Ulysses*, "Jegreek is greekjew." Or perhaps better here: "Jewchristian is christianjew."

22. "If mythical violence [that is, sovereign violence] is lawmaking, divine violence is law-destroying; if the former sets boundaries, the latter boundlessly destroys them" (Walter Benjamin, "Critique of Violence," in *Reflections: Essays, Aphorisms, Autobiographical Writings*, ed. Peter Demetz, trans. Edmund Jephcott [New York:

Schocken, 1986], 297). Above, I suggested that "Critique of Violence" can be read at least in part as a theologization of Leninism in 1917, that is, as a sort of unstable synthesis between theologization and real politics. However, the synthesis became impossible in 1940, and so "divine violence" was left free to unfold as a concept beyond any actual political consideration.

23. Jacques-Alain Miller, "Extimité," ed. M. Bracher et al. (New York: New York University Press, 1994).

Notes to Introduction

1. See Immanuel Kant, *Gesammelte Schriften*, ed. Königlich Preußische [later, Deutsche] Akademie der Wissenschaften (Berlin: Reimer; later, de Gruyter, 1900–), 3: 314; A 258 = B 313–14; *Critique of Pure Reason*, trans. Paul Guyer and Alan Wood (Cambridge: Cambridge University Press, 1997), 352, translation modified.

2. Kant, *Critique of Pure Reason*, A751–52 = B799–80.

3. See, for example, Kant, *Gesammelte Schriften*, 9: 65 and especially 7: 216, where the attempt to construct a *perpetuum mobile* (like the attempt to square the circle and comprehend the mystery of the Trinity) is placed under the sign of *Aberwitz* or *vesania*.

Chapter 1

1. Robert Musil, *The Man without Qualities*, trans. Sophie Wilkins (New York: Vintage, 1995), 41.
2. Ibid., 44.
3. Ibid., 575.
4. Ibid., 41.
5. Ibid., 43.
6. Ibid.
7. Ibid., 42.
8. Ibid.
9. Ibid.
10. Ibid., 43–44.
11. "Suppose one of you were an omniscient person and therefore new all the movements of all the bodies in the world dead or alive and that he also knew all the states of mind of all human beings that ever lived, and suppose this man wrote all he knew in a big book, then this book would contain the whole description of the world; and what I want to say is, that this book would contain nothing that we would call an *ethical* judgment or anything that would logically imply such a judgment. . . . If for instance in our world-book we read the description of a murder

with all its details physical and psychological, the mere description of these facts will contain nothing which we could call an *ethical* proposition. The murder will be on exactly the same level as any other event, for instance the falling of a stone" (Ludwig Wittgenstein, "A Lecture on Ethics," *The Philosophical Review* 74[1], 6).

12. Eithne Wilkins and Ernst Kaisser, "Foreword," in *The Man without Qualities*, by Robert Musil (London: Secker & Warburg, 1979), xxxv.

13. *The Man without Qualities*, 266.

14. Ibid., 265.

15. Ibid., 266.

16. "One must not forget that basically the scientific cast of mind is more God-oriented than the aesthetic mind, ready to submit to 'Him' the moment 'He' deigns to show Himself under the conditions it prescribes for recognizing Him, while our aesthetes, confronted with His manifestation, would find only that His talent was not original and that His view of the world was not sufficiently intelligible to rank Him with really God-given talents" (ibid., 276). Nonetheless, for the modern mind, the domain of conditioned phenomena (the "conditions it prescribes") is, by definition, indifferent to Revelation: it is clueless regarding the unconditional essence of the divine. But is this indifference, to which we are unconditionally *subdued*, indifferent in its turn? (in Musil's observation, *submission* is the name of the game). In this nonindifferent indifference, a certain religious spirit (negative, mystical) is actually invoked by "the point of view of exactitude."

17. Ibid., 327.

18. Ibid., 327–28.

19. Galileo's image of the book of the universe written in mathematical characters appears in the dialogue *Il Saggiatore*. But Galileo's Platonism, unlike the Aristotelianism against which it is forged, is already a nominalism: the book written in mathematical characters is no longer commensurable with the world because of its language (this is Aristotle's critique of Platonism, especially of its mathematical version). As Borges says in connection to a certain encyclopedia that has invaded the world, its rigor (here, the rigor of Galileo's book) would be "of chess masters, not of angels" (Jorge Luis Borges, *Labyrinths: Selected Stories & Other Writings*, ed. Donald A. Yates and James E. Irby, trans. James E. Irby [New York: New Directions, 2007], 33). And, comparing the discursive order of our world with the transcendent order of the real, Borges adds: "[I]t is useless to answer that reality is also orderly. Perhaps it is, but in accordance with divine laws—I translate: inhuman laws—which we never quite grasp. Tlön is surely a labyrinth, but it is a labyrinth devised by men, a labyrinth destined to be deciphered by men" (ibid.).

20. Alexander Koyré, *From the Closed World to the Infinite Universe* (Baltimore, MD: Johns Hopkins University Press, 1957), 4.

21. Luther's answer was supposedly this: "Unless I am convinced by Scripture and plain reason—I do not accept the authority of the popes and councils, for they have contradicted each other—my conscience is captive to the Word of God. I

cannot and I will not recant anything for to go against conscience is neither right nor safe. God help me. Amen" ("Luther at the Imperial Diet of Worms [1521]," accessed January 27, 2018, http://www.luther.de/en/worms.html).

22. Plato, *Phaedrus*, trans. Alexander Nehamas and Paul Woodruff (Indianapolis: Hackett, 1995), 79.

23. Jorge Luis Borges, "From Allegories to Novels," in *Other Inquisitions: 1937–1952*, trans. Ruth L. C. Simms (Austin: University of Texas Press, 1964), 157. I address Borges's nominalism more thoroughly in the chapter "Outline of an Ethic for Immortals."

24. This singularity, toward the side of the insignificant human reason—"the most arrogant and mendacious minute in the 'history of the world,'" as Nietzsche calls it in *On Truth and Lie in a Nonmoral Sense* (in *The Birth of Tragedy and Other Writings*, ed. Raymond Geuss and Ronald Speirs, trans. Ronald Speirs [New York: Cambridge University Press, 2007], 141)—and only toward it, shows its face of neutral objectivity.

25. By the way, each side of this split contains somehow its opposite. Thus, whoever implacably associates language and forgetfulness "knows" of a higher-order memory from which he establishes such association (this memory must in its turn appear to him as a forgetfulness, as one more reification). Conversely, the attempts to produce a reconciliation live out of the horror, so to speak, produced by the boundless landslide of memory: they have internalized its other, which thus constitutes its most intimate and decisive truth.

Chapter 2

1. Thus, the severe *Critique of Pure Reason* begins with the narration of a kind of foundational myth: the danger of the destruction of "social unity" by the action of "the skeptics, a kind of nomads who abhor all permanent cultivation of the soil" (Kant, *Critique of Pure Reason*, trans. and eds. Paul Guyer and Allen W. Wood [Cambridge: Cambridge University Press, 2000], 99; Aix).

2. Ibid., 649–50; A751–52 = B799–80.

3. Kant writes in his *Religion within the Boundaries of Mere Reason*: "Moreover, to have the one or the other disposition by nature as an innate characteristic does not mean here that the disposition has not been earned by the human being who harbors it, i.e. that he is not its author, but means rather that it has not been earned in time (that he has been the one way or the other always, from his youth on). The disposition, i.e. the first subjective ground of the adoption of the maxims, can only be a single one, and it applies to the entire use of freedom universally. This disposition too, however, must be adopted through the free power of choice [*Willkür*], for otherwise it could not be imputed. But there cannot be any further

cognition of the subjective ground or the cause of this adoption (although we cannot avoid asking about it), for otherwise we would have to adduce still another maxim into which the disposition would have to be incorporated, and this maxim must in turn have its ground. Hence, since we cannot derive this disposition, or rather its highest ground, from a first act of the power of choice in time, we call it a characteristic of the power of choice that pertains to it by nature (even though the disposition is in fact grounded in freedom)" (*Religion within the Boundaries of Mere Reason*, in *Religion and Rational Theology*, ed. Allen W. Wood and George Di Giovanni [New York: Cambridge University Press, 2001], 74; 6:25). This contradictory structure of *Gesinmung* (innate but earned; earned, but not 'in time'; chosen, but groundless) is also the essence of Nietzsche's *amor fati*, his imperative to take on destiny as if it had been freely willed, though he fully accepts its fictional and performative character. Nietzsche writes: "My formula for human greatness is *amor fati*: that one wants nothing to be different, not in the future, not in the past, not for all eternity. Not only to endure what is necessary, still less to conceal it—all idealism is falseness in the face of necessity—, but to love it" (*Ecce Homo: How One Becomes What One Is*, in *Ecce Homo and The Antichrist*, trans. Thomas Wayne [New York: Algora, 2004], 39).

 4. Immanuel Kant, *Idea for a Universal History with a Cosmopolitan Aim*, trans. Allen W. Wood, in *Anthropology, History, and Education*, eds. Günter Zöller and Robert B. Louden (Cambridge: Cambridge University Press, 2007), 109; 8:18.

 5. Ibid.
 6. Ibid., 112; 8:22.
 7. Ibid., 114–15; 8:25.
 8. Ibid., 111; 8:21.

 9. Hans Vaihinger (1852–1933), in his *The Philosophy of 'As If': A System of the Theoretical, Practical and Religious Fictions of Mankind* (1911), proposed that Kant's transcendental philosophy should be understood as a system of pragmatic fictions; an understanding that made Nietzsche his intellectual heir. Vaihinger was an outstanding Kantian scholar and the founder, in 1896, of the very prestigious journal *Kant-Studien*.

 10. Kant, *Idea for a Universal History* . . . , 109–10; 8:18–8:19.
 11. Ibid., 118; 8:29.
 12. Ibid.

 13. The utilitarianism of Hegel's contemporary Bentham (and through it, the philosophical pragmatism that follows) can be understood, not *de facto* but indeed *de jure*, as the adversary that Kant has in front of him when formulating his ethics. For utilitarianism, the good is ultimately reduced to utility. For Kantian morality, by contrast, moral duty is only such insofar as it is fulfilled for the sake of duty itself, beyond (and even against) any consideration of utility, either social or individual. As already stated above, the theological, extraordinary aspect of nature is

addressed in depth by Kant in the *Critique of the Power of Judgment*. Suggestively, along the lines of the ideas I am developing here, this aspect is connected there to the extraordinary in art.

14. G. W. F. Hegel, *The Spirit of Christianity and Its Fate*, trans. T. M. Knox, in *On Christianity: Early Theological Writings by Friedrich Hegel* (New York: Harper Torchbooks, 1961), 182.

15. Ibid., 186.

16. Ibid., 185.

17. Ibid., 187.

18. Ibid., 192.

19. Ibid., 191.

20. "The idea of arranging *all* significant points of view in such a single sequence, on a ladder that reaches from the crudest to the most mature, is as dazzling to contemplate as it is mad to try seriously to implement it" (Walter Kaufmann, *Hegel: A Reinterpretation* [Notre Dame, IN: Notre Dame University Press, 1978], 133).

21. "From Allegories to Novels," in *Other Inquisitions: 1937–1952*, trans. Ruth L. C. Simms (Austin: University of Texas Press, 1964). Borges's main thesis in this text is that the novel stems from the loss of faith in the reality of universals, which is characteristic of nominalism.

22. G. W. F. Hegel, *Phenomenology of Spirit*, trans. A. V. Miller (Oxford: Oxford University Press, 2004), 492–93. Italics are mine, and I have omitted some of Hegel's italics as well.

23. I develop this idea in chapter 8: "Outline of an Ethics of Immortality."

24. Hegel, *Phenomenology*, 178–79.

25. Karl Marx, *Economic and Philosophical Manuscripts*, in *Early Writings*, trans. Rodney Livingstone and Gregor Benton (New York: Penguin, 1992), 329.

26. He extended his admiration to its author. "There is no other road for you to truth and freedom except that leading through the brook of fire [the *Feuerbach*]. Feuerbach is the purgatory of the present times," he once wrote. See Ludwig Feuerbach, *The Fiery Brook: Selected Writings*, ed. and trans. Zawar Hanfi (New York: Verso, 1972), 172.

27. Ludwig Feuerbach, *The Essence of Christianity*, trans. George Eliot (Walnut, CA: MSAC Philosophy Group, 2008), 175.

28. Karl Marx, *Economic and Philosophical Manuscripts*, in *Early Writings*, trans. Rodney Livingstone and Gregor Benton (New York: Penguin, 1992), 329.

29. Ibid.

30. Ibid.

31. The famous section on "Commodity Fetishism" in *Capital*, Volume 1, is representative of this. Here, Marx is about to acknowledge that the objects of our knowledge might be "fetishes" in the same way as commodities. However, at the last moment, he steps back on the face of this nominalist abyss. Indeed, in

order to explain the "physically metaphysical" nature of commodities, Marx relies on the following analogy: "In the same way, the impression made by a thing on the optic nerve is perceived not as a subjective excitation of that nerve but as the objective form of a thing outside the eye. In the act of seeing, of course, light is really transmitted from one thing, the external object, to another thing, the eye. It is a physical relation between physical things. As against this, the commodity-form, and the value-relation of the products of labour within which it appears, have absolutely no connection with the physical nature of the commodity and the material [*dinglich*] relations arising out of this" (Marx, *Capital*, trans. Ben Fowkes [New York: Penguin, 1982], Vol. 1, 165). In order to avoid any misunderstanding, let us say that the nominalist abyss that Marx dodges has nothing to do with the denial of the real, but rather with its affirmation—the affirmation of its alterity, which is irreducible to the "forms of objectivity" and to the *idola* (the expressions belong to Lukács and to Bacon, respectively) that are imposed upon it. The Marx from *Capital*, by contrast, requires that objectivity be nothing but a datum. Thus, it is possible for him to make techno-scientific progress compatible with dis-alienation.

32. See chapter 7, especially the references there to George Bataille's *The Accursed Share*.

Chapter 3

1. Against this interdiction, it is often said that in everyday life, facts and values are indistinguishably imbricated. It is worth considering this objection in some detail. It stems from the factual unity of life. And, indeed, life, as it is lived in internal experience, is indivisible—and not only that: it is also nonrepresentable (representation presupposes distance). Life is not "the life," "life does not live" (Ferdinand Kürnberger, quoted by Adorno in one of the epigraphs of his *Minima Moralia*). But this objection does not realize that the division at stake is not factual, but rather normative: it constitutes, so to speak, the First Commandment, perhaps the only one, of the religion of the moderns. Modern dualism would be therefore not an obstacle that ethics must remove, but rather its condition of possibility. For instance, for Emmanuel Lévinas, it is this dualism that makes the separation and the encounter with the Other "as other" possible: justice, beyond any (false) reconciliation within history. The Holocaust and the Gulag are often used to argue against the separation of facts and values, for there, the sole factual account seems enough to trigger ethical condemnation. But, on the contrary, that which makes them condemnable, even beyond any ethics, is precisely their character of limit-experiences—catastrophes that make the limits between ethics and history collapse and which, therefore, somehow do not take place "in" history, but rather occur "to" history. The thought of Modernity certainly has been forged in the aporetic attempt to *supersede* dualism, for example, through history or art. To ignore this

by invoking the unity of "life" carries the risk of falling into the bad illusion of a Modernity without the Reformation (in which the Reformation and its legacy would be reduced to a kind of bad intellectual habit).

2. We can recognize here the "discontent of language" of Borges's Ireneo Funes in "Funes the Memorious."

3. Ludwig Wittgenstein, *Tractatus Logico-Philosophicus*, trans. D. F. Pears and B. F. McGuinness (New York: Routledge, 2002), 89.

4. Let us now clarify that as a concept, the extraordinary would be the post-Kantian, post-Wittgensteinian equivalent of the unconditioned in Kant. However, I would like for other resonances to be heard behind the concept: on the one hand, a branch of contemporary philosophy (the one associated with the "second" Wittgenstein) is called "ordinary language philosophy." The name is astonishing—truth, good, and beauty are extra-ordinary predicates of which philosophy could hardly just dispose. The academic practice of this philosophy (but not only of it), which often situates itself comfortably in the place of truth, is even more astonishing. On the other hand, "ordinary," unlike the "conditioned," has "vulgar" among its meanings. And, indeed, the modern option to explain the high as a modality of the low has a plebeian, anti-aristocratic bias, whose realization, accompanied by the symptomatizing of the concomitant discontent, is clearly present in Nietzsche. On the plebeian nature of effective history, the *wirkliche Historie* practiced by Nietzsche in his condition of genealogist, see Michel Foucault, "Nietzsche, Genealogy, History," in *The Foucault Reader*, ed. Paul Rabinow (New York: Pantheon, 1984).

5. Roland Barthes, *Mythologies*, trans. Annette Lavers (New York: Noonday, 1972).

6. Ibid., 128.
7. Ibid., 142.
8. Ibid., 121–22.
9. Ibid., 124.
10. Ibid., 127.
11. Ibid., 143.
12. Ibid., 148.
13. Ibid., 132.
14. Ibid., 132–33.
15. Ibid., 134.
16. Ibid., 132.
17. Ibid.
18. Ibid., 134.

19. Max Horkheimer and Theodor W. Adorno, *Dialectic of Enlightenment: Philosophical Fragments*, ed. Gunzelin Schmid Noerr, trans. Edmund Jephcott (Stanford: Stanford University Press, 2002), 2–3.

20. Ludwig Wittgenstein, *Tractatus Logico-Philosophicus*, trans. D. F. Pears and B. F. McGuinness (New York: Routledge, 2002), §5.1361; 47.

21. Ibid., §6.3; 80.
22. Ibid., §5.632; 69.
23. R. M. White, "Can whether one proposition make sense depend on the truth of another? (*Tractatus* 2.0211–12)," ed. Godfrey Vesey (Ithaca, NY: Cornell University Press, 1976), 19.
24. Barthes, *Mythologies*, 121.
25. Thomas S. Kuhn, *The Structure of Scientific Revolutions* (Chicago: University of Chicago Press, 2002), 181–86.
26. Ludwig Wittgenstein, *Philosophical Investigations*, trans. G. E. M. Anscombe, P. M. S. Hacker, and Joachim Schulte (West Sussex, UK: Basil Balckwell, 2009), §50; 29.
27. The deep identity between Enlightenment and myth is Horkheimer and Adorno's teaching.
28. Jean-Pierre Vernant, *Myth and Society in Ancient Greece*, trans. Janet Lloyd (New York: Zone Books, 1990), 207.
29. Ibid., 207.
30. Ibid., 203–04.
31. "[T]he freedom to believe whatever man wants is very detrimental and harmful, because it is freedom to err, and to err is a tremendously dangerous thing. For a true truth cannot be but one, everything that differs and departs from it is deception, blindness, and error; and a man's heart without this true faith, is like a ship without a government that any wind grabs and any wave takes away" (Pedro de Ribadeneira, quoted in Manuel Jiménez Redondo, "Habermas en el contexto del Pensamiento Político Moderno y la posición de Habermas en el debate Modernidad/Posmodernidad," Conference "Modernidad Terminable o Interminable" [Santiago de Chile, 2000]).
32. Jacques Monod, *Chance and Necessity: An Essay on the Natural Philosophy of Modern Biology*, trans. Austryn Wainhouse (New York: Vintage, 1972), 20.
33. Ibid., 21.
34. Ibid., 180.

Chapter 4

1. In these foundations, questions of fact and questions of value mingle in an indiscernible manner. One can see this by looking at the correspondence between Leibniz and Clarke, Newton's secretary, during the dawn of modern science. There, for example, the point of departure is a discussion about the way to explain scientifically the clash of two billiard balls. A few lines below, and without any breaks in the argumentation, the debate moves to the existence of God, his relationships with the human world, and the ethical and political consequences of each one of the possible positions.

2. Heidegger was not ignorant in scientific matters. His first university studies were in physics.

3. In strictly Heideggerian terms, which however often confuse those who are not familiar with them, this sentence would be enough: to "project" a "world picture" would be by itself a technological attitude.

4. Martin Heidegger, "The Age of the World Picture," in *The Question concerning Technology and Other Essays*, trans. William Lovitt (New York: Garland, 1977).

5. Ibid., 118–19.

6. What does it have to do in an *inherent* way, beyond mere "application"? In the last instance, this is the question that Einstein is answering with a categorical "no" when he denies that God "plays dice." Because if God played dice, there would be a gap between our cognitions, which would be intrinsically probabilistic, and unconditional truth. And it is through this gap, no matter how minimal it may be, where material, mundane conditions and interests can break in. With the best ethical intentions, but with a philosophical reasoning that was not equally good, Einstein wanted to separate his discoveries from disgusting issues such as the invention of the atomic bomb. The problem is whether ethical unconditionality (of the good) requires the unconditionality of cognitive truth, or one must rather approach things in a totally different domain.

7. Ethical unconditionality looks like an issue for metaphysical philosophers and their jargon. It is not, however. The unconditioned is the opposite of the conditioned, the empirical, which for Modernity, inheritor of the nominalism of the Late Middle Ages and of the protestant Reformation, is by itself neutral in terms of values. Aside from that, this is the content of the very scientific and modern "postulate of objectivity," which prohibits that teleological explanations of natural phenomena be considered scientific. If there are no aims and values that can be "read" from the Book of Nature, then values can only inhabit the sphere of the subject, which must necessarily be a sphere subtracted from causal explanations. Given that it is not possible to be responsible for something that is causally determined, be it a genetic, physical, economic, sociological, or physical-chemical causality, or any other imaginable, it is only possible to attribute responsibility if it is somehow possible (daunting task) to defend the existence of a sphere subtracted from causal explanations.

8. Henri Atlan, *Entre le cristal et la fumée: Essai sur l'organisation du vivant* (Pairs: Seuil, 1979), 27.

9. The idea of the commensurability between representations and the real can be projected into the realm of collective representations. Thus, for medieval culture, the commensurability between human representations and the real (the Greek cosmos, Christianized) is secured by the fact that the latter was created by a good God, and not by a malignant and deceitful genius like the one that will later appear to Descartes. What this God secures, in other words, is the *order* of the universe which, precisely because it is an order, is capable of being grasped by the

human being. Not by all human beings, only by those in whom a fully developed reason and the privilege of being Revelation's sole recipients are combined; in other words, by the Medieval ecclesiastic and political institution, which attributes itself the capacity to decipher the order of the universe and to translate it into the terms of ethical-political norms, in terms of a social order that becomes obligatory for all. The hegemony and legitimacy of the power of such institution rests upon this operation of deciphering and translating.

10. The novelty of chaos theory consists in that there is no proportionality between causes and effects: small causes can produce, when enough time has passed, enormous effects. From now on, no physical magnitude is a priori "negligible."

11. On this origin of probability and statistics in human and social sciences, see the books of Canadian philosopher Ian Hacking, *The Emergence of Probability: A Philosophical Study of Early Ideas about Probability* (Cambridge: Cambridge University Press, 2006); *The Taming of Chance* (Cambridge: Cambridge University Press, 1990).

12. Atlan, *Entre le cristal et la fumée*, 29.

13. Ibid.

14. This replacement, as Heidegger has also shown, has its philosophical expression in the transformation, from Descartes on, of the philosophy of Modernity into the "philosophy of the subject," of a subject characterized essentially by its will, culminating in Nietzsche's ontology of the "will to power." Heidegger calls our attention to the original meaning of the word "subject": *sub-jectum*, that is, what underlies (ground)—the Latin word that translates the Greek word *hypokeimenon*. The subject is not originally a human being, but rather a ground. Modernity would be that historical event by virtue of which the mind and its representations come to occupy the primordial place of ground.

15. See the work of German philosopher Hans Blumenberg, in particular his book *The Legitimacy of the Modern Age*, trans. Robert M. Wallace (Cambridge, MA: MIT Press, 1985).

16. Groundless, that is, from a logical point of view.

17. Atlan, *Le critstal et la fumée*, 32.

18. Ibid. My italics.

19. If we think more in-depth this relationship between theoretical contemplation and labor, all the Byzantine discussions that want to distinguish between manual and intellectual labor are left aside. The main source of technological labor, and of labor as such, is the human ability to make distinctions. It would be necessary to inscribe this claim within the history of the concept of labor, which exceeds the scope of this chapter.

20. Atlan formulated his Spinozism during his talks at the III School of Complex Systems, Valparaíso Institute for Complex Systems, Chile, January 2005. See Henri Atlan, *Configurations spinozistes* (Paris: Odile Jacob, 2018).

21. Baruch Spinoza, *Ethics*, ed. Seymour Feldman, trans. Samuel Shirley (Indianapolis, IN: Hackett, 1992), 166. The "preserve oneself" is Spinoza's famous

"*conatus essendi*": all things persist in their being (including the human being which, on this basis, is not distinct from animals).

22. Ibid.

23. "There is no document of civilization that is not at the same time a document of barbarism." This sentence is part of the VII thesis on the concept of history (known as "Thesis on the Philosophy of History"), which Walter Benjamin wrote shortly before his death. It is evident that Spinozism turns absurd propositions of this kind, or propositions such as Freud's.

24. Emmanuel Lévinas, *Totality and Infinity: An Essay on Exteriority*, trans. Alphonso Lingis (London: Martinus Nijhoff, 1979), 35. For an assessment by Lévinas regarding Spinoza, in which the monism that seems to be implied in Spinoza's texts such as the *Ethics* is questioned through a reading of the *Theological-Political Treatise*, see the essay "Avez-vous relu Baruch?," included in *Difficile liberté* (Paris: Le livre de poche, 2003). There, Lévinas notes that for Spinoza in the *Treatise*, the validity of the Judeo-Christian Scriptures is of another kind (ethical), *different* from the cognitive validity (truth) of philosophy and science.

25. We might also say "of normativity," insofar as the aspirations of Newton and Galileo's science are not merely inductive. It seeks to say not how things empirically are, but rather how they "ought to be." Even in the most unreachable galaxies (of which we lack all experience) the law of inertia *ought to* be valid. The problem of the unconditional can be described in terms of the difference between "facts" and "norms." There can only be inductive, empirical generalizations of facts, while norms, by contrast, seek to be universal. This is contained in the so-called "motto of the empiricists": "From an is does not follow an ought." Even in his attempts to overcome it, Kant remains loyal to this distinction.

26. Immanuel Kant, *Groundwork of the Metaphysics of Morals*, in *Practical Philosophy*, ed. Mary J. Gregor (New York: Cambridge University Press, 1999), 49; 4:393.

27. See Alenka Zupančič, *Ethics of the Real: Kant, Lacan* (London: Verso, 2000), for a Lacanian elaboration of this Kantian split. In any case, according to Kant, the choice faced by the subject points to two aspects of the will, in principle contradictory, which he designates by means of two variations made possible by the German language. There is, on the one hand, *Wille*, the will as legislator, as the site of the moral law in all its rational, unconditional rigor, and in its full capacity to break through the selfish shelves of individuals; on the other hand, *Willkür*, the will as the capacity for action, for choice in a secular world. How is this contradiction resolved? In *Religion within the Boundaries of Mere Reason* (1794), Kant finally gives an answer to this question. The conflict between *Wille* and *Willkür* is not eliminable. As in psychoanalysis, which Kant's reflection somehow anticipates, there is nothing else to do but to accept the gap inherent to modern psyche. Now, in Kant, the stage of this conflict is what he calls "disposition" (*Gesinnung*) which,

although constituted by hereditary traits and life-experiences, is the highest realization of autonomy, insofar as the individual willfully recognizes it as the outcome of his own choice. But how is it possible that inheritance and biography, which are located in the past, be taken up as creations of the will? Was not Kant already senile when he thought about this, as some readers ask? But if autonomy has any content, it does not consist in choosing this or that, this thing or another, but rather in choosing oneself in a nonreified, unconditional manner. In this, as in many other aspects, Kant is a precursor to Nietzsche and to his radical critique of the morality of *ressentiment*, the morality of those who are not capable of freeing themselves from the weight of their history by taking it on as belonging to them. In works like *The Gay Science* and *Ecce Homo*, Nietzsche develops a purified version of Kantian autonomy, which he very adequately calls *amor fati*, "love of one's own destiny." He writes, with clear words that shed light on what remained obscure in the reflections of his antecessor: "My formula for human greatness is *amor fati*: that one wants nothing to be different, not in the future, not in the past, not for all eternity. Not only to endure what is necessary, still less to conceal it—all idealism is falseness in the face of necessity—, but to *love* it" (Friedrich Nietzsche, *Ecce Homo*, in *Ecce Homo and the Antichrist*, trans. Thomas Wayne [New York: Algora, 2004], 39). Both Kant and Nietzsche acknowledge indeed that autonomous moral construction can fail. In Kant's terminology, the disposition can collapse, being reduced to a mere propensity (*Hang*), which a passage in his *Religion within the Boundaries of Mere Reason*, perhaps prophetically, links to an addiction to intoxicants. In sum: lacking the conditions for the subject to realize its autonomy in this fundamental sense—as radical moral decision—*ressentiment* takes its place, as a psychical disposition that is predominant in modern life.

28. Friedrich Nietzsche, *On the Genealogy of Morals*, ed. Walter Kaufmann, trans. Walter Kaufmann and R. J. Hollingdale (New York: Vintage, 1989), 65.

29. Wittgenstein, *Tractatus Logico-Philosophicus*, §5.632; 69: "The subject does not belong to the world: rather, it is a limit of the world." In the Spinozism / anti-Spinozism axis, we could say that Wittgenstein's first work (the *Tractatus*) belongs to the second trend, and his posthumous work (the *Philosophical Investigations*, in which all language expression is linked to a usage, to a certain "language game" and the social practices that constitute it) to the first.

30. Lévinas, *Totality and Infinity*, 95–96.

Chapter 5

1. Friedrich Nietzsche, *On Truth and Lying in a Non-Moral Sense*, in *The Birth of Tragedy and Other Writings*, eds. Raymond Geuss and Ronald Speirs, trans. Ronald Speirs (Cambridge: Cambridge University Press, 2007), 143.

2. Ibid., 146.

3. Inéditos 1881–86; Inéditos 1882/3–1888, citados por Vaihinger, Han, 1988, *La voluntad de ilusión en Nietzsche*.

4. The place of Paul Celan, for example, survivor of the *Shoah* and suicide victim of the Seine, in whose words Primo Levi heard "the gaps of an agonizing person."

5. Nietzsche, quoted in Martin Heidegger, *Nietzsche*, trans. David Farrell Krell (New York, HarperCollins), 19.

6. Ibid.

7. Emmanuel Lévinas, *Totality and Infinity: An Essay on Exteriority*, trans. Alphonso Lingis (London: Martinus Nijhoff Publishers, 1979), 43–44. Let us note that in Lévinas the term "metaphysics" is reserved for designating a desire for exteriority that Western thought, still under the identitary hegemony of ontology, would not have ceased to express (for example, the Cartesian idea of infinity). This way, Lévinas doubles down on Heidegger's bet: ontology as "destruction" of metaphysics is in its turn destroyed, exposed in the forgetting of exteriority that would be inherent to it.

8. Ibid., 44–45.

9. Ibid., 45–46.

10. "*Recapitulation*: to *stamp* Becoming with the character of Being—that is the supreme will to power." As it is known, in his lectures and texts on Nietzsche, Heidegger sought to make of him the last metaphysician, in whose work the tradition of metaphysics would have reached its fulfillment and its truth. At the end of the road, what becomes evident with Nietzsche is that this tradition was internally being shaped by the will—the will to power. However, Nietzsche's sentence, which I am quoting again here, suggests an inversion: if "to *stamp* Becoming with the character of Being" is "the supreme will to power," then such apotheosis would have its fulfillment in Heideggerian ontology and not in Nietzsche's thought, which rather anticipates it. This would be another way to justify the claim that I have made and that I have argued relying mostly on Lévinas, in the sense that hermeneutic ontology, and not scientism, constitutes the positivism of our time.

11. Let us think of this distinction between "normal" and "revolutionary" exercise of power along the lines of the distinction that Thomas S. Kuhn establishes (*The Structure of Scientific Revolutions*) between "normal" science and scientific revolutions. Under conditions of normality, science operates in a world of given entities that present themselves as natural. With revolutions, by contrast, the world of the scientists changes: other objects become distinguishable in it. In the transition from one state to another, however, it should be possible to see the illusionism of the will to power, as well as the radical alterity to which it seeks to stamp the "character of Being."

12. Further down, I will speak of "hermeneutic drift," following the same perspective. In this drift, alienation and forgetfulness as specifically modern phe-

nomena would be fulfilled—alienation and forgetfulness that also have the drift of instrumentality and of the market among its components.

13. Hans Vaihinger, *The Philosophy of "As If": A System of the Theoretical, Practical and Religious Fictions of Mankind*, trans. C. K. Ogden (London: Kegan Paul, Trench, Trubner, 1935), 344.

14. Friedrich Nietzsche, *Human, All Too Human: A Book for Free Spirits*, trans. R. J. Hollingdale (Cambridge: Cambridge University Press, 1996), 29. It could be objected that in this passage Nietzsche is referring to untruth (and truth) in a metaphysical sense. And indeed, the aphorism goes on: "For there is no longer any 'ought'; for morality, insofar as it was an 'ought,' has been just as much annihilated by our mode of thinking as has religion." But the alternative that Nietzsche proposes farther down no longer sounds really perspectivist. Indeed, if we read the aphorism further, we find that Nietzsche calls for a thinking that is no more than nature—for a "free, fearless hovering over customs, laws and the traditional evaluations of things." This call is not at all reassuring. We could speculate that, driven by its own dynamics, perspectivism can only be a stopping point for the Nietzschean critique of metaphysics. Indeed, perspectivism can only criticize metaphysics for its lack of self-consciousness. However, it is impotent for a positivist metaphysics such as Vaihinger's, which assumes that the validity of metaphysics relies ultimately on the "as if." In the aphorism prior to the one I am commenting on (33), Nietzsche attributes to the poet the capacity to endure seeing humanity (and himself) as waste. But now poets are also the target of his irony: "and poets always know how to console themselves," he writes. Briefly stated, if metaphysics and perspectivism are both devices of consolation, the one thing left is the call, inherent to genealogical thinking (as we will see later), to a sort of primordial language through which, catastrophically and beyond all humanism, the things themselves will speak.

15. Friedrich Nietzsche, *On the Genealogy of Morals*, trans. Walter Kaufmann and R. J. Hollingdale (New York: Vintage, 1989), 21.

16. *Post festum*, Hegel accurately said. Thus, all "sacred history" begins with a festivity—with a proliferation, an excess of reality that it would later try to submit, to order, and to forget.

17. Friedrich Nietzsche, *On the Genealogy of Morals*, ed. Walter Kaufmann, trans. Walter Kaufmann and R. J. Hollingdale (New York: Vintage, 1989), 21.

18. "Back to the rough ground!" is the war cry of the ordinary language philosophy practiced by the "second" Wittgenstein in his *Philosophical Investigations* (§107). Nietzsche too, in the *Genealogy*, would want to resist the "seduction of language" (and "the fundamental errors of reason that are petrified in it"), linked (see below) to the subject-predicate form. But in the "bare ground," would it be possible to keep doing philosophy? Or will this "return" be precisely the catastrophe that all philosophizing must prevent (postpone): its Other, and therefore its condition of possibility? Let this be a general observation regarding the abysmal fate of the philosophy of Modernity.

19. Nietzsche, *Genealogy*, 40.

20. Friedrich Nietzsche, *The Gay Science*, ed. Bernard Williams, trans. Josefine Nauckhoff and Adrian Del Caro (Cambridge: Cambridge University Press, 2001), 110.

21. See Michel Foucault, "Nietzsche, Genealogy, History," in *The Foucault Reader*, ed. Paul Rabinow (New York: Pantheon, 1984). The notion of *Entstehung* takes us to what we could call a "systemic" aspect of Nietzsche's thought, which unfolds through the attempt to provide a non-Aristotelian explanation of natural species. "The species needs itself to be a species, to be something that, by virtue of its very hardness, uniformity, and simplicity of form, can succeed and makes itself persevere" (*Beyond Good and Evil: Prelude to a Philosophy of the Future*, eds. Rolf-Peter Horstmann and Judith Norman, trans. Judith Norman [Cambridge: Cambridge University Press, 2001], 158). From a more contemporary perspective, we would say that, on the basis of a certain bifurcation taking place by chance, form (the limit between the system and its surroundings) is an evolutionary self-produced achievement. The species is an autopoeitic system, which continually reproduces its difference with its surroundings. Thus, the concept of species can be thought, in its non-Aristotelian dimension, as a differential concept: the species is merely the difference between the species and its surroundings (in Nietzschean language: "the species needs itself to be a species"). By the way, it follows from this that the concept of autopoeisis has its original ground not in biology, but rather in "the protest against the tyranny of the existing" that constitutes the essential *ethos* of Modernity and that contains the imperative to explain the extraordinary (form) as a sedimentation of small variations in the distribution of ordinary, uniform elements. Biology, as well as the contemporary sciences of complexity, only maximize the possibilities for explaining this logic in connection to phenomena.

22. Nietzsche, *Genealogy*, I.13.

23. Ibid., 45.

24. Ibid., 45–46.

25. G. W. F. Hegel, *Phenomenology of Spirit*, trans. A. V. Miller (Oxford: Oxford University Press, 2004), 117.

26. "The possibility of movement is supposed, rather, to be like a shadow of the movement itself," Wittgenstein says in *Philosophical Investigations* (trans. G. E. M. Anscombe, P. M. S. Hacker, and Joachim Schulte [Malden, MA: Wiley-Blackwell, 2009]), §194; 84–85. "A machine already contains its possible movements in some mysterious way," he also says (ibid., 84).

27. Nietzsche, *Genealogy*, 26; 36–37.

28. Ibid., 54.

29. From this perspective, the history of Modernity would be the history of the dislodgement of the subject. But narrated by whom? By an evanescent, speculated subject who affirms itself in negation. This subject is no longer the dominating subject of which Modernity speaks in broad daylight but rather a sort of zero-dimension homunculus located within it, who affirms it, negates it, and

writes it from the shadow. "The subject does not belong to the world, but is a limit of the world" (*Tractatus Logico-Philosophicus*, §5.632). This limit-subject would be Modernity's "subject of writing"—the one whom the *saying* of the text necessarily excludes, but who is nevertheless *shown* in the text.

Chapter 6

1. PageRank, Google's powerful algorithm, is not concerned with large-scale library indexing but with tracing links connecting each and every element within the library with each other. This very important feature is the key to Google's crushing success. However, this feature is not relevant for my claims in this chapter.

2. Virginia Woolf, *Orlando: A Biography* (Orlando: Harcourt, 2006), 185–86.

Chapter 7

1. Let us remember that this is the way that Emmanuel Lévinas (*Totality and Infinity*) interprets the primacy of being over beings in Heideggerian ontology. Believing that he has found a way out of Modernity, Heidegger would not have but fulfilled its "aphasic"—"civilization of aphasics," Lévinas himself says in *Difficile Liberté*—and totalitarian strand.

2. In philosophical thought, nominalism is the expression of this experience of incommensurability between language (reason) and reality. Therefore, nominalism can be understood as the purified (and therefore self-reflexive) form of modern alienation.

3. Jorge Luis Borges, "The Mirror of Enigmas," in *Labyrinths: Selected Stories & Other Writings*, eds. Donald A. Yates and James E. Irby, trans. James E. Irby (New York: New Directions, 2007).

4. In Borges, labyrinths, mirrors, libraries, and encyclopedias are symbols of alienation.

5. "All reification is forgetting" (Max Horkheimer and Theodor W. Adorno, *Dialectic of Enlightenment*, eds. Gunzelin Schmid Noerr and Edmund Jephcott [Stanford: Stanford University Press, 2002], 193). And indeed, in the drift of instrumentality, market, and culture, works leave behind and forget their history. This way, the problem of alienation coincides with the question of memory and forgetfulness.

6. There is an affinity between the idea of the extraordinary that I am developing here and the idea of the infinite, as Lévinas identifies it in Descartes's thought, at the foundational moment of modern subjectivity: "What remains ever exterior to thought is thought in the idea of infinity" (*Totality and Infinity: An Essay on Exteriority*, trans. Alphonso Lingis [London: Martinus Nijhoff, 1979], 25). However, in order for this exteriority to remain indeed exterior, it must not be so exterior that it is reduced to an entity that is other—it must therefore preserve its

link with the thought of which it is exteriority, without however being reduced to it. This structure (neither this, nor that, and both together), is precisely the one that characterizes the production of the extraordinary, which thus cannot be but a movement. And, in its turn, this movement has to cancel itself by becoming work, that is, the product of the alienated praxis of a subject—in other words, it requires the ordinary, precisely as that which projects it beyond itself.

7. "The beautiful in nature assures us that we are at home in the empirical world" (Jens Kulenkampff, "A Logica Kantiana Do Juizo Estetico e o Significado Metafisico Do Belo Da Naturaleza," in *200 Anos Da Critica Da Facultade Do Juizo de Kant*, ed. Valerio Rohden [Porto Alegre, Brazil: Universidade Federal do Rio Grande do Sul, 1990], p. 12). It is worth noting that the *Critique of Pure Reason* does not provide such certainty. The "account of the individual formation" of the real (that is, the problem of the commensurability between reason and Being: the order of the real), as Ernst Cassirer says, "is required more as a sheer opposition between the empirical and the particular and the abstract and universal, more as a mere stuff underlying the pure forms of thought as given by transcendental logic in some fashion not subject to further determination in detail. The empirical concept must determine the given by progressively mediating between it and the universal, since it relates the data to the universal through a continuous series of intermediate conceptual stages. . . . Were the multiplicity and dissimilarity of the empirical laws so great that it would be possible to organize individual ones under a general class concept but never to comprehend the totality of them in a unitary series ordered by degrees of generality, we would have in nature, even if we thought of it as subjected to the law of causality, just a 'crude chaotic aggregate.' But now the judgment confronts the idea of such formlessness, not with an absolute logical decree but with a maxim that acts as its incentive and guidepost in all its inquiries. It posits a progressive lawfulness of nature, which is contingent by the concepts of the understanding alone, but which it 'assumes for its own benefit'" (Ernst Cassirer, *Kant's Life and Thought*, trans. James Haden [New Haven, CT: Yale University Press, 1981], 292; 297–98).

8. The impossible and endless search for the unconditioned, as well as the paradox that is inherent to it, are paradigmatically represented in the realm of ethics by the following passage in the *Groundwork of the Metaphysics of Morals*: "In fact, it is absolutely impossible by means of experience to make out with complete certainty a single case in which the maxim of an action otherwise in conformity with duty rested simply on moral grounds and on the presentation of one's duty. It is indeed sometimes the case that with the keenest self-examination we find nothing besides the moral ground of duty that could have been powerful enough to move us to this or that good action and to so great a sacrifice; but from this it cannot be inferred with certainty that no covert impulse of self-love, under the mere pretense of that idea, was not actually the real determining cause of the will; for we like to flatter ourselves by falsely attributing to ourselves a nobler motive, whereas in fact we can

never, even by the most strenuous self-examination, get entirely behind our covert incentives, since, when moral worth is at issue, what counts is not actions, which one sees, but those inner principles of actions that one does not see" (Immanuel Kant, *Groundwork of the Metaphysics of Morals*, in *Practical Philosophy*, ed. Mary J. Gregor [New York: Cambridge University Press, 1999], 61–62; 4:407). The blindness of experience unto the "covert impulse of self-love" is the spring that will throw modern consciousness into thoroughly cataloguing those impulses—Nietzsche and Freud, genealogy and psychoanalysis, have a filiation in this passage. On the other hand, it necessarily follows from this blindness (this is Kant's reasoning in chapter 1 of the *Groundwork*) that a selfish philanthropist (a man in whose heart "nature had put little sympathy") would be closer to the unconditionality of duty than someone to whom the fulfillment of generous deeds brings joy (an "intimate pleasure"). Therefore, the "demonic" strand of Modernity—mystical ascesis through pain and suffering: de Sade, Baudelaire—has also its roots in Kant.

9. Jorge Luis Borges, *Other Inquisitions: 1937–1952*, trans. Ruth L. C. Simms (Austin: University of Texas Press, 1964), 5.

10. On the other hand, these signs only work insofar as they are identified as such. Now: this discernment (which makes a sign out of an "X": index, sign of the conditioned, and "truth" that the purportedly unconditioned would veil) is precisely the operation that fleetingly exceeds all conditioning. The performative contradiction taking place here is not an error of which modern consciousness could dispose (as Habermas thinks in his *The Philosophical Discourse of Modernity*, where the argument of the performative contradiction is used as a kind of philosophical stick against Nietzsche, Adorno, Derrida, and other purported heretics of modern orthodoxy). On the contrary, it is the specific mode of production of modern subjectivity under the conditions that Wittgenstein (*Conference on Ethics*) established in his allegory of the "book of the world." The culture described by the book of the world has gone through the experience of the limitless extension of causal explanations (physical, sociological, psychological, genetic, etc.). This way, the unconditioned (which corresponded in Kant to the experience of freedom, of the moral law) is expelled from the world: it becomes an experience of the extraordinary (the miracle, the "mystical," in Wittgensteinian terminology).

11. It is Heidegger who qualifies both Schopenhauer's and Nietzsche's readings of Kantian aesthetics as "bad" (*Nietzsche*, trans. David Farrell Krell [New York: HarperCollins, 1991], 107–14). Heidegger criticizes Nietzsche's identification of the Kantian aesthetic "disinterestedness" with the Schopenahuerian anesthetics of the will. This way, the positive conception of Kantian disinterestedness is pushed to the background. However, it is worth asking to what extent this positivity ("our capability, to the extent that we are claimed supremely in our essence, which is to say, to the extent that we ascend beyond ourselves" [ibid., 113], says Heidegger, for example) does not somehow remain naively below the "demonic" character of modern spirit (thus, the Nietzschean invocation of drunkenness as a fundamental

aesthetic state is interpreted by Heidegger as "an attunement in the sense of the supreme and most measured determinateness" [ibid.]!). Heidegger's lack of understanding for the "degenerate" art of his time seems to be implicit here.

12. Friedrich Nietzsche, *On the Genealogy of Morals*, ed. Walter Kaufmann, trans. Walter Kaufmann and R. J. Hollingdale [New York: Vintage, 1989], 104–06.

13. Ibid., 111. Regis Debray provides a contemporary version of the Nietzschean irony on Kantian aesthetics. He imagines its propositions read by the famous *marchand d'art*, "totemic figure" of contemporary art, as he says, Leo Castelli. From New York, he has "propelled pop, conceptual, and minimalist artists." When confronting the Kantian proposition "the beautiful is the object of disinterested contemplation," Debray says: "Castelli, who has always calculated prices and has always desired to possess not only the works, but even the artists themselves (for the benefit of his customers), cannot avoid thinking that if Kant were right, the history of art would not exist, because there would not have been a market for art, nor art plain and simple, which is not an operation of the Holy Spirit" (Regis Debray, *Vie et mort de l'image: Une histoire du regard en Occident* [Paris: Gallimard, 1992], 142–43). Nevertheless, Castelli/Debray thinks and says it: this way, he reproduces the very operation of the spirit that the content of his discourse would deny.

14. "The principle of sacrifice is destruction, but though it sometimes goes so far as to destroy completely (as in a holocaust), the destruction that sacrifice is intended to bring about is not annihilation. The thing—only the thing—is what sacrifice means to destroy in the victim. Sacrifice destroys an object's real ties of subordination; it draws the victim out of the world of utility and restores it to that of unintelligible caprice. When the offered animal enters the circle in which the priest will immolate it, it passes from the world of things which are closed to man and are *nothing* to him, which he knows from the outside—to the world that is immanent to it, *intimate*, known as the wife is known in sexual consumption (*consummation charnelle*). . . . The sacrifice declares: '*Intimately*, I belong to the sovereign world of the gods and myths, to the world of violent and uncalculated generosity, just as my wife belongs to my desires. I withdraw you, victim, from the world in which you were and could only be reduced to the condition of a thing, having a meaning that was foreign to your intimate nature. I call you back to the *intimacy* of the divine world, of the profound immanence of all that is'" (Georges Bataille, *Theory of Religion*, trans. Robert Hurley [New York: Zone Books, 1989], 43–44).

15. Gonzalo Díaz's exhibition unfolded the text by Andrés Bello around the room: "More trust has been placed in the law than in the judgment of parents and natural feelings. But when the latter go astray or fail, the voice of the law is powerless, its prescriptions easy to avoid, and the area in which it can expand, extremely narrow. What could laws on inheritance and donations do against the usual squandering, against the luxury of vain ostentation that endangers the future of families, against the chances of gambling that secretly wastes patrimonies? The project has limited itself to repressing the great excesses of indiscrete freedom, which,

if not the truth, which is the most fearsome thing against the just hopes of the inheritors, is the only thing that civil law can reach, without overstepping its rational boundaries, without invading the asylum of domestic affections, without dictating inquisitorial provisions which are difficult to execute, and nevertheless ineffective."

16. By the way, this is contemporary *kitsch*. There is also an artified, postmodern *kitsch* (self-conscious, of a second degree), which focuses on the parody of the former. Jeff Koons's floral, exaggerated *puppy*, exhibited at the Guggenheim Museum in Bilbao, can work as an example here.

17. A nonpropositional truth: *a-letheia*, unconcealment.

18. Georges Bataille, *Theory of Religion*, trans. Robert Hurley, vol. 1 (New York: Zone Books, 1989), 124.

19. A syndrome to which we are all prone, on the other hand, insofar as our deep convictions, located beyond any calculation and any argumentation, are deformed to the point of being unrecognizable and become inexpressible as they materialize in works—as they enter, we would say, the refractory medium of works, ruled by calculus, by the Weberian ethics of responsibility.

20. Let us note that Díaz replaced this sign with the title of his installation in neon words. Around this gesture, however, the paradoxes associated with the sacrificial strategy, which we are making manifest for the totality of the work, condense and reproduce themselves. Indeed, the name that is crossed out in this way does not disappear, but rather it acquires a spectral presence: in its absence, it shines opaquely. In this way, by the crossing, the name becomes Name. Only in this way, the museum is invested as Museum, *locus* of the extraordinary.

21. Strictly speaking, precontingent or even: nothing of that sort.

22. The murky underground of the law can be interpreted in its turn in more local terms. Indeed, Bello and Montt are aware that the efficacy of laws is inherently limited. At the same time, they are gentlemen of the twentieth century: facing such limitation, they invoke patriarchal power and nature. But, if we go to the bottom of it, what the presentation of the Civil Code makes manifest is a sort of disquieting gray area: the invocation of instances that, not being outside of the law, are not within it either, and which makes possible that the former operates "without overstepping its rational boundaries." And, under the thick veil of pious euphemisms from the nineteenth century ("judgment of the parents"; "natural feelings"), it is possible to see a sinister reality: the implacable whip of the father and the landlord; fear and domestication mythically turned into nature.

23. Max Horkheimer and Theodor W. Adorno, *Dialectic of Enlightenment*, eds. Gunzelin Schmid Noerr and Edmund Jephcott (Stanford: Stanford University Press, 2002), 2.

24. Serge Rezvani, *L'origine du monde: Pour une ultime histoire de l'art à propos du "cas Bergamme"* (Paris: Actes Sud, 2000), 26.

25. Walter Benjamin, "Theses on the Philosophy of History," in *Illuminations: Essays and Reflections*, ed. Hannah Arendt, trans. Harry Zohn (New York: Schocken, 1969), 253.

Chapter 8

1. Jorge Luis Borges, "Afterword," *The Aleph and Other Stories*, trans. Andrew Hurley (New York: Penguin, 2004), 134.

2. The story has been exemplarily read this way by Enrique Pezzoni in *Enrique Pezzoni lector de Borges: Lecciones de literatura 1984–1988* (Buenos Aires: Sudamericana, 1999), 169–87.

3. Jorge Luis Borges, *The Garden of Forking Paths*, in *Collected Fictions*, trans. Andrew Hurley (New York: Penguin, 1999), 67.

4. The metaphysicians of Tlön claim that "metaphysics is a branch of fantastic literature" ("Tlön, Uqbar, Orbis Tertius," in Jorge Luis Borges, *Labyrinths: Selected Stories & Other Writings*, ed. Donald A. Yates and James E. Irby, trans. James E. Irby [New York: New Directions, 2007], 10). This way, they resolve in favor of fiction a millenary dispute and become part of a conception proposed by Borges in some of his essays and epilogues. "Tlön, Uqbar, Orbis Tertius," the fable of a world invaded by an encyclopedia, is one among Borges's parables on the literary space, as well as on the nominalism that is at its base.

5. Borges, "The Library of Babel," in *Collected Fictions*, 112.

6. Borges, "The Immortal," in *Labyrinths*, 109.

7. Jorge Luis Borges, "From Allegories to Novels," in *Other Inquisitions: 1937–1952*, trans. Ruth L. C. Simms (Austin: University of Texas Press, 1964), 156–57.

8. Ibid., 124.

9. Borges, "Funes the Memorious," in *Labyrinths*, 64.

10. Ibid., 66. The poem "Insomnia" is also about insomnia, the inability to forget, waste ("waste of Buenos Aires"), and immortality. One could draw a parallel with the conception of sleep in Blanchot (in "The Outside, the Night," in *The Space of Literature*); also with the fundamental experience that Lévinas (*Time and the Other*) characterizes as the experience of the "*il-y-a*" (of the anonymous "there is").

11. Peter Sloterdijk, *En el mismo barco: Ensayo sobre la hiperpolítica*, trans. Manuel Fontán del Junco (Madrid: Siruela, 1994), 39–40.

12. Borges, "A New Refutation of Time," in *Labyrinths*, 233–34.

13. Ibid., 234.

14. Tautology of culture: every culture legitimates itself by offering solutions to problems that it has invented (and fails in this). The distance between the problem and the solution is the space where the task is located; failure is the evidence that the task was impossible.

15. In this regard, it should be possible and fruitful to bring Benjamin's and Adorno's saturnine, melancholic, and mystical gaze to Borges's. An inventory of Borgesian figures of exteriority (of the Real, beyond any symbolic inscription) should also include the knife (the sword) and the South (the South-American experience such as it appears in the story "The South" or in the "Conjectural Poem"): "At last

I come face to face / with my destiny as a South American," Colonel Francisco Laprida thinks while he awaits death ("the knife, so intimate, opening my throat") in the mid of "the darkness spreading across the marshes" (*Selected Poems*, ed. Alexander Coleman [New York: Penguin, 2000], 159–61).

16. Borges, "The Immortal," in *Labyrinths*, 117.

17. Ibid., 118.

18. *A Coat of Many Colors* is, according to the *King James Version*, the cloth that Jacob made for his son Joseph as a sign of affection (Genesis, 37, 3). The name "Nahum Cordovero" is obviously Sephardic. Moses Cordovero was in fact a Cabalist, a Jewish mystic from the diaspora in Safed, in the sixteenth century. Nahum, as Pezzoni observes, means "consolation." Is it the consolation granted by an illusory rescue of the figure of the author, from the deep waters of the literary space? On the other hand, who begins the tradition of reading the Bible as if it were a patchwork? Perhaps the figure of Baruch Spinoza, "free from metaphor and myth," is present behind the erudite and tenacious Nahum Cordovero (Jorge Luis Borges, *Borges, A Reader: A Selection from the Writings of Jorge Luis Borges*, ed. Emir Rodriguez Monegal and Alastair Reid [New York: Dutton, 1981], 229).

19. Borges, "The Immortal," 118.

20. Ibid.

21. Ibid., 115.

22. "Transvaloration" is the literal translation of Nietzsche's *Umwertung*. Borges's paradoxical strategy of transvaluation consists in erasing the subject of writing: "[I]f the pages of this book contained one happy verse, the reader shall forgive my impoliteness by having usurped them, previously," Borges wrote already in 1923, in the dedication to *Fervor de Buenos Aires*. But this erasure thereafter confers on him an oracular status: literature would speak through him, no more, no less.

23. Andreas Huyssen, "La cultura de la memoria: medios, política, amnesia," in *Revista de Crítica Cultural* 18, 8–15 (1999).

24. "There was no one in him; behind his face (which even in the poor paintings of the period is unlike any other) and his words, which were copious, imaginative, and emotional, there was nothing but a little chill, a dream not dreamed by anyone." So is Shakespeare in Borges's "Everything and Nothing," to whom God addresses the following words: "Neither am I one self; I dreamed the world as you dreamed your work, my Shakespeare, and among the shapes of my dream are you, who, like me, are many persons—and none" (Jorge Luis Borges, *Dreamtigers*, trans. Mildred Boyer and Harold Morland [Austin, TX: University of Texas Press, 1985], 46–47).

25. Jorge Luis Borges, "The Homeric Versions," in *The Total Library: Non-Fiction 1922–1986*, ed. Eliot Weinberger, trans. Esther Allen, Suzanne Jill Levine, and Eliot Weinberger (New York: Penguin, 1999), 70.

26. Jorge Luis Borges, "Los cuatro ciclos," in *Obras completas* (Barcelona: Emece, 1996), 504.

27. "The possibility of movement is supposed, rather, to be like a shadow of the movement itself" (Ludwig Wittgenstein, *Philosophical Investigations*, trans. G. E. M. Anscombe, P. M. S. Hacker, and Joachim Schulte [Malden, MA: Wiley-Blackwell, 2009], 84).

28. The expression is Paul Ricoeur's, referring to the thought of Marx, Nietzsche, and Freud.

29. "*Finale.*" So begins the last aphorism in Adorno's *Minima Moralia*, which continues: "[T]he only philosophy which can be responsibly practiced in face of despair is the attempt to contemplate all things as they would present themselves from the standpoint of redemption. Knowledge has no light but that shed on the world by redemption: all else is reconstruction, mere technique." This perspective, he adds, "is also the utterly impossible thing, because it presupposes a standpoint removed, even though by a hair's breadth, from the scope of existence, whereas we well know that any possible knowledge must not only be first wrested from what is, if it shall hold good, but is also marked, for this very reason, by the same distortion and indigence which it seeks to escape." However, concerning thought, "even its own impossibility it must at last comprehend for the sake of the possible" (Theodor W. Adorno, *Minima Moralia: Reflections from Damaged Life*, trans. E. F. N. Jephcott [London: Verso, 2006], 247). In other words, Modernity's critical thought knows that there is nothing but the unconditioned and that its own knowledge may not be exempted from it. Later on, two alternatives are presented to it:

1. To place itself in a "happy positivism" (Foucault) for which the distinction between the conditioned and the unconditioned and the aspiration to transcend "the scope of existence" are metaphysical, meaningless and must be left behind. There is no way to glimpse behind our language and our ordinary practices. It is pointless to ask about the real beyond this horizon. There is no possible mismatch between reason and history, not as a result of a dialectical drama *à la* Hegel, but rather because it could not be otherwise. Constructivism, ordinary language, and philosophy are paradigmatic representatives of this position.

2. To persist in "making oneself responsible in light of desperation." Then the Adornian mythical spiral is unavoidable. Suggestively, this is also the path followed by thinkers as different as Bataille or the Wittgenstein of the *Tractatus*. The latter, for the sake of preserving the possibility of ethics, is ready to accept its lack of meaning and even the finally meaningless character of the whole intellectual enterprise of his *Tractatus*. "Meaning" and "lack of meaning" (*sinnlos*) are here however in a dialectical relationship. What lacks meaning is not indeed what is merely "without meaning" (*unsinnig*): it is rather the Other of meaning, its condition of possibility (*Tractatus*, 4.461–4.4611).

30. An Absolute Book, Borges says in one of the many passages that he devotes to such a fantastic idea, would be "a book that [is] something of a Platonic archetype ("Walt Whitman: Man and Myth," *Critical Inquiry* 1[4], 709). Later, he lists those who fed this ambition, from Apollonius of Rhodes to Joyce, Eliot, and

Pound, going through Donne, Milton, Góngora, Mallarmé (*"tout aboutit à un livre"*), and Yeats. Borges himself, who more than once gestures toward a complicity with this very distinguished gallery of ambitious people, should be added to the list. An Absolute Book is indeed a book in which all "possible" readings and interpretations are prefigured and that, therefore, is its own commentary. In the same way, some stories by Borges ("The Immortal," "Tlön, Uqbar, Orbis Tertius," among others) include comments and postscripts, which are literally "postscripted," that is, dated after the date of publication. In this way, the Borgesian commentary is located in a sort of untemporal present, of which we, its readers, with our readings and interpretations, are part. The Borgesian fiction seeks to prefigure its readers, in the same manner as a text by Whitman (*"Salut au monde"*) posits, as Borges himself notes, the immorality of the poet by means of mingling with each future reader and talking in the poem with the other, with Whitman ("What are you hearing, Walt Whitman?"). Borges's reading of Whitman points, once again, to the idea of a literary space.

31. Harold Bloom, *The Anxiety of Influence: A Theory of Poetry* (Oxford: Oxford University Press, 1997); *The Western Canon: The Books and School of the Ages* (New York: Riverhead, 1995).

32. Gershom Scholem, *On the Kabbalah and Its Symbolism* (New York: Schocken, 1996).

33. Borges, "Partial Magic of the Quixote," in *Labyrinths*, 187.

34. Ibid.

35. Borges, "Nostalgia for the Present," in *Selected Poems*, 447.

36. See Tzvetan Todorov, *The Fantastic: A Structural Approach to a Literary Genre*, trans. Richard Howard (Ithaca, NY: Cornell University Press, 1975).

37. Borges, "Tlön, Uqbar, Orbis Tertius," in *Labyrinths*, 20.

38. It is a posthistorical world, as well, given that it carries with it the knowledge that history would be nothing but a literary artifice. Thus, "already a fictitious past occupies in our memories the place of another, a past of which we know nothing with certainty—not even that it is false" (ibid., 33).

Chapter 9

1. Peter Sloterdijk, *En el mismo barco: Ensayo sobre la hiperpolítica*, trans. Manuel Fontán del Junco (Madrid: Siruela, 1994), 39–40.

2. Ibid., 40.

3. Ibid., 41.

4. Ibid., 41–42.

5. Ibid., 42.

6. Friedrich Nietzsche, *On the Genealogy of Morals*, ed. Walter Kaufmann, trans. Walter Kaufmann and R. J. Hollingdale (New York: Vintage, 1989), 68–69.

7. Ibid., 69.

8. "Apart from retaining 'an unpaved open area of about ten acres in the center, there is no discernible single idea behind [Athens's] agora architecture" (Richard Sennett, *Flesh and Stone: The Body and the City in Western Civilization*, [New York: W. W. Norton: 1996], 60). Sennett, on whose distinction between agora and theater I am relying here, is quoting M. I. Finley, *The Ancient Greeks* (New York: Penguin, 1987).

9. Sennett, *Flesh and Stone*, 60.

10. Ibid.

11. Ibid.

12. The expression is Paul Veyne's, referencing the Stoic Seneca.

13. Not safe, however, from the master of suspicion, Nietzsche, who says: "the invention of 'free will,' of the absolute spontaneity of man in good and in evil, was devised above all to furnish a right to the idea that the interest of the gods in man, in human virtue, *could never be exhausted*. There must never be any lack of real novelty, of really unprecedented tensions, complications, and catastrophes on the stage of the earth: the course of a completely deterministic world would have been predictable for the gods and they would have quickly grown weary of it—reason enough for those *friends of the gods*, the philosophers, not to inflict such a deterministic world to their gods!" (Nietzsche, *Genealogy*, 69). In this line of thought, freedom operates like an element of seduction that, extending a veil over the rawness of the cosmic theater of cruelty, makes it more enjoyable—like a mask whose game both postpones and prolongs pleasure.

14. "*Enlightenment in the human being's emergence from his self-incurred minority*. Minority is inability to make use of one's own understanding without direction from another. This minority is *self-incurred* when its cause lies not in lack of understanding but in lack of resolution and courage to use it without direction from another. *Sapere aude!* Have courage to make use of your *own* understanding! is thus the motto of enlightenment" (Immanuel Kant, "An Answer to the Question: What Is Enlightenment?," in *Practical Philosophy*, ed. Mary J. Gregor [New York: Cambridge University Press, 1999], 17).

15. Let us note that none of these elements (exposed by Marx, by Max Weber, by Georges Bataille in *The Accursed Share*) can be understood as a "cause." Rather, we should think of a constellation of phenomena, none of which is meaningful in isolation but which magnify one another until they crystalize in a new social formation.

16. Michel Foucault, *Discipline and Punish: The Birth of the Prison* (New York: Vintage, 1995), 197.

17. Ibid., 198.

18. Ibid., 195.

19. Ibid., 200.

20. Ibid., 216.

21. Ibid., 200.
22. Ibid., 202–3.
23. Political life. Recalling the relationship between city and politics can seem unnecessary, a mere translation (polis=city). However, one suffers for the city. Therefore, is there not an indissoluble relationship between politics and suffering? And is not suffering the product, not of the abuse of politics, but precisely of its use? The question is in order for those who still identify politics with justice.
24. Only when there is a failure does the user become conscious, in practice, that the car has something called "gearbox," or that the computer is connected to a "server" (for examples, when the server is busy and the user bumps into a message that says something like "The server is busy. Try again later").
25. On the concept of "black box," see Herbert Simon, *The Sciences of the Artificial* (Cambridge, MA: MIT Press, 1981).
26. I should include here Sloterdijk's comment on the democratization of "megalopathic stress" in contemporary societies: "Now, it is people on the street who must have the worries that before were the concern only of a secretary of foreign affairs" (*En el mismo barco*, 68–69).
27. Adolf Loos (1870–1933), contemporary of most of the Kakanian characters who have been discussed in this text. Initially linked to the *Secession* of Gustav Klimt, Joseph Olbrich and others, created in 1897, he soon turned into its fierce enemy, repelled by the sensualist and aestheticist *pathos* that characterized the movement. Like his predecessors, architects Camilo Sitte and Otto Wagner, Loos was critical of the Viennese urban remodeling known as *Ringstrasse*, which had a number of historicist imitations of the "noble" architectures of the past. Loos called it "Potemkin City," alluding to Prince Potemkin, the favorite of Catherine the Great, who anticipating the visits of his sovereign, often built entire cities in *tromp l'oeil* in the middle of the desert. Karl Krauss wrote on Loos: "Alfred Loos and I—he in the artifacts, I in the words—have done nothing but demonstrate that there is a clear difference between a pot and a urinal, and that culture has its proper space within this difference. The others, the men with more positive perspectives, are divided into those who treat the pot like an original (the historicists) and those who treat the original like a pot (the modernists)." Just like he opposed historicism, Loos also criticized the *Glasskultur*, the culture of transparency of architectonic modernism. According to Loos, both modernism and historicism propose a false reconciliation between the private and the public.
28. Loos quotation by Karl E. Schorske, "Adolf Loos: Revuelta En Viena," in *La Emoción de Lo Moderno: Viena Del 900*, ed. Nicolás Casullo (Buenos Aires: Nueva Visión, 1991), 416.
29. Ibid., 415.
30. Indeed, there are energy exchanges with the outside (the world "transmits nothing to the interior life except light," Loos says. But "light" can encompass here other zones of the electromagnetic spectrum, other kinds of energy). Also, as in

hierarchical organizations, there are transferences of control in exceptional situations: sickness, lack of safety, etc. But none of this deprives the Loosian black box of its opacity (and of its essential transparency).

31. Foucault, *Discipline and Punish*, 200.

32. See Martin Jay, *Downcast Eyes: The Denigration of Vision in Twentieth-Century French Thought* (Los Angeles: UC Press, 1994), 85. Indeed, the camera obscura requires an opening to the outside. But this opening has the only function of capturing the images to be projected and appropriated in the panel of the mind. At the limit, the opening tends to zero. It is then that the Cartesian subject can go through the decisive experience of observing himself as an observer: "I think . . . I am."

33. Ludwig Wittgenstein, *Tractatus Logico-Philosophicus*, trans. D. F. Pears and B. F. McGuinness (New York: Routledge, 2002), 69; §5.632. It should be possible to write a history of modern philosophy understood as a sequence of strategies of concealment. Thus, Kantian ethics, presided by the categorical imperative—moral precepts are to be unconditional—would not be the outcome of an insane moral rigorism that would have overtaken a senile Kant (the one of the *Critique of Practical Reason*) but rather of a clever strategy that consists in retreating to an interiority that the gaze of science—which propagates in the medium of the conditioned—can no longer penetrate. The science that Kant knew certainly was Newtonian mechanism, which, blinking and intimidated, withdrew in the face of the remaining premodern radiance of the body and the soul. By contrast, the subsequent scientific gaze (biomedical, psychological, sociological) will not hesitate to go beyond those illusory boundaries, indefinitely extending the realm of the conditioned. But, in the face of this indiscretion, which is constitutive of both Modernity and the subject itself, the latter retreats again and again toward the inside of the inside. This unending movement of folding and retreating would constitute it.

34. Foucault, "Nietzsche, Genealogy, History," in *The Foucault Reader*, ed. Paul Rabinow (New York: Pantheon, 1984), 76.

35. Max Horkheimer and Theodor W. Adorno, *Dialectic of Enlightenment*, ed. Gunzelin Schmid Noerr and Edmund Jephcott (Stanford: Stanford University Press, 2002), 182.

36. Ibid. I believe that this paragraph is from Adorno, given its similarity with others that have only his signature. See, for example, Theodor W. Adorno, *Minima Moralia: Reflections from Damaged Life*, trans. E. F. N. Jephcott (London: Verso, 2006), §153. The following passage by Massimo Cacciari, in one of the essays that he has devoted to Loos, is also telling: "If in this age the possibility of exception dwells in the tomb, we could also say that existence has been always 'sheltered' there. It is also true that the tomb does not suggest an eternal image of the past. Only there can we still find a hope that is not a consolation or a flight, nor an ornament or an illusory harmony. . . . The power of this waiting emerges only at the peak of danger, in the fulfilment of hopelessness. And only where hearing is centered on the tomb can we expect to reach the peak" (Massimo Cacciari, "Loos,

Roth, Wittgenstein: Interior y Experiencia," in *La emoción de lo moderno: Viena del 900*, ed. Nicolás Casullo [Buenos Aires: Nueva Visión, 1991], 198).

Chapter 10

1. Jacques Monod, *Chance and Necessity: An Essay on the Natural Philosophy of Modern Biology*, trans. Austryn Wainhouse (New York: Vintage, 1972), 180.

2. Michel Foucault, *Language, Counter-Memory, Practice: Selected Essays and Interviews*, ed. Donald F. Bouchard (Ithaca, NY: Cornell University Press, 1980), 154.

3. In §96 of "The Wanderer and His Shadow" (dated 1880; *On the Genealogy of Morals* was published seven years later), Nietzsche wrote: "Grand style originates when the beautiful carries off the victory over the monstrous [*das Ungeheure*]" (*Human, All Too Human: A Book for Free Spirits*, trans. R. J. Hollingdale [Cambridge: Cambridge University Press, 1996], 334).

4. Hugo von Hofmannsthal, *The Lord Chandos Letter and Other Writings*, ed. and trans. Joel Rotenberg (New York: New York Review, 2005), 117.

5. Ibid., 122.

6. Benjamin, "Theses on the Philosophy of History" in *Illuminations: Essays and Reflections*, ed. Hannah Arendt, trans. Harry Zohn (New York: Schocken, 1969), 257.

7. Von Hofsmansthal, *The Lord Chandos Letter*, 127–28.

8. Robert Musil, *The Man without Qualities*, trans. Sophie Wilkins (New York: Vintage, 1995), 572.

9. Ibid., 573–74.

10. Ibid., 7.

11. Max Horkheimer and Theodor W. Adorno, "Le Prix du progrès," in *Dialectic of Enlightenment*, ed. Gunzelin Schmid Noerr and Edmund Jephcott (Stanford: Stanford University Press, 2002), 190–91.

12. Karl Marx, *Capital*, trans. Ben Fowkes, vol. 1 (New York: Penguin, 1982), 164–65.

13. Tomás Maldonado, *El diseño industrial reconsiderado* (Barcelona: Gustavo Gil, 1993), 14. Maldonado is a representative figure of the Ulm School, founded after World War I following the spirit of Bauhaus, which had been shut down by the National Socialist government. Ulmians seek an ethics of design, a "true" design, whose referent is function and use value, protected from inappropriate ornamental disturbances by a syntax and a rational methodology. In connection to consumption goods, this ethics assumes that use value is a piece of information that is constructed independently of the market. The evolution of capitalism, however, will sweep this independence away: styling, the trend in design that emerged in the United States as a response to the crisis of 1929, is rather characterized by the creation of needs. The conception of design that I am presenting here (design as a sort of prosthesis of

memory that compensates for the abstraction performed by the market) corresponds, evidently, to this more recent stage of capitalist Modernity.

14. Karl E. Schorske, "The Quest for the Grail: Wagner and Morris," in *The Critical Spirit: Essays in Honor of Herbert Marcuse*, ed. Kurt H. Wolff and Barrington Moore (Boston: Beacon, 1967). William Morris (1834–1896), contemporary and friend of the pre-Raphaelians, of Dante Gabriel Rossetti and Charles Algernon Swinburne, is one of the great figures of English culture in the second half of the nineteenth century, from literature to politics and including industry, applied arts, design, and architecture.

15. "Take note, too, that in the best art all these solemn and awful things are expressed clearly and without any vagueness, with such life and power that they impress the beholder so deeply that he is brought face to face with the very scenes, and lives among them for a while. . . . Its very greatness makes it a thing to be handled carefully, for we cannot always be having our emotions deeply stirred" (William Morris, *Some Hints on Pattern-Designing* [London: Chiswick, 1899], 3).

16. Anna Calvera, "La modernidad de William Morris," *Temes de disseny* 14 (1997), 70.

17. Morris, *Some Hints on Pattern-Designing*, 2.

18. Ibid.

19. Cacciari, "Loos, Roth, Wittgenstein: interior y experiencia," 422.

20. Borges, "The Zahir," *Labyrinths*, 158.

21. Ibid., 154.

22. Ibid., 157.

Chapter 11

1. Sigmund Freud, *An Outline of Psychoanalysis*, 83. By the way, the parallel that Freud draws with experimentation and inference in physics only applies to those metaphysical remainders that, less and less, coexist with the purely operational emphasis, the formalization, and the rigorous application of Occam's nominalist "razor." These elements already characterized the "hard sciences" in Freud's time, and they do so even more in ours.

2. Ibid.

3. Immanuel Kant, *Critique of Pure Reason*, ed. Paul Guyer and Allen W. Wood (New York: Cambridge University Press, 2000), 99.

4. Ludwig Wittgenstein, *Lectures and Conversations on Aesthetics, Psychology and Religious Belief*, ed. Cyril Barrett (Berkeley: University of California Press, 1967), 51.

5. In a similar vein (and also commenting on Wittgenstein, whose phrase "a powerful mythology" "can be interpreted antithetically as another involuntary tribute to Freud's mythologizing power"), Harold Bloom writes: "Speculation, rather than theory, is Freud's mode, as it was Montaigne's. It hardly matters that Montaigne

cheerfully and knowingly also confused reasons with causes, or if it matters it is only to enrich his discourse. Freudian speculation may or may not be scientific or philosophical; what counts about it is its interpretative power. All mythology is interpretation, but interpretation only become mythology if it ages productively. Interpretation that dies young or ages barrenly is exposed as gossip. Montaigne, just short of Shakespeare, is the dominant mythologist of the later Renaissance. Freud, short of no one, is the dominant mythologist of our time, whatever our time turns out to have been" (Bloom, "Freud: Frontier Concepts, Jewishness, and Interpretation," in *Trauma: Explorations in Memory*, ed. Cathy Caruth [Baltimore, MD: Johns Hopkins University Press, 1995], 113).

6. The manuscript of 1934 has the title *Der Mann Moses: Ein historischer Roman*. The title of the original published in 1939 is *Der Mann Moses und die monotheistische Religion: Drei Abhandlungen* (*Moses the Man and Monotheist Religion: Three Essays*). This title seems to emphasize two important aspects of the work: that *Moses the man* would have given his religion to the Jews and that monotheism would be a necessary moment in the development of a sort of collective neurosis of humanity which, according to Freud, is religion. Pressure by the publisher would have led Freud to opt for a simpler title in the first English translation: *Moses and Monotheism*.

7. This is at least how the text has been read in the last decades, with nuances, due especially to the work of historian Yosef Hayim Yerushalmi. In 1989, Yerushalmi, known at that point for his work on Jewish memory (*Zakhor: Jewish History and Jewish Memory*, 1982), was invited to give the Franz Rosenzweig annual lectures organized by Yale University. Under the title "Freud's Moses: Judaism, Terminable and Interminable," these lectures analyzed the issue of Judaism in Freud, precisely through a rereading of *Moses and Monotheism*. Afterwards, they brought about a series of commentaries—in which this text would humbly want to situate itself—by a number of prominent authors, among whom philosophers Jacques Derrida and Richard J. Bernstein stand out, as well as the epilogue by Jan Assmann. The lectures given by Yerushalmi (professor of Jewish history at Yale University), which were repeated in 1990 in Mount Holyoke College and Smith College, and in Paris at the École des Hautes Études en Sciences Sociales, were published by Yale University Press. In 1994, Jacques Derrida devoted his lecture at the International Colloquium "Memory: The Question of Archives" (Societé Internationale d'Histoire de la Psychiatrie et de la Psychanalyse," Freud Museum, Courtland Institute of Art, London, June 1994) to a comment on Yerushalmi's text, which was published in 1995 as *Mal d'archive: une impression freudienne*. Richard J. Bernstein published in 1998 a book (*Freud and the Legacy of Moses*) in which he comments on Yerushalmi's and Derrida's texts, focusing on the contribution of psychoanalysis to the understanding of cultural transmission of tradition and on Freud's characterization of the essence of Judaism as *der Fortschritt in der Geistigkeit* ("the progress of spirituality"), linked to strict monotheism and the prohibition of

images. Jan Assmann, on the other hand, has published *Moses the Egyptian: The Memory of Egypt in Western Monotheism.*

8. Sigmund Freud, *Moses and Monotheism*, trans. Katherine Jones (Letchworth, UK: Hogarth, 1939), 161.

9. Ibid., 143.

10. The labyrinthic structure of *Moses and Monotheism*, to which I have referred earlier, is noteworthy. Although the political situation and Freud's bad health can be useful as an explanation, it is worth providing an interpretation more suited to the thesis that I am developing here. In *Moses and Monotheism*, which seeks to account for monotheism on the basis of the original scene of the murder of the protofather, what emerges is rather the repressed in psychoanalysis itself (and in Judaism, which for Freud, as we will see later on, represents its antecedent). I attribute to this return of the repressed Freud's difficulty in expressing himself, to which Yerushalmi calls attention, each time that he tried to define the essence of (and of his own) Judaism. Thus, in the brief preface that Freud wrote in December of 1930 for the Hebrew edition of *Totem and Taboo*, one reads the following words: "No reader of this book will find it easy to put himself in the emotional position of an author who is ignorant of the language of holy writ, who is completely estranged from the religion of his fathers—as well as from every other religion—and who cannot take a share in nationalist ideals, but who has yet never repudiated his people, who feels that he is in his essential nature a Jew and who has no desire to alter that nature. If the question were put to him: 'Since you have abandoned all these common characteristics of your countrymen, what is there left to you that is Jewish?' he would reply: 'A very great deal, and probably its very essence.' He could not now express that essence clearly in words; but some day, no doubt, it will become accessible to the scientific mind" (*Totem and Taboo*, trans. James Strachey [London: Routledge, 2004], xiii). In a text published shortly after *Freud's Moses*, Yerushalmi contrasts Freud's "biblical" trust in the powers of the word with Schoenberg's attitude (a "Maimonidian" attitude, he says, in reference to Maimonides, 1135–1204, who is considered the most important intellectual figure of medieval Judaism), which emphasizes the fallibility of all verbal expression. But this contrast makes Freud's hesitation more evident, as when, in the paragraph cited above, he attempts to articulate "the essence" of Judaism, beyond any community of language, religion, or national sentiment. On this point, Yerushalmi notes: "Only twice, to my knowledge, does his confidence in verbal expression falter, both times in trying to define the nature of his Jewishness (see the address to the B'nai Brith and the preface to the Hebrew translation of *Totem and Taboo*). He did not rest, however, until he *had* found the words. The result was *Moses and Monotheism*" (Yosef Hayim Yerushalmi, "The Moses of Freud and the Moses of Schoenberg: On Words, Idolatry, and Psychoanalysis," *The Psychoanalytic Study of the Child* 47, 13). Freud's address was given to the Viennese circle of the B'nai B'rith in 1926. In it, Freud interprets his adherence to Judaism in terms of "many obscure emotional forces, which were the more powerful the

less they could be expressed in words" ("Address to the Society of B'nai B'rith," in *The Standard Edition of the Complete Psychological Works of Sigmund Freud*, ed. and trans. James Strachey, V. 20 [London: Hogarth, 1959], 274). From this perspective, we could say that in *Moses and Monotheism*, Freud recovers his *biblical* capacity of articulation, not, however, without hesitations.

11. What may have been, in its turn, the episode that triggered Egyptian monotheism? Freud's answer is, in this case, particularly "Marxist": he links the reemergence of monotheism in Egypt to the expansion of the Empire, which would have brought about the need to universalize religious beliefs.

12. Freud, *Moses and Monotheism*, 129.

13. On the (supposedly) problematic transference of concepts that seem to have their original ground in the study of the individual psyche to the domain of "mass psychology" (for example, the unconscious), Freud says that "the content of the unconscious is collective anyhow, a general possession of mankind" (ibid., 208). The distinction between the individual and the collective, let us add, is historical, not "natural." In fact, in the line of interpretation that I am developing, the foundational myth of the modern subject would find its expression in psychoanalysis: it is on this basis that its categories are more primordial, prior to the dichotomy between the individual and the collective.

14. Ibid., 178–79.

15. Freud, *Totem and Taboo*, xiii.

16. Richard J. Bernstein calls attention to the fact that Freud has chosen precisely the section of *Moses and Monotheism* titled "*Der Fortschritt in der Geistigkeit*" ("The Progress of Spirituality") to be read by his daughter Anna at the International Psychoanalytic Congress of 1938 in Paris. The section addresses the cultural meaning of the Mosaic religion and the importance of the interdiction of images (it also tells the story of Rabbi Jochanaan ben Sakkai, the founder of the first school for the study of the Torah, in times of great adversity for the Jews—immediately after the destruction of the Temple). Bernstein asks: "Why did Freud select this section to be read before the Paris International Psychoanalytic Congress? After all, it barely contains any reference or contribution to psychoanalysis." And he responds: "Let me suggest that Freud intended to leave a testament to his fellow psychoanalysts—to remind them of what he passionately believed—that psychoanalysis represented a further development in *Der Fortschritt in der Geistigkeit*. Freud, the proud godless Jew, conceived of his own discovery of psychoanalysis as continuous with the tradition introduced by 'the great man' Moses, whose legacy had decisively influenced the character of the Jewish people" (Richard J. Bernstein, *Freud and the Legacy of Moses* [Cambridge: Cambridge University Press, 1998], 82–83).

17. Anna Freud ("your Antigone," Yerushalmi "says" to Freud in the "Monologue with Freud," the final chapter of his *Freud's Moses*) surprised the International Psychoanalytic Congress, which took place in Jerusalem in 1977, by claiming at the end of the text that she submitted that psychoanalysis is a "Jewish science."

The paragraph says: "During the era of its existence, psychoanalysis has entered into connection with various academic institutions, not always with satisfactory results. . . . It has also, repeatedly, experienced rejection by them, been criticized for its methods being imprecise, its findings not open to proof by experiment, for being unscientific, even for being a 'Jewish science.' However the other derogatory comments may be evaluated, it is, I believe, the last-mentioned connotation which, under present circumstances, can serve as a title of honour" (Anna Freud, quoted by Yosef Hayim Yerushalmi, *Freud's Moses: Judaism Terminable and Interminable* [New Haven, CT: Yale University Press, 1993], 100).

18. Freud, *Moses and Monotheism*, 213. The hypothesis that Freud would have identified himself with Paul rather than with Moses has also been formulated by Jacob Tauber, *Die politische Theologie des Paulus* (Munich: Wilhelm Finn, 1993).

19. An acceptance that is however hesitant and conflictive, at least until the Council of Nicaea of 787 decided that images were legitimate (a legitimacy which would be put again into question by the Reformation). See Régis Debray, *Vie et mort de l'image: Une histoire du regard en Occident* (Paris: Gallimard, 1992), 82–86.

20. Freud, *Moses and Monotheism*, 145.

21. Ibid., 143.

22. Ibid., 215.

23. Ibid., 139.

24. Ibid., 207.

25. Ibid., 159. In *An Outline of Psychoanalysis* from 1938, also referring to the interpretation of dreams, Freud claims: "[D]reams bring to light material which cannot have originated either from the dreamer's adult life or from his forgotten childhood. We are obliged to regard it as part of the *archaic heritage* which a child brings with him into the world, before any experience of his own, influenced by the experiences of his ancestors. We find the counterpart of this phylogenetic material in the earliest human legends and in surviving customs. Thus dreams constitute a source of human prehistory which is not to be despised" (*An Outline of Psychoanalysis*, 40).

26. Freud, *Moses and Monotheism*, 162–63.

27. See Benjamin's essay "On Some Motifs in Baudelaire," in *Illuminations: Essays and Reflections*, ed. Hannah Arendt, trans. Harry Zohn (New York: Harcourt Brace Javanovich, 2007).

28. Cathy Caruth, "Trauma and Experience: Introduction," in *Trauma: Explorations in Memory*, ed. Cathy Caruth (Baltimore, MD: Johns Hopkins University Press, 1995), 8.

29. The expression is Kevin Newmark's, "Traumatic Poetry: Charles Baudelaire and the Shock of Laughter," in *Trauma: Explorations in Memory*. On the significance of Baudelaire's poetry, Giorgio Agamben writes: "Baudelaire was the poet who had to face the dissolution of the authority of tradition in the new industrial society and therefore had to invent a new authority. He fulfilled this task by turning the very

intransmissibility of culture into a new value and putting the experience of shock at the center of his artistic labor. The shock is the jolt power acquired by things when they lose their transmissibility and their comprehensibility within a given cultural order. Baudelaire understood that for art to survive the ruin of tradition, the artist had to attempt to reproduce in his work that very destruction of transmissibility that was at the origin of the experience of shock: in this way he would succeed in turning the work into the very vehicle of the intransmissible. Through the theorization of the beautiful as instantaneous and elusive epiphany (*in éclair . . . puis la nuit!* ['a flash . . . then night!']), Baudelaire made of aesthetic beauty the cipher of the impossibility of transmission" (*The Man without Content*, ed. Georgia Albert (Stanford: Stanford University Press, 1999), 106–107). It is worth pointing out the affinity between this theorization of the beautiful and the sacrificial interpretation of art that I developed before, as well as the affinity with the "transvaluing" strategy that I have identified in Borges's work.

30. Marcel Proust, quoted by Benjamin, "On Some Motifs in Baudelaire," in *Illuminations*, 158.

31. Ibid., 160.

32. Ibid.

33. Freud, *Beyond the Pleasure Principle*, 33.

34. Benjamin, "On Some Motifs in Baudelaire," 159.

35. Ibid., 175.

36. Benjamin sees in film an art that would be at the level of the traumatic, denaturalized character of modern experience (*The Work of Art in the Age of Mechanical Reproduction*). Ambiguously, Benjamin laments the loss of the aura, of the signature of the extraordinary in the work of art. But, at the same time, he highly praises its possibilities. This ambiguity regarding the aura can be traced back to Baudelaire himself. In fact, Benjamin calls attention to a text by Baudelaire (*Perte d'auréole*) that addresses precisely this issue. The poet finds himself in a "bad place," where someone he knows reproaches: "You, in a bad place! You, the drinker of spirits! You, the eater of ambrosia!" The poet's answer is telling: he attributes the loss of his aura to the fact that he had to avoid a difficult traffic jam ("moving chaos where death comes in one stroke"). The aura has been left on the mud at the road, but the poet does not regret it: "Now I can wander unrecognized, perform bad deeds, and surrender myself to the low-life, like the simple mortals. And here I am, looking completely like you, as you see!" (Charles Baudelaire, "Perte d'auréole," in *Petits poëmes en prose* [Paris: Louis Conard, 1917], 157–58). The deauratized poet of Baudelaire and Benjamin, I speculate, will wander on the streets and finally enter into a movie theater. Or otherwise he will go back to his desk to write (as Benjamin once imagined, and as Borges did, and as his "Pierre Menard, Author of the Quixote" executes eternally) a literary work conformed only by quotations, in which the modern (in)experience of de-contextualization, alienation, and shock, would find its fulfillment, its catastrophe, its (im)possible overcoming.

37. Walter Benjamin (that uprooted Jew) gladly lets himself be pulled by the flux of this errancy. Uprootedness is the common denominator of Modernity and Judaism. Indeed, Hegel deduces from Abraham's uprootedness the essence of Judaism, with its abstract universality, its prohibition of the image, and the abstract severity of its Law. In chapter 2, I mentioned the horror that Hegel experiences in the face of this abstract universality (which is the universality of Kantian thought, which Hegel wants to overcome). I also said that this horror would be at the basis of what we could now call the "Egyptian" aspect of Hegel's thought: the positing of history as the instance of actualization of a "concrete universality," free from the stigma of forgetfulness. By contrast, Jewish abstract universality, as I also said earlier, is hostile to history and to the powers invested by it. Situated within the gap between being and thinking, the modern subject seeks to extract from it the symbolic energies with which to judge history as a single block, recusing all identity between ethics and politics. On the other hand, abstract universality makes possible modern freedom, understood primordially as freedom of interpretation. Indeed, interpretation can only be located there where memory leaves gaps, where the crushing weight of the living totality has yielded to the gray lightness of writing. From that point on, Modernity is thrown into an infinite interpretation: to the infinity of interpretation, which bestows it with its specific dignity.

38. Benjamin, "On Some Motifs in Baudelaire," 169.

39. Baudelaire, "À une passante," in *Petits poëmes en prose*, 327.

40. Jacques Lacan, *Écris*, trans. Bruce Fink (New York: W. W. Norton, 2006), 324.

41. "The Law is there *ab origine*. It is therefore out of the question to ask oneself the question of origins—the Law is there precisely from the beginning, it has always been there, and human sexuality must realize itself through it and by means of it" (Jacques Lacan, *Seminar III: The Psychoses*, ed. Jacques-Alain Miller, trans. Russell Grigg (New York: W. W. Norton, 1997), 83.

42. Slavoj Žižek, *Tarrying with the Negative: Kant, Hegel, and the Critique of Ideology* (Durham, NC: Duke University Press, 1993), 116.

43. From this perspective, contemporary globalized society, in which apparently, beyond any law and any lack, everything should be possible (this infinite possibility, we would say, is its promise) would be a perverse society, oriented to *jouissance*. The outcome would be the exhaustion of desire, depression. This is the Lacanian reading of contemporary society developed by psychoanalyst Kathya Araujo ("El goce de la globalización," in *Cultura y globalización*, eds. Gonzalo Portocarrero and Iván Degregori [Lima: Red para el Desarrollo de las Ciencias Sociales en el Perú, 1999]). In any case, it is worth noting that Lacanian psychoanalysis is precisely the symbolic device by virtue of which the illusory game of desire is unmasked, exposed. Like it or not, it would be then depression itself, its self-conscious, articulated expression.

44. Jacques Lacan, *Seminar VII: The Ethics of Psychoanalysis*, ed. Jacques-Alain Miller, trans. Dennis Porter (London: Routledge, 1992), 177.

45. Lacan, *Seminar III*, 96.

46. Disenchantment or demagnification (*Entzauberung*) is, according to Max Weber, the key to Modernity, which progressively disenchants and secularizes myth. However, I have insisted throughout this book that disenchantment is, primordially, self-disenchantment—a self-reflective turn upon the mythical core of Modernity, upon the residues that this very process leaves behind. I have also developed this idea in a previous book (*El desánimo: Ensayo sobre la condición contemporánea* [Oviedo, Spain: Ediciones Nobel, 1996]), particularly in chapter 4.

47. Paul Celan, "Psalm," in *Selected Poems and Prose of Paul Celan*, trans. John Felstiner (New York: W. W. Norton, 2001), 156.

Bibliography

Adorno, Theodor W. *Minima Moralia: Reflections from Damaged Life*. Translated by E. F. N. Jephcott. London: Verso, 2006.
Agamben, Giorgio. *The Man without Content*. Edited by Georgia Albert. Stanford, CA: Stanford University Press, 1999.
Araujo, Kathya. "El Goce de La Globalización." In *Cultura y Globalización*, edited by Gonzalo Portocarrero and Iván Degregori. Lima: Red para el Desarrollo de las Ciencias Sociales en el Perú, 1999.
Atlan, Henri. *Configurations Spinozistes*. Paris: Odile Jacob, 2018.
———. *Entre Le Cristal et La Fumée: Essai Sur l'organisation Du Vivant*. Pairs: Seuil, 1979.
Barthes, Roland. *Mythologies*. Translated by Annette Lavers. New York: Noonday, 1972.
Bataille, Georges. *The Accursed Share: An Essay on General Economy*. Translated by Robert Hurley. New York: Zone Books, 1988.
———. *Theory of Religion*. Translated by Robert Hurley. Vol. 1. New York: Zone Books, 1989.
Baudelaire, Charles. *Petits Poëmes En Prose*. Paris: Louis Conard, 1917.
Benjamin, Walter. *Illuminations: Essays and Reflections*. Edited by Hannah Arendt. Translated by Harry Zohn. New York: Schocken, 1969.
———. *Reflections: Essays, Aphorisms, Autobiographical Writings*. Edited by Peter Demetz. Translated by Edmund Jephcott. New York: Schocken, 1986.
Bernstein, Richard J. *Freud and the Legacy of Moses*. Cambridge: Cambridge University Press, 1998.
Bloom, Harold. *The Anxiety of Influence: A Theory of Poetry*. Oxford: Oxford University Press, 1997.
———. "Freud: Frontier Concepts, Jewishness, and Interpretation." In *Trauma: Explorations in Memory*, edited by Cathy Caruth. Baltimore, MD: Johns Hopkins University Press, 1995.
———. *The Western Canon: The Books and School of the Ages*. New York: Riverhead, 1995.

Blumenberg, Hans. *The Legitimacy of the Modern Age*. Translated by Robert M. Wallace. Cambridge, MA: MIT Press, 1985.
Borges, Jorge Luis. *The Aleph and Other Stories*. Translated by Andrew Hurley. New York: Penguin, 2004.
———. *Borges, A Reader: A Selection from the Writings of Jorge Luis Borges*. Edited by Emir Rodriguez Monegal and Alastair Reid. New York: Dutton, 1981.
———. *Collected Fictions*. Translated by Andrew Hurley. New York: Penguin, 1999.
———. *Dreamtigers*. Translated by Mildred Boyer and Harold Morland. Austin: University of Texas Press, 1985.
———. *Labyrinths: Selected Stories & Other Writings*. Edited by Donald A. Yates and James E. Irby. Translated by James E. Irby. New York: New Directions, 2007.
———. *Obras Completas*. Barcelona: Emece, 1996.
———. *Other Inquisitions: 1937–1952*. Translated by Ruth L. C. Simms. Austin: University of Texas Press, 1964.
———. *Selected Poems*. Edited by Alexander Coleman. New York: Penguin, 2000.
———. *The Total Library: Non-Fiction 1922–1986*. Edited by Eliot Weinberger. Translated by Esther Allen, Suzanne Jill Levine, and Eliot Weinberger. New York: Penguin, 1999.
———. "Walt Whitman: Man and Myth." *Critical Inquiry* 1, no. 4 (1975).
Cacciari, Massimo. "Loos, Roth, Wittgenstein: Interior y Experiencia." In *La Emoción de Lo Moderno: Viena Del 900*, edited by Nicolás Casullo. Buenos Aires: Nueva Visión, 1991.
Calvera, Anna. "La Modernidad de William Morris." *Temes de Disseny* 14 (1997).
Caruth, Cathy, ed. *Trauma: Explorations in Memory*. Baltimore, MD: Johns Hopkins University Press, 1995.
Cassirer, Ernst. *Kant's Life and Thought*. Translated by James Haden. New Haven, CT: Yale University Press, 1981.
Celan, Paul. *Selected Poems and Prose of Paul Celan*. Translated by John Felstiner. New York: W. W. Norton, 2001.
Debray, Régis. *Vie et Mort de l'image: Une Histoire Du Regard En Occident*. Paris: Gallimard, 1992.
Feuerbach, Ludwig. *The Essence of Christianity*. Translated by George Eliot. Walnut, CA: MSAC Philosophy Group, 2008.
Finley, M. I. *The Ancient Greeks*. New York: Penguin, 1987.
Foucault, Michel. *Discipline and Punish: The Birth of the Prison*. New York: Vintage, 1995.
———. *The Foucault Reader*. Edited by Paul Rabinow. New York: Pantheon, 1984.
———. *Language, Counter-Memory, Practice: Selected Essays and Interviews*. Edited by Donald F. Bouchard. Ithaca, NY: Cornell University Press, 1980.
Freud, Sigmund. "Address to the Society of B'nai B'rith." In *The Standard Edition of the Complete Psychological Works of Sigmund Freud*, edited and translated by James Strachey, Vol. 20. London: Hogarth, 1959.

———. *An Outline of Psychoanalysis*. Edited and translated by James Strachey. New York: W. W. Norton, 1969.
———. *Moses and Monotheism*. Translated by Katherine Jones. Letchworth, UK: Hogarth, 1939.
———. *Totem and Taboo*. Translated by James Strachey. London: Routledge, 2004.
Hacking, Ian. *The Emergence of Probability: A Philosophical Study of Early Ideas about Probability*. Cambridge: Cambridge University Press, 2006.
———. *The Taming of Chance*. Cambridge: Cambridge University Press, 1990.
Hegel, G. W. F. *Phenomenology of Spirit*. Translated by A. V. Miller. Oxford: Oxford University Press, 2004.
———. "The Spirit of Christianity and Its Fate." In *On Christianity: Early Theological Writings by Friedrich Hegel*, translated by T. M. Knox. New York: Harper Torchbooks, 1961.
Heidegger, Martin. "The Age of the World Picture." In *The Question concerning Technology and Other Essays*, translated by William Lovitt. New York: Garland, 1977.
———. *Nietzsche*. Translated by David Farrell Krell. New York: HarperCollins, 1991.
Hofmannsthal, Hugo von. *The Lord Chandos Letter and Other Writings*. Edited and translated by Joel Rotenberg. New York: New York Review, 2005.
Horkheimer, Max, and Theodor W. Adorno. *Dialectic of Enlightenment*. Edited by Gunzelin Schmid Noerr and Edmund Jephcott. Stanford, CA: Stanford University Press, 2002.
Huyssen, Andreas. "La Cultura de La Memoria: Medios, Política, Amnesia." *Revista de Crítica Cultural* 18 (1999).
Jay, Martin. *Downcast Eyes: The Denigration of Vision in Twentieth-Century French Thought*. Los Angeles: UC Press, 1994.
Jiménez Redondo, Manuel. "Habermas En El Contexto Del Pensamiento Político Moderno y La Posición de Habermas En El Debate Modernidad/Posmodernidad." Santiago, Chile, 2000.
Kant, Immanuel. "An Answer to the Question: What Is Enlightenment?" In *Practical Philosophy*, edited by Mary J. Gregor. New York: Cambridge University Press, 1999.
———. *Critique of Pure Reason*. Edited by Paul Guyer and Allen W. Wood. New York: Cambridge University Press, 2000.
———. "Groundwork of the Metaphysics of Morals." In *Practical Philosophy*, edited by Mary J. Gregor. New York: Cambridge University Press, 1999.
———. "Idea for a Universal History with a Cosmopolitan Aim." In *Anthropology, History, and Education*, edited by Günter Zöller and Robert B. Louden, translated by Allen W. Wood. Cambridge: Cambridge University Press, 2007.
———. "Religion within the Boundaries of Mere Reason." In *Religion and Rational Theology*, edited by Allen W. Wood and George Di Giovanni. New York: Cambridge University Press, 2001.

Kaufmann, Walter. *Hegel: A Reinterpretation*. Notre Dame, IN: Notre Dame University Press, 1978.
Koyré, Alexander. *From the Closed World to the Infinite Universe*. Baltimore, MD: Johns Hopkins University Press, 1957.
Kuhn, Thomas S. *The Structure of Scientific Revolutions*. Chicago: University of Chicago Press, 2002.
Kulenkampff, Jens. "A Logica Kantiana Do Juizo Estetico e o Significado Metafisico Do Belo Da Naturaleza." In *200 Anos Da Critica Da Facultade Do Juizo de Kant*, edited by Valerio Rohden. Porto Alegre, Brazil: Universidade Federal do Rio Grande do Sul, 1990.
Lacan, Jacques. *Écris*. Translated by Bruce Fink. New York: W. W. Norton, 2006.
———. *Seminar VII: The Ethics of Psychoanalysis*. Edited by Jacques-Alain Miller. Translated by Dennis Porter. London: Routledge, 19992.
———. *Seminar III: The Psychoses*. Edited by Jacques-Alain Miller. Translated by Russell Grigg. New York: W. W. Norton, 1997.
Lévinas, Emmanuel. *Difficile Liberté*. Paris: Le livre de poche, 2003.
———. *Totality and Infinity: An Essay on Exteriority*. Translated by Alphonso Lingis. London: Martinus Nijhoff, 1979.
"Luther at the Imperial Diet of Worms (1521)." Accessed 27 January 2018. http://www.luther.de/en/worms.html.
Maldonado, Tomás. *El Diseño Industrial Reconsiderado*. Barcelona: Gustavo Gil, 1993.
Marx, Karl. *Capital*. Translated by Ben Fowkes. Vol. 1. New York: Penguin, 1982.
———. "Economic and Philosophical Manuscripts." In *Early Writings*, translated by Rodney Livingstone and Gregor Benton. New York: Penguin, 1992.
———. "The Economic and Philosophic Manuscripts of 1844." In *Karl Marx: Selected Writings in Sociology and Social Philosophy*, edited by T. B. Bottomore and Maximilien Rubel, translated by T. B. Bottomore. New York: McGraw-Hill, 1963.
Miller, Jacques-Alain. "Extimité." edited by M. Bracher, M. Alcorn Jr., R. J. Cortell, and F. Massardier-Kenney. New York: New York University Press, 1994.
Monod, Jacques. *Chance and Necessity: An Essay on the Natural Philosophy of Modern Biology*. Translated by Austryn Wainhouse. New York: Vintage, 1972.
Morris, William. *Some Hints on Pattern-Designing*. London: Chiswick, 1899.
Musil, Robert. *The Man without Qualities*. Translated by Sophie Wilkins. New York: Vintage, 1995.
Nietzsche, Friedrich. *Beyond Good and Evil: Prelude to a Philosophy of the Future*. Edited by Rolf-Peter Horstmann and Judith Norman. Translated by Judith Norman. Cambridge: Cambridge University Press, 2001.
———. *Ecce Homo and The Antichrist*. Translated by Thomas Wayne. New York: Algora, 2004.
———. *The Gay Science*. Edited by Bernard Williams. Translated by Josefine Nauckhoff and Adrian Del Caro. Cambridge: Cambridge University Press, 2001.

———. *Human, All Too Human: A Book for Free Spirits*. Translated by R. J. Hollingdale. Cambridge: Cambridge University Press, 1996.

———. *On the Genealogy of Morals*. Edited by Walter Kaufmann. Translated by Walter Kaufmann and R. J. Hollingdale. New York: Vintage, 1989.

———. "On Truth and Lying in a Non-Moral Sense." In *The Birth of Tragedy and Other Writings*, edited by Raymond Geuss and Ronald Speirs, translated by Ronald Speirs. New York: Cambridge University Press, 2007.

Pezzoni, Enrique. *Enrique Pezzoni Lector de Borges: Lecciones de Literatura 1984–1988*. Buenos Aires: Sudamericana, 1999.

Plato. *Phaedrus*. Translated by Alexander Nehamas and Paul Woodruff. Indianapolis: Hackett, 1995.

Rezvani, Serge. *L'origine Du Monde: Pour Une Ultime Histoire de l'art à Propos Du "Cas Bergamme."* Paris: Actes Sud, 2002.

Sabrovsky, Eduardo. *Chile, Tiempos Interesantes: A 40 Años Del Golpe Militar*. Santiago, Chile: Educiones UDP, 2013.

———. *El Desánimo: Ensayo Sobre La Condición Contemporánea*. Oviedo, Spain: Ediciones Nobel, 1996.

Schmitt, Carl. *The Concept of the Political*. Translated by George Schwab. Chicago: University of Chicago Press, 2007.

———. *Political Theology: Four Chapters on the Concept of Sovereignty*. Translated by George Schwab. Cambridge, MA: MIT Press, 1985.

Scholem, Gershom. *On the Kabbalah and Its Symbolism*. New York: Schocken, 1996.

Schorske, Karl E. "Adolf Loos: Revuelta En Viena." In *La Emoción de Lo Moderno: Viena Del 900*, edited by Nicolás Casullo. Buenos Aires: Nueva Visión, 1991.

———. "The Quest for the Grail: Wagner and Morris." In *The Critical Spirit: Essays in Honor of Herbert Marcuse*, edited by Kurt H. Wolff and Barrington Moore. Boston: Beacon, 1967.

Sennett, Richard. *Flesh and Stone: The Body and the City in Western Civilization*. New York: W. W. Norton, 1996.

Simon, Herbert. *The Sciences of the Artificial*. Cambridge, MA: MIT Press, 1981.

Sloterdijk, Peter. *En El Mismo Barco: Ensayo Sobre La Hiperpolítica*. Translated by Manuel Fontán del Junco. Madrid: Siruela, 1994.

Spinoza, Baruch. *Ethics*. Edited by Seymour Feldman. Translated by Samuel Shirley. Indianapolis: Hackett, 1992.

Tauber, Jacob. *Die Politische Theologie Des Paulus*. Munich: Wilhelm Finn, 1993.

Todorov, Tzvetan. *The Fantastic: A Structural Approach to a Literary Genre*. Ithaca, NY: Cornell University Press, 1975.

Vaihinger, Hans. *The Philosophy of "As If": A System of the Theoretical, Practical and Religious Fictions of Mankind*. Translated by C. K. Ogden. London: Kegan Paul, Trench, Trubner, 1935.

Vernant, Jean-Pierre. *Myth and Society in Ancient Greece*. Translated by Janet Lloyd. New York: Zone Books, 1990.

White, R. M. "Can Whether One Proposition Make Sense Depend on the Truth of Another? (Tractatus 2.0211–2)." edited by Godfrey Vesey. Ithaca, NY: Cornell University Press, 1976.
Wilkins, Eithne, and Ernst Kaiser. "Foreword." In *The Man without Qualities*, by Robert Musil. London: Secker & Warburg, 1979.
Wittgenstein, Ludwig. "A Lecture on Ethics." *The Philosophical Review* 74, no. 1 (1965): 3–12.
———. *Lectures and Conversations on Aesthetics, Psychology and Religious Belief.* Edited by Cyril Barrett. Berkeley, CA: UC Press, 1967.
———. *Philosophical Investigations*. Translated by G. E. M. Anscombe, P. M. S. Hacker, and Joachim Schulte. Malden, MA: Wiley-Blackwell, 2009.
———. *Tractatus Logico-Philosophicus*. Translated by D. F. Pears and B. F. McGuinness. New York: Routledge, 2002.
Woolf, Virginia. *Orlando: A Biography*. Orlando, FL: Harcourt, 2006.
Yerushalmi, Yosef Hayim. *Freud's Moses: Judaism Terminable and Interminable.* New Haven, CT: Yale University Press, 1993.
———. "The Moses of Freud and the Moses of Schoenberg: On Words, Idolatry, and Psychoanalysis." *The Psychoanalytic Study of the Child* 47 (1992): 1–20.
Žižek, Slavoj. *First as Tragedy, Then as Farce*. London: Verso, 2009.
———. *Tarrying with the Negative: Kant, Hegel, and the Critique of Ideology*. Durham, NC: Duke University Press, 1993.
Zupančič, Alenka. *Ethics of the Real: Kant, Lacan*. London: Verso, 2000.

Index

Adorno, Theodor W., 31, 79, 116, 172n29
Alexander the Great, 102
Araujo, Kathya, 184n43
Aristotle, 13, 102, 151n19
Atlan, Henri, xx, 37, 40–46
Augustine of Hippo/Saint Augustine, 107
Austro-Hungarian Empire, xv, 7. *See also* Vienna

Babel, xii, 22, 29, 62–63, 86, 115
Bacon, Francis, 30–31, 86, 155
Balzac, Honoré de, 82–83
Barthes, Roland, 28–35
Bataille, Georges, 168n14, 169n18
Bateson, Gregory, 40–41
Baudelaire, Charles, 141, 182n29, 183n36
Bello, Andrés, 72, 78–79, 168n15, 169n22
Benjamin, Walter, xix–xxii, 14, 72, 83, 120, 139–141, 184n37
Bentham, Jeremy, 109–111, 153n13
Bernstein, Richard J., 181n16
Bloom, Harold, 95, 178n5
Boltzmann, Ludwig, 40–42

Borges, Jorge Luis, viii–x, 14, 62, 68–72, 85–98, 126, 147n1, 151n19
Buenos Aires, Argentina, x, 85, 126

Cacciari, Massimo, 125, 176n36
Calvera, Anna, 125
Calvin, Jean, 76, 89, 118–125
Cassirer, Ernst, 166n7
Celan, Paul, 145
Chaucer, Geoffrey, 87–88

Darwin, Charles, 56
Debray, Régis, 168n13
Díaz, Gonzalo, 72–80
Duchamp, Marcel, 67, 68, 72

Egypt, 132–133

Feuerbach, Ludwig, 24
Foucault, Michel, 2, 47, 108–111, 114–115
Freud, Sigmund, 46, 127–141

Galilei, Galileo, xvii, 12, 56, 64, 94
Greece, 105–107, 174n8

Habermas, Jürgen, 167n10

Hacking, Ian, 159n11
Hegel, G. W. F., xiii, 20–25, 78, 89, 184n37
Heidegger, Martin, 37–39, 50–53, 159n14, 167n11
Heraclitus (pre-Socratic thinker), 103
Hobbes, Thomas, 17
Hofmannsthal, Hugo von, 31, 119–120
Homer, 91, 105
Horkheimer, Max, 31, 79
Hume, David, 27

Joyce, James, 22, 83, 88

Kafka, Franz, xii, 115
Kant, Immanuel, xii–xiv, 1–4, 17–21, 46–47, 68–71, 92–94, 128, 156n4, 160n27
Kierkegaard, Søren, 80
Koyré, Alexander, 12
Kraus, Karl, 175n27
Kuhn, Thomas S., 33, 162n11

Lacan, Jacques, 141–144
Latin America, ix–x
Leibniz, Gottfried Wilhelm, 117
Lévinas, Emmanuel, 46–48, 52–53, 155n1, 162n7
Loos, Adolf Franz Karl Viktor Maria, 112–115, 125
Luther, Martin, 13–14, 76, 89, 118

Maldonado, Tomás, 124, 177n13
Marx, Karl, xiii, 23–25, 123, 154–155n31
Matte, Rebeca, 76
Mellado, Justo Pastor, 77
Miller, Jacques-Alain, xxii
Monod, Jacques, 35–36, 56
Morris, William, 124–125

Moses, 132–136
Musil, Robert, xv, 7–10, 119–123

National Arts Museum, Santiago de Chile, 72, 76–77
Newton, Isaac, 41, 46, 92, 94
Nietzsche, Friedrich, 49–60, 71, 103–107, 115, 152–153n3, 160–161n27

Oedipus, 104, 127
Oyarzún, Pablo, 79

Paul, Saint, xix, 136
Perón, Juan Domingo, viii
Plato, xiv, 13, 64, 103
Pnyx, Athens, 105
Popper, Karl, 127–129
Prigogine, Ilya, xx–xxi
Proust, Marcel, 22, 139–141

Rezvani, Serge, 82

Schmitt, Carl, xviii, xxi
Schopenhauer, Arthur, 70–71
Schorske, Karl E., 124
Sennett, Richard, 106–107
Sloterdijk, Peter, 101–102, 175n26
Smith, William Robertson, 132, 137
Spinoza, Baruch, 45–48
Stengers, Isabelle, xx–xxi

Tarski, Alfred, 61
Thamus, 13–14

Vaihinger, Hans, xiv, 54
Vienna, 113–114, 120, 128, 131, 175n27. *See also* Austro-Hungarian Empire

Warhol, Andy, 72

Weber, Max, xv, 43, 47, 185n46
Whitman, Walt, 172–173n30
Wittgenstein, Ludwig, xi–xii, xvi, 27, 31–33, 79, 128, 130–131, 156n4, 172n29
Woolf, Virginia, 65

Yahweh, 133
Yerushalmi, Yosef Hayim, 179–180n7, 180–181n10, 181–182n17

Žižek, Slavoj, 148n6